Pushing the
Antithesis

D1247718

Pushing the Antithesis

The Apologetic Methodology of Greg L. Bahnsen

GARY DeMar, EDITOR

AMERICAN VISION PRESS
POWDER SPRINGS, GEORGIA

American Vision
EXERCISING SERVANTHOOD DOMINION

A Biblical Worldview Ministry

THE MISSION OF AMERICAN VISION, INC. IS TO PUBLISH AND DISTRIBUTE
MATERIALS THAT LEAD INDIVIDUALS TOWARD:

———

A personal faith in the one true God: Father, Son, and Holy Spirit

———

A lifestyle of practical discipleship

———

A worldview that is consistent with the Bible

———

An ability to apply the Bible to all of life

Pushing the Antithesis:
The Apologetic Methodology of Greg L. Bahnsen

Printed in The United States of America.

American Vision, Inc.
3150 Florence Road, Suite 2
Powder Springs, Georgia 30127-5385
www.americanvision.org
1-800-628-9460

Library of Congress Cataloging-in-Publication Data

DeMar, Gary, editor.
  Pushing the Antithesis / Gary DeMar, editor—1st ed.
  Includes bibliographical references and index.
  ISBN 978-0-9972402-2-1

This book is dedicated to David L. Bahnsen,
a faithful son who keeps his father's legacy alive.

Table of Contents

Foreword

By Gary DeMar

"It is never about winning, Greg. It is about exposing their inconsistency. God does everything else. Never forget the antithesis."

—Cornelius Van Til to Greg L. Bahnsen (1985)[1]

I KNOW THAT GOD must have a sense of humor since I'm writing a Foreword to a book that outlines the apologetic methodology of Dr. Greg L. Bahnsen. Even the phrase "apologetic methodology" has a distant comic ring to it considering that prior to becoming a Christian in 1973, I wouldn't have had the slightest idea what the phrase meant. If there was ever a relationship where brawn and brain identified the two participants, it was my association and friendship with Dr. Bahnsen.

The focus of my life in high school and college was athletics. Instead of studying, I spent my time training for the shot put, discus, javelin, long jump, with the greatest emphasis on the shot put. For those of you not familiar with this track and field event, think of a man pushing (not throwing) a cannon ball from the confines of a seven-foot circle in an attempt to outdistance his competitors. I spent hours every day training with weights since, in order to throw a 12-pound iron ball, you have to be big and strong. This meant eating an inordinate amount of food every day to get my weight up to 220 pounds as a high school senior. My dedicated efforts led to a new Pennsylvania state record in 1968, a fifth-place ranking in the nation with a throw of more than 64 feet, participation in the Golden West Invitational track and field meet held in Sacramento, California, as well as 50 scholarship offers to some of the best colleges in the nation. Only one thing was missing: good grades. While I trained diligently, even religiously some might say, I did all of this to the exclusion of studying.[2]

I entered college academically atrophied. But like I said, God has a sense of humor. During my senior year in college, after a steady decline in my athletic ability and interest in sports, God transformed my life spiritually and academically. I truly became a "new creation in Christ" (2 Cor. 5:17) with a transformed mind (Rom. 12:2). Realizing that I was far behind in my knowledge about so much, I began to read and study, beginning with C.S. Lewis' *Mere Christianity*, Paul L. Maier's *First Christmas*, and Josh McDowell's *Evidence that Demands a Verdict*. Hoping to accelerate my re-education, in 1974, I enrolled as a student at Reformed Theological Seminary (RTS) in Jackson, Mississippi. It was there that I came in contact with other students of like mind, a large library, a well-stocked bookstore, well-equipped professors, and the most well-equipped of them all, Dr. Greg L. Bahnsen.

When I first came to Christ, I was living in a less than ideal spiritual setting. But even this was for God's greater purpose. I learned very early that defending the Christian faith took knowledge, skill, and the work of the Holy Spirit. As long as I shared the worldview of those I lived with, there was little to debate. While I did my best to answer serious questions and outright objections thrown at me by my housemates and their friends, it was obvious that I was woefully unprepared. My Christian faith was put to the test immediately by skeptical inquiry. Their questions led me to further study, and I soon realized that the field of

Christian apologetics was an area of ministry that might actually be the call of God for my life. But who was I to defend the claims of Christ in an academic setting where history, knowledge of Greek and Hebrew, logic, debate skills, and a comprehensive knowledge of the Bible are required? I was trained as an athlete, not as an apologist. Even so, God seemed to be moving me to specialize in apologetics.

In God's unpredictable providence, I ended up at RTS where brawn met brain. This is not to say that Dr. Bahnsen did not enjoy and participate in athletics; it's just that he did not make sports the focus of his life as I did. While I graduated from Western Michigan University with a degree in Physical Education and was aspiring to coach at the college level, Dr. Bahnsen's academic accomplishments were, to put it kindly for my benefit, on the other end of the spectrum. In 1970, Dr. Bahnsen graduated *magna cum laude* from Westmont College where he received his B.A. in philosophy and was awarded the John Bunyan Smith Award for his overall grade point average. From there he pursued advanced degrees at Westminster Theological Seminary in Philadelphia, Pennsylvania, where he studied under Cornelius Van Til (1895–1987) and solidified his understanding and appreciation of the presuppositional methodology of apologetics developed by Van Til. When he graduated in May 1973, Dr. Bahnsen simultaneously received two degrees, Master of Divinity and Master of Theology, as well as the William Benton Greene Prize in apologetics and a Richard Weaver Fellowship from the Intercollegiate Studies Institute. After completing seminary, he began academic work at the University of Southern California (USC), where he studied philosophy, specializing in the theory of knowledge (epistemology). In 1975, after being ordained in the Orthodox Presbyterian Church, he became an associate professor of Apologetics and Ethics at Reformed Theological Seminary in Jackson, Mississippi. While there, he completed his doctoral studies at USC, receiving his Ph.D. in 1978 at the age of 30.[3]

As a new Christian living in the den of unbelief during my final semester of college, I found that every time someone raised objections about the authority of the Bible—the reality of miracles, the problem of evil, or the existence of God—and I attempted to answer them, I would be hit with another objection. When I was stumped, as I often was, I spent time researching and returned a day or two later with answers from my study of Scripture and additional information culled from books in my growing library. Sometimes I would get a nod of agreement from my skeptical friends on points I had made, but then out would come a new objection. There had to be a better way to defend the Christian faith than in a "bits and pieces" fashion. I soon learned that there was a better *biblical* way that follows Peter's admonition to "sanctify Christ as Lord in your hearts, always being ready to make a defense to everyone who asks you to give an account for the hope that is in you, yet with gentleness and reverence" (1 Pet. 3:15). Peter makes it clear that defending the faith is not for a special breed of Christian. We must all be ready. Certainly some are better equipped than others, but there is still the requirement for all Christians to be ready to make a defense. This means that the methodology must be basic enough for any Christian to master.

The "bits and pieces" method I was using relied heavily on evidences. This methodology is best articulated by Josh McDowell in *Evidence that Demands a Verdict*, the book I was encouraged to consult by my new Christian friends to make my case for the authenticity of the biblical record and my Christian testimony. Evidences of a factual nature are certainly important in the defense of the Christian faith,[4] but I would soon learn that they should never be viewed independently of a person's worldview. The evidentialist approach assumes facts are neutral, that they "speak for themselves," and that those evaluating the facts are without biases or operating worldview assumptions in their interpretation of the facts. If a skeptic begins with the premise that miracles don't happen, then all the evidence in the world will not convince him otherwise. His operating anti-supernatural starting point will assume that there must be some naturalistic explanation that was not understood by those writing in a pre-scientific time. The anti-supernaturalist might argue: (1) Maybe Lazarus was not really dead when he was entombed. He could have been in a coma and was misdiagnosed by his family and friends who had little medical knowledge. (2) Later writers of the gospel accounts made up stories about Jesus' life and work in order to make Him look like a miracle worker to those who were asked to join the new religion. (3) In terms of what we know about science, it just isn't possible to bring dead people back to life.

For those set in their anti-supernatural worldview ways, there will always be some naturalistic reason why miracles are impossible, and no amount of evidence will convince them otherwise. Consider the following humorous story to make the point that evidences only make sense within the context of a person's already accepted worldview:

> Once upon a time there was a man who thought he was dead. His concerned wife and friends sent him to the friendly neighborhood psychiatrist. The psychiatrist determined to cure him by convincing him of one fact that contradicted his belief that he was dead. The psychiatrist decided to use the simple truth that dead men do not bleed. He put his patient to work reading medical texts, observing autopsies, etc. After weeks of effort the patient finally said, "All right, all right! You've convinced me.

xiv   *Pushing the Antithesis*

Dead men do not bleed." Whereupon the psychiatrist stuck him in the arm with a needle, and the blood flowed. The man looked down and contorted, ashen faced and cried: "Good Lord! Dead men bleed after all!"[5]

Sounds ridiculous, but as we'll see, there are real-life examples of people who argue in a similar way. The facts for this "dead man" were not convincing because of his operating presupposition. The evidence presented to him was incontrovertible for someone who operated within a worldview with the starting assumption that only living people bleed. In order to maintain the legitimacy of his worldview, our patient only had to make a few adjustments to his worldview to fit in a new "fact" unknown to him before—dead men do bleed. The doctor and the patient were looking at the same fact—the flow of blood—but their operating worldviews cause them to come to different conclusions as to what the evidence meant.

We've all experienced this. The debate over abortion is not just about the evidence. It can't be since the evidence is the same for pro- and anti-abortionists. The same is true in the creation-evolution debate. Biologists, anthropologists, chemists, and philosophers from both positional sides are looking at the same evidence, but they come to different conclusions. What makes the difference? A prior commitment to a set of presuppositions. Consider the following from evolutionist Richard Lewontin:

> We take the side of science *in spite of* the patent absurdity of some of its constructs, *in spite of* its failure to fulfill many of its extravagant promises of health and life, *in spite of* the tolerance of the scientific community for unsubstantiated just-so stories, because we have a prior commitment, a commitment to materialism. It is not that the methods and institutions of science somehow

compel us to accept a material explanation of the phenomenal world, but, on the contrary, that we are forced by our a priori adherence to material causes to create an apparatus of investigation and a set of concepts that produce material explanations, no matter how counterintuitive, no matter how mystifying to the uninitiated. Moreover, that materialism is absolute, for we cannot allow a Divine Foot in the door.[6]

There you have it! I couldn't have made the point any better. Oftentimes it's difficult to convince people that science is not the objective field of study it's made out to be. Even when the facts don't make sense, the unproven prior commitment to materialism must be embraced at all cost, no matter what the facts might say. To loosen the grip just a little means that God must be considered as the prime factor in the equation, and this will never do for the materialist even if it means being irrational and unscientific to protect a worldview that needs God to account for the logic that is used to keep Him out.

The goal in apologetics, as Dr. Bahnsen taught his students, was to approach a person at the level of his worldview, a worldview that is built on a set of operating assumptions about the source and nature of knowledge that gives meaning to the facts and experiences he encounters. Dr. Bahnsen offers the following helpful summary of the methodology:

Everybody thinks and reasons in terms of a broad and fundamental understanding of the nature of reality, of how we know what we know, and of how we should live our lives. This philosophy or outlook is "presupposed" by everything the unbeliever (or believer) says; it is the implicit background that gives meaning to the claims and inferences drawn by people. For this reason, every apologetical encounter is ultimately a conflict of worldviews or

xvi   *Pushing the Antithesis*

fundamental perspectives (whether this is explicitly mentioned or not).[7]

Consider the resurrection. Since the universe was created by
God out of things that are not visible (Heb. 11:3), and man was
formed "of dust from the ground" (Gen. 2:7), then reanimating
a dead body would not be a major task for God. Paul makes the
point to King Agrippa: "Why is it considered incredible among
you people if God does raise the dead?" (Acts 26:8). The logic is
simple: Since God creates; He can certainly recreate. Accounts
of supernatural (from our point of view) events found in the
Bible are easily accounted for when the operating presupposition is that the Creator of the cosmos is behind the events.
The Bible *begins* with the operating presupposition that "God
created the heavens and the earth" (Gen. 1:1). If this is not the
starting point, then nothing makes sense. There is no way to
account for reason, logic, love, goodness, personhood, or meaning of any kind in a random, matter-only cosmos. "In short,"
Dr. Bahnsen argued, "presuppositional apologetics argues for
the truth of Christianity 'from the impossibility of the contrary.'
Someone who is so foolish as to operate in his intellectual life as
though there were no God (Ps. 14:1) thereby 'despises wisdom
and instruction' and 'hates knowledge' (Prov. 1:7, 29). He needs
to be answered according to his folly—demonstrating where his
philosophical principles lead—'lest he be wise in his own eyes'
(Prov. 26:5)."[8]

So then, instead of beginning with the bits and pieces of a
worldview (evidences for this or that doctrine, or this or that god),
the starting point is more fixed and fundamental. "Thus, when
all is said and done," Dr. Bahnsen makes clear to us, "apologetics
becomes the vindication of the Christian worldview as a whole,
not simply a piecemeal defense of isolated, abstractly defined,

religious points."[9] It's with this operating presupposition that Dr. Bahnsen called his students to "push the antithesis," that is to force the unbeliever to live consistently with his rationalistic and materialistic presuppositions that underlie and seemingly support his worldview. It's this push that exposes the inherent faultlines in naturalistic worldviews that begin with the supposed sovereignty of the creature rather than the Creator, which is the essence of the antithesis. "Without the ingredient of *antithesis*, Christianity is not simply anemic, it has altogether forfeited its challenge to all other worldviews."[10] Dr. Bahnsen continues:

> Abraham Kuyper well understood that all men conduct their reasoning and their thinking in terms of an ultimate controlling principle—a most basic presupposition. For the unbeliever, this is a natural or naturalistic principle, in terms of which man's thinking is taken to be intelligible without recourse to God. For the believer, it is a supernatural principle based on God's involvement in man's history and experience, notably in regeneration—[a] perspective that provides the framework necessary for making sense of anything. These two ultimate commitments—call them naturalism and Christian supernaturalism—are logically incompatible and seek to cancel each other out.[11]

When pushed to be consistent with the operating assumptions of their worldview, naturalists soon learn that matter-only presuppositions don't work and lead to nihilism. R. C. Sproul puts it well when he writes, "Although I do not embrace presuppositional apologetics, I do recognize that the existence of God is the supreme *proto*-supposition for all theoretical thought. God's existence is the chief element in constructing any worldview. To deny this chief premise is to set one's sails for the island of nihilism. This is the darkest continent of the darkened mind—the ultimate paradise of the fool."[12]

Dr. Bahnsen left a lasting legacy that is bearing considerable fruit. As the quotation by R.C. Sproul demonstrates, it's hard to shake the implications and effectiveness of the presuppositional model defended, practiced, and popularized by Dr. Bahnsen. The presuppositional method of apologetics is being acknowledged in other works on the subject. Joe Boot applies the presuppositional methodology in his book *Why I Still Believe*.[13] Doug Powell's *Guide to Christian Apologetics* carries an entire chapter on apologetic methodology where he quotes Cornelius Van Til, John Frame, and Greg Bahnsen in a succinct and reliable way. Powell does an excellent job in describing and distinguishing the various approaches to apologetics and includes well designed graphics to illustrate the antithesis between Christian and non-Christian thought.

On a personal note, Dr. Bahnsen helped turn an athlete into an apologist, someone who continues to study so that (with God's help) he will be always ready to defend the faith. What began as a teacher to student relationship grew into friendship and a professional relationship. Dr. Bahnsen was the anchor speaker for the three years that American Vision hosted the "Life Preparation Conference" (1991–1993). He and I presented papers at the "Consultation on the Biblical Role of Civil Government" that was held at Geneva College in Beaver Falls, Pennsylvania, on June 2 and 3, 1987. Our articles, along with those of the other participants, were published in *God and Politics: Four Views on the Reformation of Civil Government*.[14] In order to help advance Dr. Bahnsen's teaching ministry and biblical approach to apologetics to a wider audience, I commissioned him to write several articles for American Vision's *Biblical Worldview Magazine*. These were later published in "Section Five" of *Always Ready: Directions for Defending the Faith*.[15] Dr. Bahnsen's influence on my life demonstrates the truth of what Dr. Gary North wrote on the dedication page of his economic commentary on Numbers:

> This book is dedicated to Gary DeMar
> who has proven that there *is* life beyond shot-putting.[17]

With religion so prevalent in the news today, and with the rise of the "New Atheism" movement led by the unholy trinity of Richard Dawkins, Daniel C. Dennett, and Sam Harris, those of us who saw Greg in action as a debater lament that he is no longer with us to push the antithesis with these men. He left a legacy in the people who God providentially brought under his teaching. There are many who are well equipped to handle the onslaught of unbelieving thought today because Greg showed us how to "push the antithesis" in a thoughtful and cogent way.[16] While his legacy continues with the ever growing number of men and women who have came under his teaching, there was only one Greg L. Bahnsen. All of us who knew Greg sure do miss him. "That same mysterious Providence that gave us Dr. Bahnsen also called him home at the early age of 47—he went to be with his Lord on December 11, 1995."[17]

Notes

1. A conversation between Cornelius Van Til and Greg L. Bahnsen as reported by David L. Bahnsen, "Twenty Years Ago Tonight: The Bahnsen/Stein Debate": www.dlbthoughts.com/Articles.aspx?IDCol=91

2. For additional background, see Gary DeMar, "Ron Semkiw: A Short But Strong Career," 14:3 *MILO* (December 2006), 49–53 and Gary DeMar, "The Steroid Culture" (December 9, 2004): www.americanvision.org/articlearchive/12-09–04.asp

3. For a brief biography of Dr. Bahnsen, see David L. Bahnsen, "The Life of Dr. Greg L. Bahnsen," *The Standard Bearer: A Festschrift for Greg L. Bahnsen*, ed. Steven M. Schlissel (Nacogdoches, TX: Covenant Media Press, 2002), 9–27.

4. Thom Notaro, *Van Til and the Use of Evidence* (Phillipsburg, PA: Presbyterian and Reformed, 1980).

5. John Warwick Montgomery, *The Altizer-Montgomery Dialogue* (Chicago, IL: InterVarsity Press, 1967), 21–22. For a different illustration of this phenomenon, see the Introduction in Gary DeMar, *Thinking Straight in a Crooked World: A Christian Defense Manual* (Powder Springs, GA: American Vision, 2001).

6. Richard Lewontin, "Billions and billions of demons," *The New York Review* (January 9, 1997), 31.

7. Greg L. Bahnsen, *Van Til's Apologetic: Readings and Analysis* (Phillipsburg, NJ: Presbyterian and Reformed, 1998), 30.

8. Bahnsen, *Van Til's Apologetic*, 6.

9. Bahnsen, *Van Til's Apologetic*, 31.

10. Greg L. Bahnsen, "At War with the Word: The Necessity of Biblical Antithesis," *Antithesis*, 1:1 (January/February 1990), 6.

11. Bahnsen, "At War with the Word," 48.

12. R. C. Sproul, *The Consequences of Ideas: Understanding the Concepts that Shaped our World* (Wheaton, IL: Crossway Books, 2000), 171.

13. Joe Boot, *Why I Still Believe (Hint: It's the Only Way the World Makes Sense)* (Grand Rapids, MI: Baker Books), 2006.

14. Gary Scott Smith, ed., *God and Politics: Four Views on the Reformation of Civil Government* (Phillipsburg, NJ: Presbyterian and Reformed, 1989).

15. Greg L. Bahnsen, *Always Ready: Directions for Defending the Faith*, ed. Robert R. Booth (Nacogdoches, TX: Covenant Media Foundation, 2006).

16. Gary DeMar, "'The Brights': A Worldview with No Light of Their Own," *Biblical Worldview Magazine* 22:10 (October 2006), 4–6 and Gary DeMar, "The Invisible God Called 'Reason,'" *Biblical Worldview Magazine* 22:11 (November 2006), 4–6, 8.

17. Gary North, *Sanctions and Dominion: An Economic Commentary on Numbers* (Tyler, TX: Institute for Christian Economics, 1997), v.

18. Robert R. Booth, "Editor's Preface," *Always Ready*, x.

Dr. Bahnsen
"Pushing the Antithesis"

THE FOLLOWING IS an excerpt from "The Great Debate: Does God Exist?," a formal debate between Dr. Greg L. Bahnsen and Dr. Gordon S. Stein that was held at the University of California (Irvine) on February 11, 1985. Dr. Bahnsen begins the cross examination:

Dr. Bahnsen: "Are all factual questions answered in the same way?"

Dr. Stein: "No, they are not. They're answered by the use of certain methods, though, that are the same—reason, logic, presenting evidence, and facts."

Dr. Bahnsen: "All right. I heard you mention logical binds and logical self-contradictions in your speech. You did say that?"

Dr. Stein: "I said. I used that phrase, yes."

Dr. Bahnsen: "Do you believe there are laws of logic, then?"

Dr. Stein: "Absolutely."

Dr. Bahnsen: "Are they universal?"

Dr. Stein: "They're agreed upon by human beings. They aren't laws that exist out in nature. They're consensual."

Dr. Bahnsen: "Are they simply conventions, then?"

Dr. Stein: "They are conventions, but they are conventions that are self-verifying."

Dr. Bahnsen: "Are they sociological laws or laws of thought?"

Dr. Stein: "They are laws of thought which are interpreted by men and promulgated by men."

Dr. Bahnsen: "Are they material in nature?"

Dr. Stein: "How can a law be material in nature?"

Dr. Bahnsen: "That's a question I am going to ask you."

Dr. Stein: "I would say no."

Moderator: "Dr. Stein, you now have an opportunity to cross-examine Dr. Bahnsen."

Dr. Stein: "Dr. Bahnsen, would you call God material or immaterial?"

Dr. Bahnsen: "Immaterial."

Dr. Stein: "What is something that is immaterial?"

Dr. Bahnsen: "Something not extended in space."

Dr. Stein: "Can you give me an example of anything other than God that is immaterial?"

Dr. Bahnsen: "The laws of logic."

Moderator: "I am going to have to ask the audience to hold it down please. Please. Refrain from laughter and applause. Can you hold that down please?"

Introduction

Pushing the Antithesis is based on Dr. Greg L. Bahnsen's lecture series titled *Basic Training for Defending the Christian Faith*. The talks were given at American Vision's first "Life Preparation Conference" in 1991 held at the University of Alabama. High school and college students from around the United States converged on the UA campus for a week of intensive **worldview** study. They had the privilege of sitting under one of the most accomplished Christian apologists the Church has produced. The video tapes of the series sat untouched for more than 15 years until they were noticed sitting in a storage box at American Vision's offices. Considering the advances in technology, we did not have high hopes in the quality of the video production. To our surprise, the production quality was very good. A video series was produced and has enjoyed great success as people who have only read Dr. Bahnsen's books and listened to him on audio tapes and CDs have been introduced to the more personal side of a gifted teacher.

Pushing the Antithesis deals with **apologetics**, a word derived from the combination of two Greek words: *apo* ("back, from") and *logos* ("word"), meaning "to give a word back, to respond" in defense. We find this Greek word in several New Testament texts. When Paul was in the temple in Jerusalem (Acts 21:27), some Jews in Asia Minor aroused the city against him (21:30a). The crowd dragged him out of the temple in an attempt to kill him (21:31). The Roman soldiers intervened and arrested him, taking him into protective custody (21:32–33). He was soon allowed to address the Jews to present his defense (21:39–40). He opens with these words: "Brethren and fathers, hear my defense [Gk., *apologias*] which I now offer to you" (Acts 22:1).

In his first epistle, Peter instructs all Christians how they should conduct themselves. In chapter 3 he exhorts them to be faithful even when persecuted (1 Pet. 3:9-13). Rather than becoming fearful and withdrawing from the opposition or becoming angry and responding in kind, he urges them to: "sanctify Christ as Lord in your hearts, always being ready to make a defense [Gk., *apologian*] to everyone who asks you to give an account for the hope that is in you, yet with gentleness and reverence" (3:15). This becomes the key scriptural passage urging Christians to defend their faith.

In his important work on apologetics, Dr. Bahnsen quotes Cornelius Van Til's succinct and helpful definition of "apologetics": "Apologetics is the vindication of the Christian philosophy of life against the various forms of the non-Christian philosophy of life."[1] Biblical apologetics does not teach that we are apologizing, as if admitting moral wrong or mental error, when we defend the Christian faith.

In the video series, Dr. Bahnsen uses the American Standard Version of 1901. He favored this translation because of its literal approach to translation theory and practice. Since this particular translation is difficult to find today, the New American Standard Bible will be used. This conservative, evangelical translation that follows the original ASV in attempting to be as literal as possible. Of course, no translation is without bias.

You may find that some key words and technical terms may be unfamiliar, requiring definition. Any term being defined in this study guide will display as **bold** to set it off from the rest of the text. This will alert you to a definition that will appear either in the main text or in a footnote. A "Glossary of Terms and Phrases" has also been provided beginning on page 271. Learning the jargon of apologetics will increase your understanding of the method of apologetics itself. In fact, in his last chapter, Dr. Bahnsen will mention the importance of defining terms any time you are debating.

As you study each lecture, the same basic outline will be followed. Dr. Bahnsen's **Central Concerns** will be summarized and then fleshed out with additional detail. Concentrating on central issues is important to understanding and biblically warranted. Jesus directed the Pharisees to understand the central significance of Scripture when He urged them to focus on Him (John 5:39; cf. Luke 24:25–27). He rebuked them for highlighting minutiae and forgetting the central, weightier issues: "Woe to you, scribes and Pharisees, hypocrites! For you tithe mint and dill and cummin, and have neglected the weightier provisions of the law: justice and mercy and faithfulness; but these are the things you should have done without neglecting the others" (Matt. 23:23).

After this, **Exegetical Observations** will be provided on important biblical texts relevant to the study, driving home the biblical warrant for Dr. Bahnsen's instruction.[2] This is in keeping with Paul's commendation that we be diligent in "handling accurately the word of truth" (2 Tim. 2:15). Luke commends the Bereans, noting that they "were more noble-minded than those in Thessalonica, for they received the word with great eagerness, examining the Scriptures daily, to see whether these things were so" (Acts 17:11). This is important, for as Max Reich (1867–1945) once wrote, "the Christian who is careless in Bible reading will be careless in Christian living."

Then we will ask **Review Questions** to reinforce your memory of the material. God often calls us to remember things (e.g., Ps. 105:5; Eccl. 12:1; Isa. 46:8). He even memorializes certain redemptive issues by providing "review lessons" through ceremonial rituals (e.g., Ex. 12:14; 1 Cor. 11:23–25). Review enhances memory.

Following this we will offer **Practical Applications** of the material to enhance your educational experience as a Christian. Your Christian commitment requires both understanding and doing (James 1:22; Matt. 7:24–27; Luke 6:46–49). This course work will stick with you better if you actively work through the lessons and their application assignments.

Finally, we will provide a **Recommended Reading** list to supplement your study of the issues. As a Christian, you should be eager to gain greater knowledge of the issues through research. The Lord encourages searching out things, when he teaches you: "Ask, and it shall be given to you; seek, and you shall find; knock, and it shall be opened to you" (Matt. 7:7).

"Come, then, let us reason together" (Isa. 1:18).

Notes

1. Greg L. Bahnsen, *Van Til's Apologetic: Readings and Analysis* (Phillipsburg, NJ: Presbyterian and Reformed, 1998), 34.

2. "Exegesis" is based on two Greek words: *ex*, which means "out of" (we derive our English word "exit" from it) and *ago*, which means "to go." That is, "exegesis" is that which "goes out from" the text. It is the meaning rooted in the text which is carefully drawn out of it (not read into it) through proper interpretive procedures.

1

The Myth of Neutrality

*He who is not with Me is against me; and he who
does not gather with Me scatters.*

(Matt. 12:30)

1. Central Concerns

YOU ARE A Christian. You believe in Jesus Christ as your Lord
and Savior. You worship Him in all that you do. You seek
to obey His Word. You want to honor Him in all that you do.
And as a child of God you want others to believe in Christ and
serve God. You want to know *how* to challenge others who do
not believe in Jesus Christ and Lord and Savior to submit their
lives to Him also.

The main question to consider is how you can best witness
for the Lord. America was founded as a Christian nation,[1] and
most people today claim to be Christians. There are churches
on almost every corner, and many of the people you person-

---

[1]Gary DeMar, *America's Christian History* (Powder Springs, GA: American Vision, 1995); Gary DeMar, *America's Christian Heritage* (Nashville:
Broadman and Holman, 2003); David J. Brewer, *The United States: A Christian Nation* (Powder Springs, GA: American Vision, [1905] 1996); Charles B.
Galloway, *Christianity and the American Commonwealth: The Influence of
Christianity in Making This Nation* (Powder Springs, GA: American Vision,
[1898] 2005).

ally know probably claim to be Christians.[2] Yet you know that many more people do not believe God exists. How can you reach such people? How should you reason with them? What method must you follow to show them that God exists? This is what this book is about.

Setting up the Issue

It is important to understand that the *proper manner*, the *right method*, and the *correct procedures* for proving God's existence to skeptics, doubters, and unbelievers are essential to the defense of the Christian faith. Not just any old method will do.

We must first consider a critical question: Should you be *neutral* regarding your Christian commitment while arguing for the existence of God to an unbeliever? Many Christians attempt to reach either the atheist or the agnostic[3] by saying something to this effect: "I will set aside my belief in God so that I can prove to you that He exists. I will not depend upon my faith, so that I can show you that God's existence is reasonable and not just my personal bias." These "neutral" apologists will also maintain: "I believe that there are good, independent, unbiased reasons that can lead you to the conclusion that God exists." Unfortunately, this "neutral" approach is neither biblical nor effective. Christians must be committed to *biblically-warranted* procedures for defending the faith. The biblical defense is not only different from the attempted neutrality approach, but it is the *exact opposite*. That's a pretty big difference! Christians must

---

[2]According to recent Gallup polls, about 82% of Americans claim to be Christians. http://speakingoffaith.publicradio.org/programs/godsofbusiness/galluppoll.shtml

[3]An **atheist** denies the existence of God. The word "atheist" is derived from two Greek words: *a* means "no," and *theos* means "god." An "agnostic" is one who *doubts* the existence of God; or rather, he holds that any god who may exist is unknowable. The word "agnostic" is from the Greek *a*, which means "no" and *gnostos* which means "known," that is, God can't be known or we don't have enough knowledge

not set aside their faith commitment *even temporarily* in an attempt to approach the unbeliever on "neutral ground."

Because Jesus Christ is the solid foundation of every believer, Christians must reject the "myth of neutrality" and affirm that God alone is the *starting point* in their reasoning. Unbelievers, of course, will protest this rejection of neutrality with responses like the following:

- "That's not fair! How can you assume what you are supposed to prove?"
- "You're prejudicial! You can't take Christianity for granted!"
- "Since we have conflicting viewpoints as to whether or not God exists, both of us must approach the matter from a position of neutrality."
- "You must employ standards that are common to all men, not standards generated out of your Christian convictions."

The unbeliever will challenge you to build your case for God on *neutral* ground, without building on your foundation in God. Be warned! If you don't start with God as your basic assumption, *you can't prove anything.* The assumption of God's existence is essential to *all* reasoning.

Documenting the Evidence

The neutrality principle is the alleged operating assumption in *all* unbelieving argumentation, just as it is unfortunately in most evangelical apologetic systems. You must recognize this nearly universal practice in modern thought. Neutrality and its twin, doubt, have long been unchallenged principles in the modern world's conflict with Christianity. This has been true especially since the **Enlightenment.**[4] Note the following calls to neutrality and doubt:

---

[4] According to the *Merriam Webster's Collegiate Encyclopedia*: The **Enlightenment** was the "European intellectual movement of the seventeenth and eighteenth centuries in which ideas concerning God, reason, nature, and man were blended

- David Hume (1711–1776): "Nothing can be more unphilo-sophical than to be positive or dogmatical on any subject."
- William Hazlitt (1778–1830): "The great difficulty in philoso-phy is to come to every question with a mind fresh and un-shackled by former theories."
- C. C. Colton (1780–1832): "Doubt is the vestibule which *all* must pass before they can enter into the temple of wisdom."
- William H. Seward (1801–1872): "The circumstances of the world are so variable, that an irrevocable purpose or opinion is almost synonymous with a foolish one."
- Oliver Wendell Holmes (1841–1935): "To have doubted one's own first principles is the mark of a civilized man."
- Alfred North Whitehead (1861–1947): "In philosophical dis-cussion, the merest hint of dogmatic certainty as to finality of statement is an exhibition of folly."
- Bertrand Russell (1872–1970): "In all affairs it's a healthy thing now and then to hang a question mark on the things you have long taken for granted."
- Wilson Mizner (1876–1933): "I respect faith, but doubt is what gets you an education."
- Alan Bloom (1930–1992): "The most important function of the university in an age of reason is to protect reason from itself, by being the model of truly openness."

The modern mindset claims neutrality as its general operating as-sumption, and two influential applications of contemporary thought evidence this: evolution and deconstructionism.

---

into a worldview that inspired revolutionary developments in art, philosophy, and politics. Central to Enlightenment thought were the use and celebration of reason. For Enlightenment thinkers, *received authority*, whether in science or religion, was to be *subject to the investigation of unfettered minds*." Emphasis added.

Evolution

The world's hostility to certainty and absolutes as required in the Christian system has become increasingly apparent, especially in the foundational and all-controlling commitment which dominates all of modern Western thought and culture: evolution.

Modern science teaches that man is not the apex of creation, but the ex-ape of evolution. Evolutionary theory is taken for granted *throughout* the college curriculum, just as it is in all aspects of modern thought and experience. Evolution not only influences biological and earth sciences as is to be expected, but also psychology, anthropology, sociology, politics, economics, the media, the arts, medicine, and all other academic disciplines as well.

By the very nature of the case, evolutionary theory resists stability and certainty, which are demanded in the biblical outlook. Instead, it necessitates relentless, random development over time leading to fundamental and wholesale changes in systems. Oliver Wendell Holmes, former Chief Justice of the U. S. Supreme Court (1899–1902), expressed well the modern evolutionary commitment when he asserted, "Nothing is certain but change." As is so often the case, this even harkens back to antiquity. The Greek philosopher Heraclitus (540–480 B. C.) declared something nearly identical when he stated the following more than 2,500 years ago: "Nothing endures but change."

Deconstructionism

One influential contemporary application of evolutionary thinking is called **deconstructionism**. This complicated new philosophy has not been widely known outside of scholarly circles, but it is strongly influencing intellectuals in various fields of study, and it is having an impact in the college classroom. Deconstructionism first appeared as a theory for interpreting literature in 1973 in the writings of the French philosopher, Jacques Derrida (1930–2004). His approach to literary criticism gave rise in America to what is called the Yale School of Deconstruction. But what is "deconstructionism"?

Deconstructionism is a principle of modern language analysis which asserts that language refers only to itself rather than to an external reality. It challenges any claims to ultimate truth and obligation by attacking theories of knowledge and ultimate values. This philosophy attempts to "deconstruct" texts to remove all biases and traditional assumptions. Deconstructionists argue, therefore, that no written text communicates any set meaning or conveys any reliable or coherent message. Written texts are always subject to differing interpretations which are affected by one's culture, biases, language imprecision, and so forth and will always falsify the world due to these and other factors. Consequently, *all* communication is *necessarily* subject to differing, conflicting, and changing interpretations, all of which are irreconcilable. This critical approach is a form of **relativism**[5] or **nihilism**.[6] It has spilled over the academic borders of literary analysis to become a broader principle in much modern philosophy and social criticism.

Deconstructionism directly confronts the Christian commitment to Scripture.[7] We believe the Bible is the unchanging, authoritative, truthful Word of God. For instance, the psalmist confidently declares: "The words of the Lord are pure words; as silver tried in a furnace on the earth, refined seven times" (Ps. 12:6). Christ teaches

---

[5]**Relativism** teaches that knowledge, truth, and morality are not absolute. Rather, they vary from culture to culture and even from person to person. This is due to the limited state of the mind and that there can be no absolutes to give a set meaning or value to any human thought or action.

[6]**Nihilism** teaches that the world and man are wholly without meaning or purpose. The world and man are so absolutely senseless and useless that there is no comprehensible truth. The word "nihilism" is derived from the Latin *nihil*, which means "nothing."

[7]See the following articles in *Journal of the Evangelical Theological Society* 48:1 (March 2005): Andreas J. Köstenberger, "'What is Truth?' Pilate's Question in Its Johannine and Larger Biblical Context"; R. Albert Mohler, "What is Truth?: Truth and Contemporary Culture"; "Truth, Contemporary Philosophy, and the Postmodern Turn"; Kevin J. Vanhoozer, "Lost in Interpretation? Truth, Scripture, and Hermeneutics."

that "the Scriptures cannot be broken" (John 10:35b). Paul informs us that rather than being unreliable and lacking any coherent message, "all Scripture is inspired by God and *profitable* for *teaching*, for *reproof*, for *correction*, for *training* in righteousness; that the man of God *may be adequate, equipped* for every good work" (2 Tim. 3:16–17).

But the overt teaching of these two unbelieving systems is not the only problem confronting the Christian student. There are others you must prepare for.

Hidden Opposition

Even when a college professor or media spokesperson is not *directly* attacking Christianity's truth claims, he is, nevertheless, *indirectly* warring against them *in principle*. Throughout our secularized culture— especially in the university—anti-Christian principles are taken for granted. Many issues might appear to be wholly unrelated to Christian concerns and seem unopposed to Christian truth claims. Yet because of their hidden nature they often can be the most alluring to the Christian and the most injurious to true faith. They represent powerful erosive forces quietly seeping into the mind of the believer. They gradually wash away the very foundations for the Christian life and commitment to God and His Word. Like an undetected cancer they eat away at the believer's faith by importing unbelieving assumptions into his thinking. *The Christian Post* reports the following:

> Focus on the Family's Teen Apologetics Director Alex Mc-
> Farland has been involved in youth ministry for the last 16
> years. He says students are generally ill-equipped to fend for
> their Christian faith because they lack a good understand-
> ing of the facts behind Christianity—scientific, historical, or
> logical.

According to McFarland, "Teens have a sincere child-like faith but have not been exposed to good apologetics," which he says is "so necessary to being able to defend their faith."

He warns parents, "I have counseled with many a distraught, even heartbroken, family, who spent 18 years raising a child in the ways of God only to have that faith demolished through four years at a secular university."

Studies have shown that when students lack good defenses, their faith erodes. And two-thirds will forsake Christianity by their senior year of college. On the other hand, solid faith helps students in all aspects of life.[8]

What a student does not know *will* hurt him. Here are three examples:

1. Selective considerations. Even when a college professor does not *directly* criticize the Christian faith, he quietly challenges foundational Christian assumptions. Modern education is effectively **subliminal**[9] advertising for atheism. The professor decides which options are serious, which questions are worthwhile, what evidence should be put before his class. He selects the reading assignments according to his own outlook which locks out Christian principles. The Christian student eventually becomes adapted to that process and begins leaving large fields of study detached from his faith beliefs. This is a subtle form of secularization.

2. Neutral tolerance. The university and the media supposedly encourage neutrality by urging tolerance of all views. The call to tol-

---

[8]"What Parents Can Do When College Students Lose Faith," *The Christian Post* (December 18, 2005): www.christianpost.com/article/ministries/1660/section/what.parents.can.do.when.college.students.lose.faith/1.htm

[9]**Subliminal** derives from two Latin words: *sub* ("below") and *limmen* ("threshold"). It speaks of that which is below the threshold of consciousness, that which is just out of conscious perception. Advertisers have discovered that people unconsciously pick up on and are influenced by flashes of information just below the normal limits of perception. It is claimed that some advertisers have quickly flashed images of their product on a movie screen to unconsciously suggest to the viewer an urge to buy the product.

eration is simply the application of the neutrality principle to moral issues. But we are all aware that the Christian view is seldom given equal tolerance. In fact, the call to tolerance is even self-contradictory in the non-believing system. It is intolerant of views that do not tolerate such things as homosexual conduct or feminism or abortion, for instance. As Tom Beaudoin, assistant professor of religious studies at Santa Clara University, put it: "**Generation X**[10] is not tolerant of an intolerant God."

3. *Censorship claims.* Libraries claim to resist censorship in the name of neutrality. But some form of censorship is always at work in building a library's book collection. By necessity the library must select some books over others—unless that library contains all books ever written in the whole world. Consequently, some set of principles *will* apply to book selection. Neutrality is a false illusion in libraries.

Demonstrating the Problem

Many knowledgeable Christians fall prey to the neutrality myth: "teachers, researchers, and writers are often led to think that honesty demands for them to put aside all distinctly Christian commitments when they study in an area which is not directly related to matters of Sunday worship."[11] This practice must be avoided. Cornelius Van Til[12] always challenged the unbeliever at the very foundations of his

---

[10]**Generation X** consists of those whose teen years were touched by the 1980s, i.e. those born in the 1960s and 1970s. The term was popularized by Douglas Coupland's novel *Generation X: Tales for an Accelerated Culture*. In Coupland's usage, the X referred to the difficulty in defining a generation whose only unifying belief was the rejection of the beliefs of their Baby Boomer parents. Although not the first group of Americans to grow up with television, Gen Xers were the first group that never knew life without one.

[11]Greg L. Bahnsen, *Always Ready: Directions for Defending the Faith* (Nacogdoches, TX: Covenant Media Publications, 1996), 3.

[12]Cornelius Van Til (1895–1987) wrote on apologetics, philosophy, ethics, and theology. For a complete bibliography, see Greg L. Bahnsen, *Van Til's Apologetic: Reading and Analysis* (Phillipsburg, NJ: Presbyterian and Reformed, 1998), 735–740.

thought. In a philosophical debate, believers *must* begin with biblical commitments.

As Christians we must understand the fundamental importance, wide-ranging implications, and destructive character of the claim to neutrality. We must do so if we are to engage a truly biblical apologetic in a manner that is faithful to God and his revelation in Scripture. Too many apologetic programs require that we suspend our faith commitment in order to allow for a neutral "meeting of the minds" with the unbeliever. This suspending of faith might truly be called a "suspension bridge" to the world of unbelief. Unfortunately, this "bridge" will get you into the world of unbelief, but will not bring you back.

You must not set aside your faith in God when you consider *anything*—even the proof of the existence of God. Such "neutralist thinking would erase the Christian's distinctiveness, blur the **antithesis**[13] between worldly and believing mind-sets, and ignore the gulf between the 'old man' [our inborn, fallen, sinful nature] and the 'new man' [our new birth-generated redeemed nature]. The Christian who strives for neutrality unwittingly endorses assumptions which are hostile to his faith."[14]

Simply put, you cannot adopt a position of neutrality toward God if you are to remain faithful to Christ. Our Lord never encourages or even allows suspending your faith in order to do anything. Those Christians who attempt neutrality in apologetics actually build their apologetic house on "sinking sand." Christ, however, teaches that "everyone who hears *these words of Mine*, and *acts upon them*, may be compared to a wise man, who built his house upon the rock." He

---

[13]**Antithesis** is based on two Greek words: *anti* ("against") and *tithenai* ("to set or place"). "Antithesis" speaks of opposition or a counter point. As Christians we must recognize the fundamental disagreement between biblical thought and all forms of unbelief at the foundational level of our theory of knowing and knowledge. See Chapter 6 for a discussion of the biblical notion of antithesis.

[14]Bahnsen, *Always Ready*, 23.

goes on to warn that "everyone who hears these words of Mine, and does not act upon them, will be like a foolish man, who built his house upon the sand" (Matt. 7:24, 26). A wise apologetic method recognizes its Christian foundations and implements them.

Why must you not attempt neutrality in apologetics? The answer is: Because of man's fall into sin, the world is inherently hostile to the Christian faith. From the time of the fall, enmity is the controlling principle separating the believer and unbeliever (Gen. 3:15; John 15:19; Rom. 5:10; James 4:4).

The Christian message is not congenial to the unbeliever, for it confronts him as a guilty sinner who is at war with his righteous Creator and Judge. The Apostle Paul even goes so far as to declare:

> The wrath of God is revealed from heaven against all ungodliness and unrighteousness of men, who *suppress the truth in unrighteousness*, because that which is known about God is evident within them; for God made it evident to them. For since the creation of the world His invisible attributes, His eternal power and divine nature, have been clearly seen, being understood through what has been made, so that *they are without excuse*. For even though they knew God, they did not honor Him as God, or give thanks; but they became *futile in their speculations*, and their *foolish heart was darkened* (Rom. 1:18–21).

This certainly does not sound as if Paul would endorse the neutrality principle in dealing with unbelievers. He teaches that men are *not* neutral, but are actively *hostile* to God Whom they know deep down in their hearts.

To make matters worse for the neutralist approach, Christianity's founding document, the Bible, claims infallible and obligatory authority which *demands* commitment to its truth claims and obedience to its moral directives: "The conclusion, when all has been heard, is: *fear God* and *keep His commandments*, because this applies to every person. For God will bring every act to judgment, everything which is hidden, whether it is good or evil" (Eccl. 12:13–14). This absolute demand to fear the true and living God and to obey His obligatory law-word grates on the sinner's central ambition. His sinful desire is "to be as God" determining good and evil for himself, without submitting to God's command (Gen. 3:5; Rom. 8:7). Indeed, "whatever is not from faith is sin" (Rom. 14:23) for "without faith it is impossible to please Him" (Heb. 11:6).

Sinners seek to escape the *dogmatic truth claims* and *obligatory moral directives* of Scripture by resorting to (an alleged) neutrality in thought. Such neutrality actually amounts to *skepticism* regarding the existence of God and the authority of His Word. Unbelievers complain that "nobody knows for sure, therefore the Bible cannot be what it claims to be." Interestingly, the biblical narrative explains the fall of man as arising out of the neutrality principle which encourages doubt about God's absolute authority. You must remember that God clearly commanded Adam and Eve *not* to eat of the tree of the knowledge of good and evil (Gen. 2:16–17; 3:3). Satan, however, came to them with the temptation to doubt God by assuming a position of neutrality regarding God's command: "Yea, has God said?" (Gen. 3:1b).

Satan tempted Eve to approach the question of eating from the forbidden tree in a neutral, unbiased fashion. He suggested that she must remain neutral in order to decide who was right, God or Satan. She did not accept God's word as authoritative and conclusive, but as a true neutralist, determined for herself which option to take (Gen. 3:4–6). Such "neutrality" is dangerous, for as Robert South (1634–1716) expressed it: "He who would fight the devil with his own weapons, must not wonder if he finds himself overmatched."

Paul relates this historical temptation of Eve to our spiritual failures in our devotion to Christ: "I am afraid, lest as the serpent deceived Eve by his craftiness, your minds should be led astray from the simplicity and purity of devotion to Christ" (2 Cor. 11:3). Elsewhere he writes of Eve's attempted neutrality as a failure brought about by Satanic "deception" (1 Tim. 2:14). As Edwin Hubbel Chapin (1814–1880) stated, "Neutral men are the devil's allies." You must remember that the devil presents himself as an "angel of light" (2 Cor. 11:14).

You *must not* build your defense of the faith on the principle that led to the fall of mankind. That approach not only failed, but it brought sin, death, destruction, and despair into the world.

> As Van Til labored to teach throughout his career . . . , *there simply is no presupposition-free and neutral way to approach reasoning*, especially reasoning about the fundamental and philosophically momentous issues of God's existence and revelation. To formulate proofs for God that assume otherwise is not only foolish and futile, from a philosophical perspective, but also unfaithful to the Lord. Reasoning is a God-given gift to man, but it does not grant to him any independent authority. The Christian concept of God takes Him to be the highest and absolute authority, even over man's reasoning: such a God *could not* be proved to exist by some other standard as the highest authority in one's reasoning. That would be to assume the contrary of what you are seeking to prove.[15]

> * * * *

> We live in a culture which has for so long been saturated with the claims of intellectual autonomy and the demand for neutrality in scholarship that this ungodly perspective [of neutrality] has been ingrained in us: like the "music of the spheres," it is so constant and we are so accustomed to it that we fail to discern it. It is common fare, and we simply expect it.[16]

---

[15]Bahnsen, *Van Til's Apologetic*, 614.
[16]Bahnsen, *Always Ready*, 31.

So then, the key point is this: Christian apologetics must not and cannot be neutral. To operate from a position of neutrality is to have surrendered the Christian faith in advance, before any argumentation takes place. We must avoid *the myth of neutrality*, not adopt it.

A busy academic and social schedule in college can easily pull the Christian away from God's Word. But remember: The Bible calls all believers to the apologetic task. You cannot defend God and his Word if you are not sanctified (set apart) for Him by means of contact with His Word. Too many Christian students drift away from the faith in college because they have not been prepared for the spiritual and apologetical battles they will face. Dr. Gary North once wrote an article advertising a Christian college. The article showed a dejected father who had sent his son off to a secular college. It stated: "I spent $40,000 to send my son to hell."

Learning to count is not as important as knowing what counts. Christians must keep themselves before the Lord in Scripture reading and prayer. Unfortunately, as Charles Colson observes: "Our educational establishment seeks to instill a passion for intellectual curiosity and openness, but allows for the existence of no truth worth pursuing."[17] While in college, Christians should not be passive sponges merely absorbing the material, but instead be active filters sorting out the issues through a biblical grid.

It is essential to think biblically, to reason as Christians in a "principial" (i.e., principle-based) fashion, to think God's thoughts after Him, rather than setting aside God's thoughts as called for with the neutrality principle. God's Word should be foundational in all thinking and living, for we have been "bought with a price" (1 Cor. 6:20; 7:23) and are "a people for God's own possession" (1 Pet. 2:9).

Seek to discern the professor's underlying motives and principles. Biblical apologetics is designed to teach Christians to think *as*

---

[17]Charles Colson, *Against the Night: Living in the New Dark Agaes* (Ann Arbor, MI: Vine Books, 1989), 85

Christians, not as neutral observers. No area of life is neutral; even your intellectual life must be surrendered to Christ's authority. A truly biblical apologetic representing the sovereign Creator of all things requires the surrender of all authority to Christ from the very starting point. First Corinthians 10:31 states that *even whether we eat or drink* we must do so to God's glory (cf. Col. 3:17; 1 Pet. 4:11).

Furthermore, the Bible teaches that *every* Christian should be able to deal with *every* problem at *any* time. God *expects* you to deal with any form of opposition to the Christian faith. The New Testament writers challenge their original audiences—and *you*—to be defenders of the faith. In the verse that serves as the cornerstone of Christian apologetics, Peter commands: "Sanctify Christ as Lord in your hearts, always being ready to make a defense to everyone who asks you to give an account for the hope that is in you" (1 Pet. 3:15; see also Jude 3). Note that Christians-as-such (not just the philosophically-minded among us!) are commanded "always" to answer "every man." Sadly, few evangelical students learn this in their home churches. The believer must learn apologetics for his or her own spiritual well-being, as well as for becoming an agent of reform for the untrained Christian.

All of this is effectively portrayed for us in Deuteronomy 6: "You shall teach [God's statutes] diligently to your sons and shall talk of them when you sit in your house and when you walk by the way and when you lie down and when you rise up. And you shall bind them as a sign on your hand and they shall be as frontals on your forehead. And you shall write them on the doorposts of your house and on your gates" (Deut. 6:7–9). This speaks of God's law-word guiding our daily labors (governing our "hand"), our thought processes (governing our "head"), and our mundane living for Him in lying down, rising up, sitting, and walking.

2. Exegetical Observations

Look at the following important biblical passages impacting our apologetic method. Hopefully this study will enhance our understanding of these texts of Scripture, underscoring the biblical apologetic method and a few additional exegetical observations. The Christian apologist must know God's Word to function properly.

Mark 12:30

Mark 12:30 reads, "you shall love the Lord your God with all your heart, and with all your soul, and with all your mind, and with all your strength." This statement is taken from Deuteronomy 6:5 immediately after Moses declares that "the Lord is one" (Deut. 6:5). Israel is reminded that only one God exists, in contrast to the numerous competing "gods" in the ancient pagan world surrounding her.[18] Since there is one God (who created and controls all things), there is one truth system, rather than competing systems of explanation. The ancient world had a god for the
sun, for fertility, for this and for that. Consequently, their worldview was fragmented and their knowledge lacked coherence.[19]

We should note that Christ emphasizes His call to love God in all things. He does not simply say: "You shall love the Lord your God with all your heart, soul, mind, and strength." Rather, He emphasizes the totality of your love for God by repeating "all" before each noun: "You shall love the Lord your God with *all* your heart, and with *all* your soul, and with *all your mind,* and with *all* your strength." This repetitious emphasis strengthens His call to lovingly obey God in *all* things. Of course, our special concern in apologet-

---

[18]For instance, God's ten plagues on Egypt were directed at Egypt's so-called gods (Ex. 12:12; 18:11; cf. Num. 33:4).

[19]Francis A. Schaeffer, *How Should We Then Live? The Rise and Decline of Western Thought and Culture* (Old Tappan, NJ: Revell, 1967).

ics is on the call to love God with "all your *mind.*" Non-neutrality is inherent in this charge by Christ.

1 Peter 3:15

We find the classic apologetics text in 1 Peter 3:15: "Sanctify Christ as Lord in your hearts, always being ready to make a defense to everyone who asks you to give an account for the hope that is in you, yet with gentleness and reverence." This text is clearly opposed to the neutrality principle.

Notice that Peter commands that you "sanctify Christ as Lord in your hearts" in order to defend the faith. To "sanctify" means to "set apart, to separate, to distinguish." A truly biblical apologetic does not *set aside* Christ *from* our hearts, but *sets apart* Christ *in* our hearts. In fact, it sets aside Christ *as Lord* or master. As Paul put it, Christ must "come to have first place in *everything*" (Col. 1:18). Your starting point in reasoning with the unbeliever must be Christ.

You must not miss Peter's specific point: He is calling on you to set apart Christ *in the very process of defending the faith.* His main point is to call you to "make a defense" and "to give an account" of your hope in Christ. Apologetics is not a side issue here; it is the central point. Again, he makes the point by urging that you set apart Christ in your hearts—in your inner-most being.

These are only two samples from God's Word; there are many more to study. But the fact is, the Bible presents a theological outlook and practical worldview which clearly deny that neutrality exists in fallen man and his thinking. The Bible demands that Christians recognize that neutrality is a myth and resist it.

3. Questions Raised

Attempt to answer the following questions on your own before looking at the text or consulting the **Answer Key**.

1. What is "apologetics"? Define the term and explain the derivation of the word "apologetics."

2. What is the central point of the first chapter?

3. How is the very principle of evolutionism (even apart from the scientific/biological statement of evolutionary theory) opposed to the Christian faith?

4. What is "deconstructionism"? Where did this philosophy first arise? How does it conflict with basic principles of the Christian faith?

5. List some passages of Scripture that assert the certainty and authority of God's Word.

6. How does the unbelieving college professor's worldview subtly confront your faith, even when the professor is not directly mentioning Christianity per se?

7. What is the meaning of the "myth of neutrality"?

8. What statements by Christ discount the possibility of neutrality?

9. Where in Scripture do you first see neutrality regarding God and His Word attempted?

10. Is the attempt at neutrality simply a methodological issue, or is it a moral one as well? Explain.

4. Practical Application

Now what are some practical things you can do to re-enforce what you have learned? How can you promote this apologetic method among Christian friends?

1. Frequently remind yourself of the nature of spiritual warfare. In order to prepare yourself for your college classes, at the beginning of each semester you should re-read the biblical passages that demonstrate the active antagonism of the unbelieving world against your Christian faith. You must not forget the nature of the unbeliever's challenge to your holistic faith.

2. Develop a devotional life that reinforces your call to apologetics. Make a list of the biblical passages used in this study and read them for your devotions.

3. Diligently seek to evaluate every thing you are being taught from a principled Christian perspective. After classes each day, jot down comments on the contradictions to the Christian faith which you encountered. Keep them in a notebook. Writing things down is the best secret to a good memory. Reflect on biblical answers to these supposed contradictions.

4. Develop small Bible study and accountability groups with other Christian students on campus. A part of defending the faith involves promoting its defense even among believers. As a Christian in fellowship with other Christians, you should urge fellow believers to realize their spiritual obligation to defend the faith before an unbelieving world.

5. Seek out any Christian campus ministries that are strongly committed to the Bible and are developing the Christian life. Attend their meetings and involve yourself in their ministries.

6. Find a good church in the area of your college. Commit yourself to attend church regularly. As Christians, we must not be "forsaking our own assembling together, as is the habit of some, but encouraging one another" (Heb. 10:25).

7. Where possible use class assignments to present the Christian perspective on issues. We would recommend that you avoid narrow testimonial types of papers. You should rather discretely develop worldview oriented themes that work basic Christian principles into the picture. In-your-face testimonials might be an affront to your professor and may appear to be a challenge to him. But working out your biblical principles might alert him to the philosophical implications of Christianity and will certainly help you flesh out your own understanding. You must be about "making the most of your time" while in college (Eph. 5:16).

While you are enrolled in college you are in a full-time, formal educational environment. You are seeking, therefore, to be educated. Dr. Van Til teaches that if education is to be practical it must mold the developing mind of the student so that he is put in the best possible relationship to his environment. Then he explains that man's ultimate environment is God Himself, because "in Him we live and move and exist" (Acts 17:28; cf. Job 12:10; Ps. 139:7–17; Dan. 5:23). You certainly will not find your professors assigning papers that encourage your Christian faith. But you must seek the opportunities—when they are allowed.

8. As a well-rounded Christian seeking to glorify Christ, you must approach your academic studies in a mature and diligent fashion. You are both paying hard-earned money for a college education and spending your God-given time in college; make the most of your investment. Do not cut corners in your studies or simply try to "get by." Christ calls you to excellence. Some students are naturally lazy, others suffer from voluntary inertia. Do not allow your educational experience to inadvertently teach you to be intellectually lazy. Such laziness is disloyalty to Christ.

Most colleges are liberal arts colleges that are supposed to give you a well-rounded education—even when you are obligated to take a required course that you do not particularly enjoy. As G. K. Chesterton (1874–1936) mused: "Education is the period during which you are being instructed by somebody you do not know, about something you do not want to know." Remember also that it will affect your overall grade point average and therefore impact your witness as a Christian student. Besides, you will discover, to your surprise later on, that the knowledge you gained even in that course will prove useful.

The following anonymous comments should cause you to smile at their uncovering of foolishness; they should not summarize your approach to education:

- "College is a fountain of knowledge where some students come to drink, some to sip, but most come just to gargle."
- "All college students pursue their studies, but some are further behind than others."
- "Some students take up the arts in college, some take up the sciences, while others just take up space."

5. Recommended Reading

To enhance your understanding of the antagonism of the unbelieving mind and the dangers of neutrality, we recommend the following additional reading.

Bahnsen, Greg L., *Always Ready: Directions for Defending the Faith* (Nacogdoches, Tex.: Covenant Media Foundation, 1996), chapters 1–2.

DeMar, Gary, *Thinking Straight in a Crooked World: A Christian Defense Manual* (Powder Springs, GA: American Vision, 2001)

Gentry, Kenneth L., Jr., *Defending the Faith: An Introduction to Biblical Apologetics*, 3rd ed. (Fountain Inn, SC: KennethGentry.Com, 2001)

Newport, Frank, "A Look at Americans and Religion Today": (http://speakingoffaith.publicradio`.org/programs/godsofbusiness/galluppoll.shtm.

Pratt, Richard L., Jr., *Every Thought Captive* (Phillipsburg, NJ: Presbyterian and Reformed, 1979), chapters 1, 2, 4, 6.

Van Til, Cornelius, "Why I Believe in God": (www.reformed.org/apologetics/index.html?mainframe=http://www.reformed.org/apologetics/why_I_believe_cvt.html

Destroying Philosophical Fortresses

The weapons of our warfare are not of the flesh, but divinely powerful for the destruction of fortresses. We are destroying speculations and every lofty thing raised up against the knowledge of God, and we are taking every thought captive to the obedience of Christ.
(2 Cor. 10:4–5)

1. Central Concerns

THERE ARE TWO important truths which impact our apologetic method when dealing with the problem of (alleged) neutrality. One matter is factual, the other is moral: (1) Factually, we must recognize that the unbeliever is *not* neutral. To overlook this is to approach the unbeliever from a starting point that actually acknowledges his skeptical worldview while neutralizing the biblical worldview. (2) Morally, we must understand that the believer *should not* be neutral. If we do not realize this we will engage the defense of the faith in a non-faithful way.

The Unbeliever Is Not Neutral

Despite their loud and frequent claims to the contrary, unbelievers do not practice neutrality in approaching the question of God's existence. In fact, they do not approach any issue neutrally. Any claim to neutrality is a pretense, and it is philosophically impossible.

As a Christian you believe God's Word is true. You also have a Savior who prays for your sanctification (your being set apart for God and His service) by means of God's Word. He declares that God's sanctifying Word is absolute truth: "Sanctify them in the truth; Thy word is truth." And that very Word of God deals directly with the matter of neutrality in the unbeliever's outlook.

The Unbelieving Mind is Hostile toward God

The Bible points out that the unbeliever is *not* neutral towards the question of God. But it goes further, declaring that he is actually *hostile* toward it:

> This I say therefore, and affirm together with the Lord, that you walk no longer just as the Gentiles also walk, in the futility of their mind, being darkened in their understanding, excluded from the life of God, because of the ignorance that is in them, because of the hardness of their heart. (Eph. 4:17–18)

Observe that Paul does *not* speak of the unbeliever's mind or heart as neutral. To the contrary, he declares the absolute "futility" of the unbelieving mind. The non-Christian's mind is actually "darkened," not dim. It is even "excluded" from God, not "on the fence" regarding God. This is because of his "ignorance," not confusion. His heart is "hardened" against God, not indifferent toward Him. These observations are just what you should expect in light of the fall of man into sin (Gen. 3:1–7; Rom. 3:10ff; 5:12ff) and God's curse in Genesis 3:15.

Rather than allowing the believer to adopt the unbeliever's mind (which is characterized in Eph. 4:17–18), Paul states that the believer has *not* so "learned Christ" (Eph. 4:30). That is, you as a believer did not come to a sure knowledge of Christ through fallen thought processes. Such a method, then, is inappropriate for apologetics. Because of this, Paul calls upon you to *put away* the former ways by renewing your mind:

> In reference to your former manner of life, you lay aside the
> old self, which is being corrupted in accordance with the
> lusts of deceit, and that you be renewed in the spirit of your
> mind, and put on the new self, which in the likeness of God
> has been created in righteousness and holiness of the truth.
> (Eph. 4:22–24)

Ephesians 4:17 teaches that you are either set aside for God or alienated from Him. No third option exists, no middle ground— men simply are *not* "neutral." Men will either follow the world or the Word. They either have the mind of Christ (1 Cor. 2:16; cf. Eph. 4:23–24) or a mind of futility (Eph 4:17). His thoughts are either "captive" to Christ (2 Cor. 10:5) or are "hostile" to Him (Col. 1:21). Note that some of Paul's images of the two minds imply warfare: The Christian's mind is "captive"[1] to God, whereas the unbeliever remains "hostile"[2] to him. Here we see the enmity of Genesis 3:15 separating the unbelieving mind from the believing.

Simply put: the mind is not neutral. As Jesus said, "No one can serve two masters; for either he will hate the one and love the other, or he will hold to one and despise the other" (Matt. 6:24), and "He who is not with Me is against Me" (Matt. 12:30).

Paul presents the same problem in Romans 1. This is not a stray thought in his understanding of man's condition. Notice his forceful depiction of the fallen mind as hostile to God and actively working to suppress the truth within:

---

[1] The Greek word is *aichmalotizo*, which is a part of a word group often used of war captives (see Luke 21:24; Eph. 4:8; Rev. 13:10). In fact, Paul speaks of the "weapons" of our "warfare" and the "destruction" of "fortresses."

[2] The word "hostile" is a translation of the Greek *echthros*, which is often translated "enemy," see Luke 1:74; 10:19; 1 Corinthians 15:25–26.

> For the wrath of God is revealed from heaven against all ungodliness and unrighteousness of men, who *suppress the truth in unrighteousness*, because that which is known about God is evident within them; for God made it evident to them. For since the creation of the world His invisible attributes, *His eternal power and divine nature, have been clearly seen, being understood* through what has been made, so that *they are without excuse*. For even though *they knew God*, they did not honor Him as God, or give thanks; but *they became futile in their speculations*, and their foolish heart was darkened. Professing to be wise, they became fools. . . . For *they exchanged the truth of God for a lie* (Rom. 1:18–22, 25).

Later in Romans Paul also declares that "the mind set on the flesh is hostile toward God; for it does not subject itself to the law of God, for it is not even able to do so" (Rom. 8:7).

Any apologetic method that does not recognize the hostility of the fallen mind is not only gravely mistaken but is resisting the teaching of the very Scriptures which apologetics should be defending! Christians must recognize the reality of non-neutrality in the actual world.

Contrary to the grievously impoverished theology in much of modern evangelicalism, the Scriptures teach what is known as the "**noetic**" effect of sin. "Noetic" is derived from the Greek word *nous*, which means "mind" (see: Luke 24:45; Rom. 7:23; Phil. 4:7). This is one aspect of the doctrine of "total depravity," which declares that the fall reaches deep down into a man's very being, even to his mind, his reasoning processes. "The noetic effect of sin (the depravity of man's intellect) does not imply, for Van Til, that the unbeliever cannot have a keen intellect. He may be very smart indeed, and thus all the more dangerous to himself and others. Depravity gives a distorted and destructive *orientation* to the sinner's mental functions."[3] This is evident in Paul's writings quoted above.

---

[3] The word "hostile" is a translation of the Greek *echthros*, which is often trans-

The Unbelieving Mind Denies Reality

Neutrality strikes at our *faith* in another way. Our faith declares that all things were made by and belong to God, so that there can be no neutrality in such a world. Consider the following biblical truths:

God made all things. The doctrine of creation is a foundational biblical doctrine which shows God as the Creator and the universe as His creation. The Bible rightly opens with the doctrine of creation, and the New Testament affirms it. "In the beginning God created the heavens and the earth" (Gen. 1:1). "All things came into being by Him, and apart from Him nothing came into being that has come into being" (John 1:3).[4]

Paul uses the doctrine of creation to condemn men for failing to worship Him as their *Creator* (Rom. 1:16–25). God created *everything* in the universe from its smallest atomic particle to its farthest flung galaxy. As God's creatures living in His world you cannot legitimately be neutral regarding your Creator's existence. This is especially true because man has been created in God's image (Gen. 1:26; 9:6; 1 Cor. 11:7; James 3:9).

God made all things for himself. The God of Scripture is not the God of **deism**.[5] That is, God did not simply create the world and withdraw Himself from it. He created it for Himself and positively for His own glory. "For from Him and through Him and *to Him* are all things. *To Him be the glory forever*" (Rom. 11:36). "All things have been created by Him *and for Him*" (Col. 1:16d).[6] God does not welcome neutrality in His creation, for neutrality denies God's glorious

---

lated "enemy," see Luke 1:74; 10:19; 1 Cor. 15:25–26.

[4]See also Exodus 20:11; Nehemiah 9:6; Psalm 104:24; 148:1–5; Isaiah 40:22–28; 44:24; 45:12, 18; Ephesians 3:9; Colossians 1:16–17; and Hebrews 11:3.

[5]**Deism** is a natural religion view of God which was very prevalent in the seventeenth and eighteenth centuries. This belief about God is derived solely from natural revelation and reason and not special revelation. The god of deism created the world but does not interfere with it by means of providence, miracle, incarnation, or any other Christian affirmation.

[6]See Psalm 82:8; Proverbs 16:4; 1 Corinthians 8:6; Hebrews 2:10; Revelation 4:11.

purpose. Caleb Colton (1780–1832) once commented that "Neutrality is no favorite with Providence, for we are so formed that it is scarcely possible for us to stand neutral in our hearts."

God owns all things. One recurring theme in Scripture is found in the words: "The earth is the Lord's, and all it contains, the world and those who dwell in it" (Ps. 24:1).[7] No man can trespass on another's property and claim he is neutral to the other man's ownership. Neither may man claim such in the earth, which is "the Lord's." Human property rights are protected in God's Law (e.g., Ex. 20:15; Lev. 19:11; Acts 5:4). You well know God's special redemptive ownership of believers (1 Cor. 6:20; 7:23; Acts 20:28; 1 Pet. 1:18). God has property rights over all that He has created, and He has created all things.

God governs all things. The world and the universe do not operate randomly by blind chance or under their own inherent power. God actively controls all things and continuously directs them to His own wise end. Everything exists and has its meaning and place because of God. He "*declares the end from the beginning* and from ancient times things which have not been done, saying, '*My purpose* will be established, and I will accomplish all *My good pleasure*'" (Isa. 46:10). Christ "is before all things, and in Him all things hold together" (Col. 1:17). Christ "is the radiance of His glory and the exact representation of His nature, and upholds all things by the word of His power" (Heb. 1:3a). We "have been predestined according to His purpose who works all things after the counsel of His will" (Eph. 1:11).[8] Thus, everything is controlled by the will of God for *His purpose*, not for the sake of neutrality.

---

[7]See Genesis 14:19; Exodus 9:29; 19:5; Leviticus 25:23; Deuteronomy 10:14; 1 Chronicles 29:11, 14; Job 41:11; Psalm 24:1; 50:12; 89:11; 104:24; 1 Corinthians 10:26, 28.

[8]The Westminster Confession calls the doctrine of predestination a "high mystery" (WCF 3:8). It is a difficult doctrine to understand, but a very biblical one. See: Loraine Boettner, *The Reformed Doctrine of Predestination* (Phillipsburg, NJ: Presbyterian and Reformed, 1932).

God will judge all men. As creatures of God existing in His image, we are responsible to Him and His will. "God will bring *every* act to judgment, *everything* which is hidden, whether it is good or evil" (Eccl. 12:14). "He has fixed a day in which He will judge the *world* in righteousness through a Man whom He has appointed" (Acts 17:31a).[9] In fact, you will even give account for *every* "idle word" that you speak (Matt. 12:36). None of your words is neutral; each one is subject to God's evaluative judgment. Your apologetic methodology, then, will even be subject to God's searching assessment. God's judgment is inescapable in all of life, as David discovered when he tried to flee God's presence (Ps. 139:1–17). Bahnsen explains it this way:

> Herein lies the problem: neutrality is impossible. Secularists have no claim to neutrality because everyone has a set of presuppositions that guide their moral and ethical analyses. Contending for any position depends upon this framework in that it is through one's presuppositions that facts are interpreted and related. No one lives or operates in a vacuum where the mind is a "blank slate" and facts are uninterpreted. Were that the case, "brute facts" would exist independently of God and have no logical relation to one another. Accordingly, man could not know them.[10]

Bahnsen's first point is affirmed in Scripture: We must not work from the assumption of neutrality in man's thinking. The unbeliever is not neutral; why should you be?

Christians Should Not Be Neutral

As a Christian you are obligated to *deny* neutrality in your apologetic methodology. This should naturally follow from your understanding of sin. Man is not neutral; he is a sinner. Quite obviously you should

---

[9]See also Ecclesiastes 3:17; Matthew 10:28; Acts 17:31; Romans 14:11; Philippians 2:10; Hebrews 12:23; and Revelation 20:12.

[10]Bahnsen, *Van Til's Apologetic*, 38.

not adopt a position that contradicts the biblical doctrine of sin. We may, however, go further than this in speaking against the neutrality principle. Notice this point from Bahnsen's *Always Ready*:

> No such compromise is even possible. "*No* man *is able* to serve two lords" (Matt. 6:24). It should come as no surprise that, in a world where all things have been created by Christ (Col. 1:16) and are carried along by the word of His power (Heb. 1:3) and where all knowledge is therefore deposited in Him who is The Truth (Col. 2:3; John 14:6) and who must be Lord over all thinking (2 Cor. 10:5), *neutrality is nothing short of immorality.* "Whosoever therefore would be a friend of the world makes himself an enemy of God' (James 4:4)."[11]

Note that the call to neutrality "strikes at the very heart of our faith and of our faithfulness to the Lord."[12] That is, you must balance your objective *faith* (that which Scripture reveals, such as the doctrine of sin and any other revealed doctrine) with your subjective *faithfulness* (that which the Scripture commands, such as your obedience to Christ in all of life); you must balance truth and obedience. As the gospel hymn declares, you must "trust and obey, for there is no other way."

As noted above, your "faith" warns of the reality of sin which teaches that the fallen mind is not neutral. How then may you discount this fact when developing your method for defending the faith? Now consider your positive obligation: your call to "faithfulness" directs you spiritually to pursue that which is right and good. This positive obligation also forbids adopting the position of neutrality. How is this so?

You are commanded to fear God in order positively to gain knowledge. Attempting neutrality toward God undermines your quest for knowledge. The Scriptures teach that "the fear of the Lord"—*not*

---

[11] Bahnsen, *Always Ready*, 9.
[12] Bahnsen, *Always Ready*, 3.

neutrality—"is the beginning of knowledge" (Prov. 1:7; cf. 9:10; 15:33; Job 28:28; Ps. 111:10). In that God has created all things, in His light "we see light" (Ps. 36:9). Therefore, His "word is a lamp to my feet, and a light to my path" (Ps. 119:105). How can we put this light under a bushel basket (Matt. 5:15) and expect apologetic success? Despite the unbeliever's assumption, God is not irrelevant to the world and life.

As a Christian you are to "avoid worldly and empty chatter and the opposing arguments of what is falsely called 'knowledge'" (1 Tim. 6:20). Therefore, in your apologetic method you must "hold fast the faithful word which is in accordance with the teaching, that [you] may be able both to exhort in sound doctrine and to refute those who contradict" (Titus 1:9).

People who do not have hearts for God do not know anything *truly*. "Faith is . . . prerequisite for a genuinely rational understanding of anything" for "faith is the necessary foundation or framework for rationality and understanding."[13] We are not saying unbelievers "know nothing." We are saying that they do not know anything "*truly*," because they do not recognize the most fundamental reality: All facts are God-created facts, not brute facts. Things do not simply exist as the result of random evolutionary forces. They are given meaning and significance because they exist in God's plan, for His purpose, and in order to bring Him glory. Indeed, unbelievers do not acknowledge the biggest fact of all reality—God.

Paul teaches that in Christ "are hidden *all* the treasures of wisdom and knowledge. . . . See to it that no one takes you captive through philosophy and empty deception, according to the tradition of men, according to the elementary principles of the world, rather than according to Christ" (Col. 2:3, 8). He warns about being taken captive by "empty deception," "the tradition of men," and "the elementary principles of the world." The Scripture here calls you

---

[13] Bahnsen, *Van Til's Apologetic*, 272, 273.

to non-neutrality when seeking to promote the knowledge of the truth.

We are commanded to bow in submission to the Lord in all things. Neutrality strikes at our *faithfulness* because we are called to submit to God and Christ in *all things*, not just some things or inner personal matters, so-called "religious things."

In too many places to cite, the New Testament calls God and Christ "Lord."[14] In fact, both God the Father and God the Son may be called the "Lord of lords" (1 Tim. 6:15; Rev. 17:14; 19:16). The word "Lord" is a translation of the Greek word *kurios*, which means "master, owner."[15] Just as the slave must not neutrally weigh the master's commands, neither should we who are God's "servants" (Rom. 1:1; 6:22; 1 Cor. 7:22; 1 Pet. 2:16). For instance, Paul commands hearty, total obedience to actual slaves in his day:

- Slaves, be obedient to those who are your masters according to the flesh, with fear and trembling, in the sincerity of your heart, as to Christ; not by way of eyeservice, as menpleasers, but as slaves of Christ, doing the will of God from the heart (Eph. 6:5–6; cf. Col. 3:22).
- Let all who are under the yoke as slaves regard their own masters as worthy of all honor so that the name of God and our doctrine may not be spoken against (1 Tim. 6:1).

On this master/servant relation, Paul also discounts any compromise with the world through a neutrality principle when he writes: "For am I now seeking the favor of men, or of God? Or am I striving to please men? If I were still trying to please men, I would not be a bond-servant of Christ" (Gal. 1:10). You are to be a "slave of Christ, doing the

---

[14]The word "Lord" occurs 497 times in the New Testament. The honorific title "Lord Jesus" occurs eighty-nine times.

[15]Interestingly, the English word "church" is derived from the Greek word *kuriakos*, which means "the Lord's." Christians gathered into the "church" are the "Lord's." (Do not be confused in this: The Greek word which is *translated* "church" in our English Bibles is *ecclesia*. We are here, however, talking about the English *word* "church," not the *translation*.)

will of God *from the heart*" (Eph. 6:6). You are even positively warned *not* to adopt the ways of the world such as the neutrality principle: "Do not love the world, nor the things in the world. If anyone loves the world, the love of the Father is not in him" (1 John 2:15). "Do not be conformed to this world, but be transformed by the renewing of your mind, that you may prove what the will of God is, that which is good and acceptable and perfect" (Rom. 12:2).

As noted before, your Savior calls you to "love the Lord your God with all your heart, and with all your soul, and with *all your mind*, and with all your strength" (Mark 12:30). Your mind—*and all of its principles and methods*—must display love of God, not neutrality toward him.

Since you have been "bought with a price" you must "not become slaves of men" (1 Cor. 7:23; cf. 6:20). You are saved in order to "walk in *newness* of life" (all of life) that you "no longer be slaves to sin" (in any area) (Rom. 6:4, 6). This involves your not being "conformed to this world, but [being] transformed by the *renewing of your mind*" (Rom. 12:2a). Paul commanded that you "walk no longer just as the Gentiles also walk, in the futility of *their mind*" (Eph. 4:17) but "that you be *renewed in the spirit of your mind*, and put on the new self, which in the likeness of God has been created in righteousness and holiness of *the truth*" (Eph. 4:23–24).

In fact, "whether, then, you eat or drink or whatever you do" you must "do *all* to the glory of God" (1 Cor. 10:31)—even your reasoning processes are to be for God's glory. Whether you speak or act you must do so "that in *all things* God may be glorified through Jesus Christ" (1 Pet. 4:11). You must "walk in a manner worthy of the Lord, to please Him in *all respects*, bearing fruit in every good work and increasing in the knowledge of God" (Col. 1:10; cf. 1 Thess. 2:12).

This leads you to hear the classic call to obedience *in your very thoughts*: "We are destroying speculations and every lofty thing raised up against the knowledge of God, and we are taking every thought captive to the obedience of Christ" (2 Cor 10:5). You are to

challenge "every lofty thing" which is raised up "against the knowledge of God" so that you take "every thought captive" to "the obedience of Christ." This plainly and forcefully calls you to obey Christ
in the entirety of our thought processes, including your method for
defending the faith of Christ.

To adopt neutrality in apologetics is unfaithful. You must not
forget the nature of the unbeliever's challenge:

> We live in a culture which has for so long been saturated
> with the claims of intellectual autonomy and the demand for
> neutrality in scholarship that this ungodly perspective [of
> neutrality] has been ingrained in us: like the "music of the
> spheres," it is so constant and we are so accustomed to it
> that we fail to discern it. It is common fare, and we simply
> expect it.[16]

Everywhere around you lurks the hidden assumption that life can
and should be compartmentalized into religious and non-religious
realms. And that the religious issues are narrowly defined within the
context of formal Christian worship and various obvious religious
exercises. The world believes that these religious exercises are fine—
if kept to yourself or within your church life. But in the work-a-day
world of everyday cultural activity, life must be neutral towards religious matters. Herein lies the lure to secularism. "More and more
people care about religious tolerance as fewer and fewer care about
religion" (Alexander Chase, 1966).

Never forget this. You must frequently remind yourself that you
are engaged in spiritual warfare that seeks to undermine the absolute,
universal Lordship of the Triune God. The Bible views the situation
just this way:

---

[16]Bahnsen, *Always Ready*, 31.

- Romans 1:18–32 details the unbeliever's active suppression of the knowledge of God and the moral results of that suppression.
- Ephesians 2:1–10 shows the reality of sin, the nature of redemption, and the Christian's high calling to walk in good works according to *God's* pattern.
- Ephesians 4:17–32 highlights the nature of unbelieving thought and practice and sets these over against the way we "learn" Christ.
- Ephesians 6:10–20 speaks of your equipment for spiritual warfare, reminding you that ultimately your fight is against Satan himself.
- 1 Peter 2:11–25 directs you how to react when under persecution, so that you can follow Christ's example and leave a strong witness for him.
- 1 Peter 3:15 obligates you to sanctify Christ in your hearts by being prepared to answer those who deny or challenge our faith.

Christians Must be Humble in Their Boldness

In all of this you must not only inculcate knowledge, conviction, and courage, but also humility and wisdom in yourself and your fellow Christians. Unfortunately, sometimes when the Christian recognizes the power of the Christian faith, he can develop a boastful or arrogant attitude. Paul condemns prideful boasting: "Let us not become boastful, challenging one another, envying one another" (Gal. 5:26; cf. Rom. 3:27; 1 Cor. 1:29; Gal. 5:26).

A boasting spirit and price must be avoided at all costs. "For who regards you as superior? And what do you have that you did not receive? But if you did receive it, why do you boast as if you had not received it?" (1 Cor. 4:7). The call to apologetics requires humility: "Sanctify Christ as Lord in your hearts, always being ready to make a defense to everyone who asks you to give an account for the hope that is in you, *yet with gentleness and reverence*" (1 Pet. 3:15).

This danger of pride and arrogance is especially a danger in college students. As the humorist Will Rogers (1879–1935) once remarked: "College is wonderful because it takes the children away from home just as they reach the arguing stage." The derivation of the term "sophomore" is from the compound of two Greek words: *sophia*, which means "wise," and *moron*, which means "fool" (see Rom. 1:22; 1 Cor. 1:20, 25, 27; 3:18 for both words). The second year college student now has a full year of college level academic training; it can go to his head.

As James Barnes (1806–1936) amusingly observed, "You can always tell a Harvard man, but you can't tell him much." Max Beerbohm (1872–1956) once confessed, "I was a modest, good-humored boy. It is Oxford that has made me insufferable." These observations should not characterize Christians.

2. Exegetical Observations

Let's focus a little attention on a key passage that helps flesh out more of the conflict Christians face. In Paul's powerful statement in 2 Corinthians 10:3–5, he speaks in terms of a battle. It is a battle with an enemy who is arrayed against Christians in deep enmity and violent hostility: "For though we walk in the flesh, we do not *war* according to the flesh, for the *weapons* of our *warfare* are not of the flesh, but divinely powerful for the *destruction* of *fortresses*. We are *destroying* speculations and every lofty thing raised up against the knowledge of God, and we are taking every thought *captive* to the obedience of Christ." His repeated emphasis underscores the depth of the enmity that exists between the children of God and the children of the devil from the time of the fall (Gen. 3:15; cf. John 8:44; Eph. 2:1–2; 1 John 3:10).

Here Paul specifically calls upon you to employ "divinely powerful"[17] weapons, not weapons that derive from our fallen flesh

---

[17]"Divinely powerful" is the translation of *dunata to theo*, "powerful to God."

such as the neutrality postulate. These intellectual weapons arise from your renewed mind in Christ. Nor does Paul commend *neutrality* in the battle, but vigorous, all-out warfare. In fact, he seeks the absolute *destruction* of the opposing thought patterns. The word for "destroying" (*kathaireo*) is used in Acts 13:19 of God's destroying the seven nations of Canaan. It speaks of total conquest, not slightly damaging—and certainly not of compromising through neutrality. In this war, then, we must seek the unconditional surrender of the unbelieving sinner.

The warfare Paul mentions is not a physical battle, to be sure. It is a battle of the minds. He calls upon Christians to wage war against "speculations" and "every lofty thing raised up against the *knowledge of God.*" Notice the plurality of "speculations" (or "reasonings[18]"): *all* speculations that resist God are targeted for destruction, *any* "lofty thing" raised up against the "knowledge" of God. Nor does he urge only a destructive warfare, but a re-constructive one: The old fallen world must be overthrown *so that* a new master may be established: We are to take "every *thought* captive to the *obedience of Christ.*"[19] Nothing in all of this suggests his accepting neutrality in the realm of thought; everything suggests otherwise. Bahnsen quotes Van Til's powerful statement in this regard:

> It is Christ as God who speaks in the Bible. Therefore the Bible does not appeal to human reason as ultimate in order to justify what it says. It comes to the human being with absolute authority. Its claim is that human reason must itself be taken in the sense in which Scripture takes it, namely, as created by God and as therefore properly subject to the authority of God . . . . The two systems, that of the non-Chris-

---

[18] The Greek word translated "speculations" is *logismous*. It appears as "thoughts" in Romans 2:15. It speaks of careful thought and deliberate reflection, as when translated "considered" in Hebrews 11:19 and 2 Corinthians 10:11, or "take account" in John 11:50.

[19] Herbert Schlossberg wrote an excellent critique and rebuttal of secular humanism titled *Idols for Destruction: The Conflict of Christian Faith and American Culture* (Wheaton, IL: Crossway, [1983] 1993).

tian and that of the Christian, differ because of the fact that their basic assumption, or presuppositions differ. On the non-Christian basis man is assumed to be the final reference point in **predication**.[20] . . . The Reformed method . . . begins frankly "from above." It would "presuppose" God. But in presupposing God it cannot place itself at any point on a neutral basis with the non-Christian."[21]

3. Questions Raised

Attempt to answer the following questions on your own before looking at the text or consulting the **Answer Key**.

1. Why is the unbelieving mind "hostile" to the Christian worldview? What evidence is there to support this claim?

2. On the subject of neutrality, what are the two important truths about the unbeliever's claim of neutrality in reasoning?

3. What statements by Christ discount the possibility of neutrality?

4. Why do we say that men cannot be neutral toward God? Provide at least three biblical lines of argument supporting your answer.

5. What do we mean by the "noetic effect" of sin?

6. Does Scripture teach that even the mind of man and his reasoning processes are affected by sin? Prove your answer by citing Scripture.

7. In that unbelievers have contributed much to human thought, science, and culture, what does Dr. Bahnsen mean when he states that faith in God is a pre-requisite to truly understanding?

---

[20]**Predication** is a logical concept borrowed from grammar. In logic, predication is either the affirming or denying of something. It is the attributing or negating of something to the subject of a proposition. For instance, consider the following two statements of predication: "The sun is hot"; "The dark side of the moon is not hot." The first affirms (predicates) hotness of the sun; the second denies hotness of the dark side of the moon.

[21]Bahnsen, *Always Ready*, 18 citing Cornelius Van Til, *A Christian Theory of Knowledge* (Phillipsburg, NJ: Presbyterian and Reformed, 1969), 15ff.

8. Read 2 Corinthians 10:4–5. With Christian friends, discuss its meaning and significance for apologetics.

4. Practical Application

Now what are some practical things you can do to reinforce what you have read? How can you promote this apologetic method among Christian friends?

1. Organize an apologetics club for the purpose of encouraging fellow Christians to understand the significance of apologetics and to pool your intellectual resources.

2. Discuss with Christian friends the doctrine of sin and its implications in defending the faith. In this study, show the practical usefulness of understanding biblical doctrine.

3. Look for articles on secular websites regarding neutrality and the unbiased mind. Formulate some responses to those assertions, using the material in the first two chapters.

4. Urge members of your apologetics club to jot down professors' statements or class assignments that either assume or assert neutrality. Train yourself to be alert to the presumption of the necessity of neutrality.

5. Begin collecting books on apologetics. Build a small lending library.

6. Have a book-of-the-month discussion in your apologetics club. Assign one person to lead each month; encourage members to review and come ready to discuss books at the meetings.

5. Recommended Reading

To enhance your understanding of the antagonism of the unbelieving mind and the dangers of neutrality, we recommend the following additional reading.

Flashing, Sarah J., "The Myth of Secular Neutrality: Unbiased Bioethics?" (The Center for Bioethics and Human Dignity) This web article deals with supposed neutrality in the Terry Shiavo case in Florida in 2005: www.cbhd.org/resources/bioethics/flashing_2005-08-12_print.htm)

Kruger, Michael J., "The Sufficiency of Scripture in Apologetics" in *The Master's Theological Journal*, 12:1 (Spring, 2001), 69–87: (http://websearch.cs.com/cs/boomerang.jsp?query=neutrality+and+apologetics&page=1&offset=0)

Oliphant, K. Scott, "The Noetic Effects of Sin," in *The Westminster Theological Journal*, 63:1 (2001): 199–202: (http://mywebpages.comcast.net/oliphint/Writings/Moroney%20review%20for%20wtj.htm)

Woodward, Thomas E., "Staring Down Darwinism: A Book Review": www.apologetics.org/articles/staring.html)

3

Defining Worldviews

*For from Him and through Him and to Him are all
things. To Him be the glory forever. Amen.*

(Rom. 11:36)

No one ever is—or even can be—neutral when approaching issues such as the existence of God and the creation of the universe. Neutrality is impossible according to *both* careful philosophical method *and* to sound biblical study (exegesis). That is, both reason and Scripture underscore that neutrality is a myth.

Furthermore, as a Christian you *shouldn't* even attempt neutrality. Many Christians attempt what they believe is an "unbiased" approach to a discussion of facts and the evaluation of worldviews in the hope of establishing neutral ground upon which to reason with the unbeliever. When they do so, they are not only contradicting reality (since no one can be neutral), but are denying the Creator of all reality (by not bowing before His absolute Lordship). Such an attempt is both vain and immoral, both illogical and unfaithful.

We will now focus on the *nature* and *function* of worldviews and how a sound defense of the faith must proceed by means of worldview analysis, setting the Christian worldview over against the non-Christian worldview in any of its various and multitudinous forms. The *unbeliever* must be shown that neutrality is impossible.

1. Central Concerns

You certainly have heard of worldviews. But have you ever really studied what they are? Are you aware of the significance of worldviews to your reasoning process—even your common daily actions? Have you considered the implications of worldview-thinking for defending the Christian faith? If you desire to be an effective apologist for the Christian faith, you should.

In our hurried world of instant messaging, three minute rock-and-roll recordings, five paragraph newspaper articles, and 600 mph airliners, we are not inclined to devote the time or effort necessary for analyzing such intellectual complexities as worldviews. For the average contemporary American evangelical, if your theology won't fit on a bumper sticker, it is simply too much trouble. In fact, many Christians are so anticipating the Lord's "snatching" them out of this world by an "any moment" Rapture that they see no sense in the long term implications of worldview analysis. What is worse, they not only expect Jesus to return *soon* (blocking any long term outlook for the future) but also that He will personally set up a full-blown, fully-functioning political kingdom—without their having to lift a finger. This blocks any necessity for extensive reflection on the cultural and political implications of the Christian faith.[1]

Let's buck the intellectual laziness trend of our culture by looking into this question of worldviews. Let's consider the definition of a **worldview**, and then see how this has important implications for our defending our faith:

> A worldview is a network of presuppositions which are not tested by natural science and in terms of which all experience is related and interpreted.

And a slightly enhanced definition:

---

[1] Gary DeMar, *Last Days Madness: Obsession of the Modern Church*, 4th ed. (Powder Springs, GA: American Vision, 1999).

A worldview is a network of presuppositions (which are not verified by the procedures of natural science) regarding reality (metaphysics), knowing (epistemology), and conduct (ethics) in terms of which every element of human experience is related and interpreted.

Worldview Network

First, a worldview forms a network of presuppositions, an entire system of assumptions. This network is a *complex web* of *numerous beliefs* organized in an interlocking, interdependent, self-contained truth system.

Unfortunately, many evangelical Christians generally think in a piecemeal fashion, focusing on stray individual doctrines and facts rather than a full-scale, coordinated system of beliefs. They tend to view the Christian faith as a random *assortment* of free-standing doctrines rather than as a coherent *system* of interlocking truth claims.[2] In fact, we see this problematic tendency in the more popular "evidentialist" method of apologetics which defends the faith by focusing on this or that doctrine—for instance, on the "resurrection argument" or the "creation argument." We must recognize that the Christian faith is a complex system of mutually-supported, intertwined beliefs filling out a broader interdependent worldview.

You must defend the Christian faith as a package deal. Every particular human experience, thought, or sensation must be seen and understood within the context of a broader system of interpretation of those things. Each part of a worldview must relate to every other part. As Dr. Van Til insisted, there are no **brute facts**, no uninterpreted facts that stand alone without reference to other facts, principles of interpretation, and especially to God.

---

[2] Or to use another image, Van Til speaks of Christian doctrine as a "seamless garment." This image warns against trying to pull out individual threads, for such would ruin the "garment" of faith.

We exist in what we call the "Universe." This term speaks of all created things as a collected, integrated whole. It indicates that we live in a single unified and orderly system which is composed of many diversified parts. These parts function coordinately together as a whole, rational system. We do not live in a "multiverse." A multiverse state-of-affairs would be a dis-unified, totally fragmented, and random assortment of disconnected and unconnectable facts. These unconnectable facts would be meaninglessly scattered about in a chaotic disarray and ultimate disorder, being more like an explosion in a mattress factory than coherent Universe.

Worldview Presuppositions

Second, a worldview—*any* worldview, Christian *or* secular—is founded on *special kinds* of beliefs known as "presuppositions." This does not mean that it is established on just any collection of one's favorite assumptions, but rather on premises of a very special kind, known as "presuppositions."

But just what is meant by a **presupposition**? Defining presuppositions will be extremely important for your understanding of the biblical approach to apologetics. In fact, this apologetic method is popularly known as "Presuppositional Apologetics," or more simply: "Presuppositionalism." In the book *Van Til's Apologetic*, presupposition is defined this way:

> A "presupposition" is an elementary assumption in one's reasoning or in the process by which opinions are formed. . . . [It] is not just any assumption in an argument, but a personal commitment that is held at the most basic level of one's network of beliefs. Presuppositions form a wide-ranging, foundational *perspective* (or starting point) in terms of which everything else is interpreted and evaluated. As such, presuppositions have the greatest authority in one's think-

ing, being treated as one's least negotiable beliefs and being granted the highest immunity to revision.[3]

A presupposition is, therefore, an "elementary" (i.e., basic, foundational, starting point) assumption about reality as a whole. An elementary presupposition serves as an essential condition necessary to one's outlook on the world and life. It is a necessary precondition for human thought and experience, without which logical reasoning would be impossible and human experience unintelligible. Let us flesh this out a little more so that you can see the significance of your presuppositions.

Presuppositions are often hidden assumptions that you reflexively depend upon for such foundational issues of human experience as the nature and structure of reality, the possibility and method of knowledge, and the standards and universality of morality. These basic presuppositions about the world and life guide you in discovering and resolving problems, planning for the future, and more; they provide the very standards for interpreting all of life. They govern the way you think and act, all the way down to how you select and employ specific facts from the countless number of facts ceaselessly flowing through your senses and into your mind each and every moment of the day. They form the very basis for your world-and-life view.

Worldview Universality

Third, "a worldview is a network of presuppositions . . . in terms of which *all* experience is related." This definition assumes and the correlating argument asserts that Christians are not the only ones holding a worldview, as if this were some sort of narrowly religious

---

[3]Greg L. Bahnsen, *Van Til's Apologetic: Readings and Analysis* (Phillipsburg, NJ.: Presbyterian and Reformed, 1998), 2, note 4. See Gary DeMar, *Thinking Straight in a Crooked World: A Christian Defense Manual* (Powder Springs, GA: American Vision, 2001).

approach to life. *Every* person must have—*does* have!—a framework through which he understands the world as a system and his relation to it. Everyone by necessity has a particular way of looking at the world which serves to organize ideas about the world in his mind. Any rational act *by definition* operates in terms of a particular outlook on the world. (Incidentally, all of this serves as additional evidence regarding the myth of neutrality.)

Lacking an interpretive worldview would be like reading a Bible verse for the first time without any context. By way of example, consider 1 Chronicles 26:18: "At Parbar westward, four at the causeway, and two at Parbar" (KJV). This verse is virtually unintelligible apart from its context.

Consider this example from a lecture given on the importance of "concepts" for all humans who operate in the world. To set up his discussion the speaker asked two questions: "If I set before you a black metal and plastic box, about two feet square, with a glass screen on the front, buttons below the screen, and a long cord extending out of the back, what would you immediately recognize this to be?" Obviously the answer is: "A television set."

Then he asked his second question: "If I took the television to an Aborigine tribe in the Australian Outback and asked them what it was, how would they respond?" One clever student in the back of the class responded: "A microwave?" The point was, of course, our modern technological concepts help us recognize such things as televisions without having to analyze them.

Worldview Interpretation

Fourthly, "a worldview is a network of presuppositions . . . in terms of which all experience is related *and interpreted*." Presuppositions hold the highest level of authority in one's worldview and are the basis by which we interpret and understand reality. Consequently, they are the convictions you're least likely to give up. Look at the following explanation:

> Every thinker grants preferred status to *some* of his beliefs and the linguistic assertions which express them. These privileged convictions are "central" to his "web of beliefs," being treated as immune from revision—until the network of convictions itself is altered. . . . The reality of human nature and behavior should be recognized: our thoughts, reasoning and conduct are governed by presuppositional convictions which are matters of deep personal concern, which are far from vacuous or trivial, and to which we intend to intellectually cling and defend "to the end."[4]

By the very nature of the case, your worldview—everyone's worldview—must be founded on basic presupposed ideas held as truth and which are immune from revision. We begin with certain presuppositions and build from there in our learning, communicating, behaving, planning, and so forth. Presuppositions provide the authoritative standards by which you evaluate life issues.

In your network of beliefs, those convictions more distant from your core beliefs (your presuppositions) are more susceptible to challenge, more open to failure, and more subject to dismissal. The closer you get to core presuppositions governing your thinking, the less likely you are to reject them. They give meaning to all your other thoughts and experiences and are therefore more basic and indispensable.

The necessity of presuppositions for operating in the real world is illustrated by considering how you even get up and get started in the morning. When you awaken in the morning you do not go through some sort of computer-like, boot-up scheme where you procedurally run through various system settings and open partic-

---

[4]Bahnsen, *Always Ready*, 218.

ular programs that will govern your activities for the day. No! You arise with all of your presuppositions intact and operating so that you do not have to think through such problems, allowing you to function easily in life. Some important presuppositions about the world and life to consider when using this illustration are:

- The reality of an objective external world: Am I sure that I am not just a mind imagining that matter exists?[5]
- The reliability of memory: Can I trust my memory as a basic personal function necessary for living?
- The relationship of the immaterial mind and the material body: How *does* the intangible mind interact with and govern the chemical processes of the tangible body?
- Your continuing personal identity over time: Are you sure you weren't created five minutes ago with a full memory program in place?
- The reality of cause-and-effect relations: May I expect that my physical actions will impact the material world round about me?

All of these issues—*and more*—are absolutely *essential* for understanding and operating in the world around us. Your presuppositions handle the constant in-flow of sensory information so that you can interpret the real world around you without having to self-consciously grapple with these issues one-by-one as they become necessary. Thank God for presuppositions, for without them we would be constantly exhausted and never able to function in the world!

---

[5]Chinese philosopher Chuang-Tzu (fourth century B.C.) stated that "I do not know whether I was then a man dreaming I was a butterfly, or whether I am now a butterfly dreaming I am a man."

Worldview Immunity

Fifth, "a worldview is a network of presuppositions *which are not tested by natural science.*" Presuppositions can't be counted, weighed, or measured; they are not seen, heard, or felt. In fact, they are the foundations upon which science stands and sensory experiences are understood. Just as the scientist stands on the floor of a laboratory to perform his experiments, so science itself stands on the floor of presuppositions in order to analyze the world.

When you go off to college or when you head out to your job, you will meet people who hold points of view antagonistic to your own Christian convictions and perspective. In order to challenge them to believe in God, it will be necessary that you understand *their* worldview presuppositions as well as your own. You will not be challenging them on the basis of random features of their worldview which are expendable. You will be undermining the very foundations of their worldview and providing for them, instead, a more sure foundation in Christ and the Christian worldview.

Conclusion

It is important that you realize that since Christianity is a worldview, the implications go beyond how you do apologetics. Christian worldview considerations require that if you are committed to Christ in one particular area of life, you must be committed to Him at every point in life. Christianity is not concerned merely with a narrow range of human experience, involving only your prayer life, devotional reading, or worship. In our last study we noted that the biblical cry "Christ is Lord" requires that you submit to Him in all areas of life. Too many believers are "Sunday only" Christians who quarantine religious faith from the "real," everyday life issues.

Since Christianity is a world-and-life view, it has a distinctive approach to reasoning, human nature, social relations, education, recreation, politics, economics, art, industry, medicine, and every other aspect of human experience. To be truly committed to Christ for salvation is to be committed to Christ in all of life. In our next lesson we will focus on *key issues* for any worldview, issues that only the Christian worldview makes intelligible.

2. Exegetical Observations

Our worldview analysis approach to apologetics focuses on the real world and human experience. It involves a view of the nature of reality, which requires a distinctive view of origins. Let us reflect briefly on the opening chapter to the Bible as a key component of our Christian worldview.

Genesis 1:1

The Bible opens with this simple but majestic declaration: "In the beginning God created the heavens and the earth." These sublime words not only form the foundation for the entire Bible and redemptive history, but establish the very cornerstone for an all-encompassing worldview.

We can unpack numerous marvelous truths from this statement. We will consider just three: God exists, He is the creator of all things, and the world is not eternal. Each of these is important for our worldview and our apologetic challenge to the unbeliever.

First, Genesis 1:1 asserts that God exists. When Genesis opens with the simple declaration "In the beginning God," it does not *argue* for God's existence; it *assumes* and *asserts* it. It is the grand presupposition of the creation narrative. In the believing worldview, the infinite, eternal, personal God absolutely exists and is the ground of all being.

Interestingly, the way this verse appears in the text serves as a subtle rebuttal to the wide-spread idolatry and **polytheism**[6] of Moses'

---

[6]**Polytheism** is derived from the French, *polythiesme*, which is based on the combination of two Greek words: *polu* ("many") and *theos* ("god"). Polytheism is the belief

day: there is only one true God, that is all the text mentions. Elsewhere the Scriptures reflect upon the message of Genesis 1 in confronting the mythical gods of the nations: "Thus you shall say to them, 'The gods that did not make the heavens and the earth shall perish from the earth and from under the heavens'" (Jer. 10:11). "For all the gods of the peoples are idols, but the Lord made the heavens" (Ps. 96:5; cf. 1 Chr. 16:26).

Second, Genesis 1:1 declares God is the creator of *all* things. The Hebrew language doesn't possess a single word for "universe." It denotes the universe by the phrase "the heavens and the earth." This verse introduces and the following verses forthrightly declare that the God of Scripture created the entirety of the earth and the whole universe. Here we discover an essential implication of our worldview—a two-leveled reality. That is, we have the uncreated, infinite, eternal, personal God and then all else: created reality including angels, men, animals, and matter.

In the original Hebrew of Genesis 1:1, God is called *elohim*. This is a frequently recurring name for God in the Old Testament, although it often appears in abbreviated form as *el* (and is almost always translated in English as "God"). This name stresses the idea of might, strength, and power. *Elohim* is the plural of *el* and since it refers to the *one* true God, it is called a "plural of majesty," thereby intensifying the multiplied strength implied in the name. In the New Testament Paul speaks of God's "eternal power" (Rom. 1:20).

This name for God appears throughout Genesis 1 where Moses presents the awe-inspiring account of the creation of the entire universe. This name of power is especially appropriate for identifying the Creator of all things.[7] All the might, enormity, and glory of the Universe was created by *Elohim*.

---

in many gods, wherein particular gods are thought to govern specific aspects of the world and life.

[7]Genesis 2 focuses more specifically and fully on the creation of man and his immediate surroundings. At that point we see God referred to by another name—

The universe is what it is because of the unlimited power of God. His might is exhibited throughout the text, not only in summarizing the *results* of His creative acts (showing, for instance, that He created the land, ocean, sun, moon, stars, animals, and man), but the *ease* of His creative activity by His mere spoken word. Elsewhere the psalmist declares: "For He spoke, and it was done; He commanded, and it stood fast" (Ps. 33:9). God merely speaks, and it was done.

The statement "God created the heavens and the earth" is expanded upon in the following verses where we learn that these things appeared because "God said" and declared "let there be." And it was performed in the span of six days.[8] The psalmist later reflects on the glorious ease of creation: "By the word of the Lord the heavens were made, and by the breath of His mouth all their host" (Ps. 33:6). In a similar way, the New Testament states: "By faith we understand that the worlds were prepared by the word of God, so that what is seen was not made out of things which are visible" (Heb. 11:3).

Third, Genesis 1:1 declares that the universe is not eternal. Of course, this has already been implied in the preceding comments. But here we will emphasize that the text specifically mentions "in the beginning." This locates a starting point for the creation. The universe has not always existed; God alone eternally exists (Deut. 33:27; Rom. 16:26; 1 Tim. 1:17). The universe is not self-existent or self-explanatory. It had a beginning in the powerful activity of God. This presents a tremendous problem for the modern evolutionary cosmology: Where did matter come from?

"Lord" (e.g., Gen. 2:4, 5, 7, 8, 9). This word translates the Hebrew *yahweh*, which is God's special covenant name which speaks of his intimate, loving concern (Ex. 6:2–3).

[8]For scientific studies on Six-Day Creation, see Wayne Frair, *Biology and Creation: An Introduction Regarding Life and Origins* (Creation Research Society, 2002) and Don B. DeYoung, *Physical Science and Creation: An Introduction* (Creation Research Society, 1998). For a biblical argument for literal Six-Day Creation as over against the Framework Hypothesis which denies the days are literal, see Kenneth L. Gentry, Jr. and Michael R. Butler, *Yea, Hath God Said?: The Framework Hypothesis/Six-Day Creation Debate* (Eugene, OR: Wipf & Stock, 2002).

Thus, Genesis 1:1 teaches at the very outset of biblical revelation, that the entire universe is "pre-interpreted." God creates every aspect of the universe, sets it in its proper place, and defines its proper function. For example, He creates our sun so that it might provide us light and measure our time (Gen. 1:17–18). Even though every element of creation is not specifically assigned roles in the biblical record, we know that God controls them all and places them where He will and for His own purpose. They have no meaning apart from Him and His plan. In Job 38–41 we find a marvelous, poetic depiction of God's pre-interpretive creative work. No element of creation is intelligible apart from the great presupposition of God.

3. Questions Raised

Attempt to answer the following questions on your own before looking at the text or consulting the **Answer Key**.

1. Define "worldview."

2. Why is it important that we understand the idea of a worldview?

3. Does everyone have a worldview? Or is this just a Christian concept? Explain your answer.

4. Why is understanding our worldview as a "network of beliefs" important to a biblical approach to apologetics?

5. What is a "presupposition"?

6. How do your presuppositions fit into your "network of beliefs"? That is, what role do they play in your worldview network?

7. Are presuppositions easily changed or dismissed? Why do you say this?

8. What are some presuppositional issues that we have latent in our thinking and generally do not think about, but which are absolutely essential to rational living?

4. Practical Applications

1. Engage in an in-depth study of Genesis 1 and 2, while keeping in mind the material we have been studying in this lesson. Become more familiar with this foundational chapter to Scripture. Follow out some of the marginal references in your Bible to flesh out the meaning of Genesis 1. Jot down worldview implications of the biblical narrative of creation.

2. Carefully read Job 38–41 to gain a sense of the magnificence of God's creative power and of man's puny condition.

3. Discuss the idea of a worldview with your Christian friends. Show them that they have a worldview even if they do not think about it as such.

4. Discuss with your Christian friend the importance of understanding his worldview. Show him the significance of worldview thinking for living faithfully before the Lord as a Christian.

5. Talk with an unbelieving friend. Ask him if he has ever thought about the idea of a worldview. Get him to discuss how he understands and approaches the world and life as a rational person.

6. Having gotten your unbelieving friend to consider the idea of a worldview, challenge him to recognize and consider the implications of his presuppositions for his worldview.

5. Recommended Reading

Bahnsen, Greg L., "On Worshipping the Creature Rather Than the Creator": www.cmfnow.com/articles/PA012.htm

Hurd, Wesley, "Me and My Worldview": www.mckenziestudycenter.org/philosophy/articles/wrldview.html

Moore, T. M., "Beyond Creation vs. Evolution: Taking the Full Measure of the Materialist Challenge": www.cmfnow.com/articles/PA101.htm

Nickles, James, *Mathematics: Is God Silent?* (Vallecito, Calif.: Ross House): www.carm.org/issues/elements.htm

Sarfati, Jonathan, "Genesis: Bible Authors Believed it to be History": www.answersingenesis.org/docs2005/1101genesis_history.asp

Slick, Matthew J. "Elements of a Christian Worldview": www.carm.org/issues/elements.htm

Solomon, Jerry, "Worldviews": www.probe.org

Sproul, R. C. *Lifeviews* (Old Tappan, NJ: Revell, 1986).

Stump, James, "Science, Metaphysics, and Worldviews": www.leaderu.com/aip/docs/stump.html

Worldview Features

The heavens are telling of the glory of God; and their expanse is delcaring the work of His hands. Day to day pours forth speech, and night to night reveals knowledge. (Ps. 19:1–2)

IN OUR FIRST study of worldviews, we analyzed the basic concept of a worldview. We noted that everyone has a worldview, that they are founded on elementary presuppositions, and that they are essential for helping us to function in the world. It is important to understand that this presuppositional method of defending the faith is a worldview-level apologetic, which avoids the piecemeal analysis of isolated facts and challenges the unbeliever's whole worldview with the Christian's worldview.

Now that we are well aware of the meaning and necessity of a worldview, let us consider the key issues with which every worldview must reckon.

1. Central Concerns

We have introduced three fundamental matters all worldviews must be able to handle. Technically speaking, they are metaphysics, epistemology, and ethics. Though these involve complex philosophical issues, they are ultimately very practical matters that we can simplify and apply to our everyday situations and use in our apologetic encounters with unbelievers:

> When we talk to unbelievers about their views—especially their worldviews—we should be especially sensitive to hear or discern what their controlling assumptions are about the nature of reality (metaphysics), about the nature of knowledge (epistemology), and about what is right or wrong in human behavior (ethics).
>
> Although not everyone thinks clearly and specifically about such matters in the abstract (according to underlying principles), and although not everyone will be able openly and explicitly to state what his operating assumptions are, nevertheless *everybody* utilizes some basic perspective regarding reality, knowledge and conduct. As we say, everybody "does" philosophy, but not everybody does it well—not everybody reflects self-consciously about such matters and seeks a cogent and consistent outlook.[1]

Let us consider each of these three worldview building blocks.

Metaphysics

The word **metaphysics** is derived from the Latin word *metaphysica*, which is based on the compound of two Greek words: *meta* ("after, beyond") and *physika* ("physics, nature"). It literally means "beyond the physical," that is, beyond the physical world of sense perception. Here is a helpful, succinct definition of "metaphysics": "The study of the ultimate nature of reality, the origin, structure, and nature of what is real."

Metaphysics informs us what the world is like and what man's place is in that world. It looks behind the external world of sense experience, seeking to discern what *accounts for* the physical world.

---

[1] Greg L. Bahnsen, *Always Ready: Directions for Defending the Faith*, ed. Robert R. Booth (Atlanta: American Vision, 1996), 141.

Obviously then, metaphysics is an extremely important consideration for any worldview, in that it deals with the question of the nature and structure of reality. Metaphysics asks such questions as:

- What *does it mean* to exist? What sorts of things exist?
- What is the nature of man? Is he free? Good? An animal?
- What is the nature of the universe? Is it objectively real? Or is it simply appearance?
- Does God exist? What is His nature? What is God's relation to the universe?
- Is there change or development? How do things change? How is development possible? What is history?
- What is the character of the laws or concepts that govern reality? Are they changing? Universal? What are the limits of possibility?

Metaphysicians seek to understand the world as a whole. They attempt to discover and apply fundamental principles necessary for systematizing and explaining the way in which we look at, operate in, and relate to the world around us. Whether the average person is even aware of metaphysics or not, he most definitely has a metaphysical outlook at work in his life. This is because he has at least a general understanding of what he believes the world is all about. If he did not, he wouldn't be able to make sense out of his experience and couldn't function in the external world.

As ultimate issues relating to reality, the metaphysical questions listed above are concerns for both secular and Christian worldviews. They can also be expressed in terms of Christian doctrines, such as Creation, Fall, and Consummation. Since apologetics is concerned with the question of God, it necessarily deals with God and His relation to man, man's obligation to God, how God regulates the world, man's moral predicament, and the question of man's freedom in a God-created and -controlled world.

What metaphysicians study is actually Christian theology in secular dress. This is not just because both the Christian and unbelieving worldviews must deal with the same ultimate issues regarding reality, and because man is intrinsically a religious creature, having been created in the image of God (Gen. 1:26; 9:6), but also because God has created all things and those things can only be properly understood in terms of God and His plan. Therefore, unbelievers have their secularized versions of the Christian doctrines of Creation, Fall, and Consummation. The vocabulary differs, but the issues are the same.[2] As Van Til expresses it: "There is a philosophy of fact in the Bible that we use for the interpretation of every fact of our lives."[3]

Though you are now aware that you are not on *neutral* ground with the unbeliever, you must understand that you do have *common* ground with him. That is, Christians have a "point of contact" with the unbeliever. You need to understand this point of contact in order to engage him properly. A good Christian apologist will be alert to basic metaphysical issues as he challenges the unbeliever's worldview.

The Christian faith involves a holistic worldview. Christianity does not differ with anti-Christianity over only a few items, or even over several. It disagrees with the unbelieving worldview across the board—*in principle*. It offers an entire, self-contained system of life. As such it has a definite metaphysical outlook, a way of looking at and understanding ourselves and the world. As a defender of the faith, you must be aware that the Scriptures reveal numerous truths that fill out and frame the Christian metaphysic.

As we noted in our previous study, the Bible majestically opens with the foundational statement of the very origin of the Universe. It

---

[2]For more discussion of this, see Greg L. Bahnsen, *Van Til's Apologetic: Readings and Analysis* (Phillipsburg, NJ: Presbyterian and Reformed, 1998), 58–62.

[3]Cornelius Van Til, *An Introduction to Systematic Theology* (Phillipsburg, NJ: Presbyterian and Reformed, 1974), 15.

reveals that it was created in its massive entirety by the all-powerful creative word of God (Gen. 1; cf. John 1:3; Heb. 11:3). All of Scripture rests on the assumption that the tangible world actually exists and that it is what it is because of God's original creative activity and continuing providential governance (Col. 1:17; Heb. 1:3). It teaches that all things were created by and for God (Rom. 11:36; Rev. 4:11) and directs you in properly understanding and interpreting the world as a God-created and -governed system.

You live in God's world as God's highest creature (Ps. 8:4–9). Proverbs underscores your obligation, as Van Til puts it, to "think God's thoughts after Him;" that is, you are not to think neutrally or to dismiss God from consideration when evaluating yourself or the world:

> Incline your ear and hear the words of the wise,
>
> And apply your mind to my knowledge;
>
> For it will be pleasant if you keep them within you,
>
> That they may be ready on your lips.
>
> So that your trust may be in the LORD,
>
> I have taught you today, even you.
>
> Have I not written to you excellent things
>
> Of counsels and knowledge,
>
> To make you know the certainty of the words of truth
>
> That you may correctly answer him who sent you?
>
> (Prov. 22:17–21)

As a Christian you must recognize the unchallengeable authority of God's Word and understand the psalmist's praise of God in
this regard: "In your light we see light" (Ps. 36:9b). Only from God's
perspective do you have the proper light to understand the world
aright. As Solomon expressed it: You must avoid viewing the world
and life from a limited perspective "below the sun" (e.g, Eccl. 1:3, 9;
3:16; 4:1) or "under heaven" (e.g., Eccl. 1:13; 2:3; 3:1) so that you may
understand the world accurately and live life properly.[4]

As a Christian, you are committed to a revealed metaphysic outlined in Scripture and founded upon the infinite, personal Creator,
rather than upon impersonal, irrational chance (as in the prevailing
unbelieving worldview in our culture today):

> The Scripture teaches us that 'there is one God, the Fa-
> ther, by whom are all things . . . and one Lord, Jesus Christ,
> through whom are all things' (1 Cor. 8:6). All things, of all
> sorts, were created by Him (John 1:3; Col. 1:16). But He is be-
> fore all things, and by means of Him all things hold together
> or cohere (John 1:1; Col. 1:17). He carries along or upholds
> all things by the word of His power (Heb. 1:3). Therefore, to
> exist is to be divine or created. In God we live and move and
> have our being (Acts 17:28). He, however, has life in Himself
> (John 5:25; Ex. 3:13). The living and true God gives the dis-
> tinguishable unity or common natures to things (Gen. 2:19),
> categorizing them by placing His interpretation on them
> (e.g., Gen. 1:5, 8, 10, 17; 2:9). It is He who also makes things
> to differ from each other (1 Cor. 4:7; Ex. 11:7; Rom. 9:21; 1
> Cor. 12:4–6; 15:38–41). Similarity and distinction, then, re-
> sult from His creative and providential work. Both the exis-

---

[4]Ecclesiastes is comparing and contrasting two approaches to life: A life
lived without reference to God, wholly from an "under the sun" perspective, as
over against a life lived by faith in God who exists above the sun. This explains
the negative bent of Ecclesiastes. Solomon is not expressing a *believer's* despair
of the world, but the despair that arises from an unbelieving approach to life. For
a worldview exposition of Ecclesiastes, see Kenneth Gentry, "Ecclesiastes" (www.
kennethgentry.com).

tence and nature of things find their explanation in Him—whether causal (Eph. 1:11) or **teleological** (Eph. 1:11). God is the source of all possibility (Isa. 43:10; 44:5; 65:11) and thus sets the limits of possible reality by His own will and decree.[5]

In this regard important metaphysical revelation about God's being includes the following:

- God is uncaused and eternally self-existent. There is nothing prior to God accounting for His origin and existence (Gen. 1:1; Deut. 33:37; Isa. 45:5–6, 18; Eph. 3:19; 1 Tim. 1:17).
- God is self-contained, needing nothing outside of Himself to prolong His existence. He is absolutely self-sufficient; He alone is self-definitional[6] (Ex. 3:14; John 5:26; Acts 17:25).
- God is absolutely independent and self-sufficient in thought (Job 11:7; 40:1–8; Isa. 55:8–11; Rom. 11:33-34), counsel (Ps. 33:11; Isa. 40:12–14), will (Dan. 4:35; Rom. 9:19; Eph. 1:5), and power (Ps. 115:3; 135:6; 40:21–26).
- God is the ultimate ground of all reality. Everything outside of God ultimately derives from His creative power (Gen. 1:1; Ex. 20:11; Neh. 9:6; Rev. 4:11).

Therefore, God and God alone defines the world and reality. He is the floor of all reality and must be the foundation of our metaphysi-

---

[5]Bahnsen, *Always Ready*, 179. The word "teleological" is derived from the Greek word *telos*, meaning "end" or "purpose" and *logos* ("word" or "study of"). A teleological argument argues for the existence of God based on evidence of order, purpose, design and/or direction in the created order.

[6]In Scripture, the act of *naming* something involves exercising authority over that person or thing that is named, like when parents name their children. In creation week we see the Creator naming the various aspects of creation (e.g., Gen 1:5, 8, 10). Following up on this, Scripture teaches that God names the stars (Isa. 40:26). In that Adam was created in God's image to reflect him (Gen. 1:26), he "names" the other creatures, exercising authority over them (Gen. 2:19–20, even naming his wife in that he was her head (Gen. 2:23; cf. 1 Cor. 11:3, 8, 9). At dramatic events in the lives of certain saints, God directly renames them. For example, Abram becomes Abraham (Gen. 17:5; Neh. 9:7), Jacob becomes Israel (Gen. 32:28; 35:10), Simon becomes Peter (Matt. 16:17–18). Therefore, no one names God; He names Himself. He alone is self-definitional: no authority exists over Him.

cal outlook and program. When asked to give the basis and starting point for the orderly universe and all external reality, the Christian points to the self-contained, omnipresent all-powerful, all-wise, personal God of Scripture.

As we will see later, when the non-Christian is asked to provide his foundation for the orderly universe and external reality, he points literally to nothing. It has been amusingly expressed that "an atheist is a man who has no invisible means of support" (John Buchan, 1857–1940). In his view, all has risen from nothing by the irrational mechanism of chance. When asked if something can miraculously pop into being from nothing in an instant, the non-Christian vigorously responds in the negative. Instant miracles are out of the question! But when asked if something can come out of nothing if given several billion years, the non-Christian confidently responds in the affirmative. But as Van Til has noted, the non-Christian overlooks the fact that if one zero equals zero, then a billion zeros can equal only zero. The non-Christian attempts to base the rational upon the irrational, the rational Universe on irrational chance.

Epistemology

Another key issue in any worldview is epistemology. The term **epistemology** is based on two Greek words: *episteme* ("knowledge") and *logos* ("word, discourse"). Dr. Bahnsen defines epistemology as "the study of the nature and limits of human knowledge; it addresses questions about truth, belief, justification, etc."[7] It investigates the origin, nature, methods, and limits of knowledge, discovering what we know and how we come to know it. Epistemological inquiry focuses particularly on four classes of questions:

- What is the nature of truth and of objectivity?

---

[7]Greg L. Bahnsen, *Van Til's Apologetic: Readings and Analysis* (Phillipsburg, N.J.: Presbyterian and Reformed, 1998), 4, note 8.

- What is the nature of belief and of knowledge? What are their relationships? Can we *know* and yet not *believe*?
- What are the standards that justify beliefs? How do we know what we know? What is the proof or evidence that is acceptable?
- What are the proper procedures for science and discovery? How are they evaluated? What standards do they offer?

In Christian theology epistemology corresponds with divine revelation. Revelation is the personal, supernatural act of God's self-communication by which He actively makes Himself and His will known to man. We have knowledge of God and the world revealed to us through three basic means:

General Revelation: The doctrine of **general revelation** teaches that God reveals Himself in the created order (nature). It is that creational revelation which addresses man as man (the creaturely image of God, Gen. 1:26; 9:6). It reveals God's existence (Rom. 1:20), glory (Ps. 19:1), power (Rom. 1:20), holiness (2:14–16), and wrath (1:18). This revelation is undeniably known by man, thus rendering him morally accountable to God (1:20; 2:1). This form of revelation is directed to all men (thus it is called "general" revelation). Although God's revelation in nature does not show man the way of salvation, the Trinitarian nature of God, and many other such divine truths, it does show that God exists, that He is powerful, and that man is responsible to Him.

David speaks of general revelation in Psalm 19:1–2, noting that the revelation in nature is clear and universal:

The heavens are telling of the glory of God;

And their expanse is declaring the work of His hands.

Day to day pours forth speech,

And night to night reveals knowledge.

Paul reflects the same idea while emphasizing man's moral culpability arising from this knowledge:

> For the wrath of God is revealed from heaven *against all ungodliness and unrighteousness* of men, who *suppress the truth in unrighteousness,* because that which is known about God is evident within them; for God made it evident to them. For since the creation of the world His invisible attributes, His eternal power and divine nature, have been clearly seen, being understood through what has been made, so that they are without excuse (Rom. 1:18–20).

The idea of general revelation in nature will be very important to our apologetic method. This is because Scripture teaches that all men do in fact know God—even atheists—though they attempt to "suppress that truth" (Rom. 1:18). Because of general revelation, we do have a point of contact with the unbeliever: he is the image of God and sees the glory of God in nature so that he knows deep down in his heart-of-hearts that God exists.

The apologetic import of general revelation is found in three significant implications:

1. All the universe *necessarily* reveals God. Van Til argues, "Not one single fact in this universe can be known truly by man without the existence of God."[8] He further adds that "Every fact proves the existence of God because without the presupposition of God and His counsel, no fact has any distinguishable character at all."[9] God's world reveals God; the creation shows forth the Creator. This insures our point of contact with the unbeliever: We both live in God's world—and the unbeliever knows it deep within.

2. All facts and laws of the universe are only properly comprehended in terms of their relation to God as divinely created facts

---

[8]Cornelius Van Til, *An Introduction to Systematic Theology* (Phillipsburg, NJ: Presbyterian and Reformed, 1974), 14.

[9]Van Til, *Systematic Theology,* 17.

and laws. All facts are pre-interpreted by God, which means everything in the Universe has meaning within the overarching, divinely-ordained, all-encompassing plan of God in which they exist (Col. 1:17; Heb. 1:3). The unbeliever will not be able rationally to account for the orderly universe which he experiences, since he is committed to the ultimacy of chance. (We will discuss later how to press home this issue. For now, he is simply laying the foundations for such apologetic assertions.)

3. The universe is an intensely personal environment in that it is permeated with the presence of God (Jer. 23:23–24; Acts 17:27–28) and controlled by His wise purpose (Isa. 46:10; Eph. 1:11). As the Puritan Thomas Watson commented regarding God's **omnipresence**,[10] "God's center is everywhere, His circumference is nowhere." The universe is not an impersonal environment awaiting the interpretation of man and devoid of purpose and meaning apart from human activity. It is the God-created, God-permeated, God-controlled environment of man.   In the unbeliever's worldview, he is standing quite alone in a cold, impersonal, and meaningless universe:

- "The universe is indifferent. Who created it? Why are we here on this puny mud-heap, spinning in infinite space? I have not the slightest idea, and I am quite convinced that no one has the least idea" (André Maurois, 1885–1967).
- "Why shouldn't things be largely absurd, futile, and transitory? They are so, and we are so, and they and we go very well together" (George Santayana, 1863–1952).
- "All existing things are born for no reason, continue through weakness and die by accident. It is meaningless that we are born; it is meaningless that we die" (Jean-Paul Sartre, 1905–1980).
- "Life is a bad joke" (Voltaire, 1694–1778).

---

[10]**Omnipresence** is derived from the Latin words *omni* ("all") and *praesens* ("present"). It speaks of God's personal, simultaneous presence everywhere throughout the universe.

- "All is relative" (Auguste Comte, 1798–1857).
- "How am I, an a-temporal being imprisoned in time and space, to escape from my imprisonment, when I know that outside space and time lies nothing, and that I, in the ultimate depths of my reality, am nothing also?" (Samuel Beckett, 1906–1989).

Special Revelation: God also reveals Himself directly and propositionally to the mind of man in Scripture. **Special revelation** is that disclosure that is given to God's people (hence, it is "special"). It comes from God by means of direct, personal, verbal (or visual) communication, either through special, prophetically endowed messengers or through the written record of those messengers.

As we learn from Scripture: "No prophecy was ever made by an act of human will, but men moved by the Holy Spirit spoke from God" (2 Pet. 1:21). "All Scripture is inspired by God and profitable for teaching, for reproof, for correction, for training in righteousness; that the man of God may be adequate, equipped for every good work" (2 Tim. 3:16–17).

Special revelation's apologetic import is felt in that the presupposition of Scripture's truth is the absolutely indispensable pre-condition for true and proper knowledge and science.

Incarnational Revelation: Revelation through **incarnation** is a unique form of special revelation.[11] When Christ was on the earth in the first century He brought the highest revelation of God in Himself. He was literally God walking on the earth, though shielding His glory in human form (Phil. 2:6–8). He only displayed His majesty in fullness on one occasion: at the transfiguration (Matt. 17:1–2). Peter recalls this glorious event:

---

[11] The word **incarnation** is from the Latin *incarnare*, "to become flesh." This is based on two Latin words: *in* ("in") plus *carn* ("flesh"). It speaks of the coming of the invisible, spiritual God in bodily form in Jesus Christ.

For we did not follow cleverly devised tales when we made known to you the power and coming of our Lord Jesus Christ, but we were eyewitnesses of His majesty. For when He received honor and glory from God the Father, such an utterance as this was made to Him by the Majestic Glory, "This is My beloved Son with whom I am well-pleased" (2 Pet. 1:16–17).

John's Gospel informs us that "No man has seen God at any time; the only begotten God, who is in the bosom of the Father, He has explained Him" (John 1:18). "Jesus said to him, 'Have I been so long with you, and yet you have not come to know Me, Philip? He who has seen Me has seen the Father; how do you say, 'Show us the Father'?" (John 14:9). Today we do not personally witness the incarnational presence of Christ among us. However, the record of this special form of revelation is summarized for us today in Scripture.

The Christian establishes his theory of knowledge on the all-ordering omniscient God of Scripture. God's knowledge is instantaneous (He does not learn it piecemeal over time), true (He is not confused over any aspect of reality), and exhaustive (He knows all things perfectly and fully). He is "perfect in knowledge" (Job 37:16; cf. Rom. 11:33–36). Indeed, "known unto God are all his works from the beginning of the world" (Acts 15:18). And He has revealed to man in the Bible the comprehensive principles necessary for a sure foundation for reality, knowledge, and experience (2 Tim. 3:16–17). Such a foundation insures that what man does know (although he cannot know all things) he can know truly. Knowledge does work because man's mind as created by God is receptive to external reality and is given validity by God himself.

So then, we have three modes of revelation from God: indirectly through nature, directly through Scripture, and personally in Christ. These frame in our Christian theory of knowledge, with special revelation in Scripture being particularly important for us today, as God's direct interpretation of the world and life.

As we will see point out later, the non-Christian must establish his theory of knowledge on the same foundation upon which he established reality: nebulous, chaotic, irrational chance. If followed out *consistently* the non-Christian theory of knowledge would utterly destroy the very possibility of knowledge, causing it to drown in the turbulent ocean of irrationalism. *There is no way to account for reason in the non-Christian system.* The concepts of probability, possibility, order, rationality, and so forth, are impossible in a random and chance system. Thus, the Christian has a sure foundation for knowledge, whereas the non-Christian has none.

Ethics

Ethics is the branch of philosophy known as moral philosophy. It studies right and wrong attitudes, judgments, and actions, as well as moral responsibility and obligation. Here are four questions of special concern for the ethicist:

- What is the nature of good and evil?
- What are the standards for ethical evaluation?
- What about guilt and personal peace?
- How do we attain or produce moral character?

For the Christian, morality is founded upon the all good, all-knowing, everywhere present, all-powerful, personal, and eternal Creator God of Scripture. His will, which is rooted in His being and nature, is man's standard of right. Since God is all good (Ps. 119:137; Mark 10:18b) and all-knowing (Ps. 139:2–27; Prov. 15:3), moral principles revealed in Scripture are always righteous and always relevant to our situation. Since God is eternal (Ps. 90:2; 102:12), His moral commands are always binding upon men. "Let us hear the conclusion of the whole matter: Fear God, and keep his commandments: for this is the whole duty of man. For God shall bring every work into judgment, with every secret thing, whether it be good, or whether it be evil" (Eccl. 12:13–14).

For the non-Christian there is no sure base for ethics. Since reality is founded on nothing and knowledge is rooted in irrationalism, morality can be nothing other than purely arbitrary, relativistic, personal preference. The relativist holds that "the Golden Rule is that there are no golden rules" (George Bernard Shaw, 1856–1950). Of course, this is self-contradictory: for if there are no rules, then this cannot be a rule.

Against the non-believing perspective D. M. Baillie (1857–1954) commented: "Either our moral values tell us something about the nature and purpose of reality or they are subjective and therefore meaningless." Richard Purtill observed that "if our rationality and morality do not come from God they come from chance permutations of some basic stuff or from the working of mindless forces. In either case, they have no validity."

In the unbelieving system presupposed by non-Christians, there are no—indeed, there can be no—ultimate, abiding moral principles. Everything is caught up in the impersonal flux of a random universe. Random change is an ultimate in such a system, consequently ethics is reduced to pure relativism. Non-Christian thought can offer no justification for any moral behavior whatsoever. This is dangerous, for as Fyodor Dostoevsky (1821–1881) commented, "If God does not exist, then everything is permitted." Christian scholar Steve Kumar, demonstrated that there is no neutrality, suggested an appropriate creedal formulation for atheists:

There is no God.

There is no objective Truth.

There is no ground for Reason.

There are no absolute Morals.

There is no ultimate Value.

There is no ultimate Meaning.

There is no eternal Hope.

2. Exegetical Considerations

Two particular theological issues of consequence for us are the absolute being of God and His authoritative revelation contained in Scripture. Let us analyze some key texts dealing with these doctrines.

Exodus 3:14

Fundamental to the Christian worldview and apologetic is the absoluteness of God. All our presuppositions for life are anchored in Him. Unfortunately, all sorts of nebulous and mushy views of God cloud the minds of evangelicals today. To help clarify the glory of God's being, we will briefly analyze one particularly powerful verse. This verse is found in God's statement to Moses at the Burning Bush. Exodus 3:13–14 reads:

> Then Moses said to God, "Behold, I am going to the sons of Israel, and I shall say to them, 'The God of your fathers has sent me to you.' Now they may say to me, 'What is His name?' What shall I say to them?' And God said to Moses, 'I AM WHO I AM'; and He said, 'Thus you shall say to the sons of Israel, 'I AM has sent me to you.'"

The statement of particular interest is: "I am Who I am." This passage is the historical source of God's special covenantal name Yahweh (or Jehovah), which appears 6,823 times in the Old Testament. The name is spelled with four Hebrew consonants (and no vowels) and is sometimes called the "Tetragrammeton" ("four letters": YHWH). It is generally spelled "LORD" with all caps in English versions, so as to distinguish it from "Lord" (*Adonai*). A world of theology is packed into this divine self-revelatory name.

1. "I am Who I am" is the verb "to be" found in the imperfect tense in Hebrew. The imperfect tense indicates uncompleted action, thus involving an ongoing reality. When names are formed from this tense they are distinguishing a constantly manifested quality. The name speaks of God's self-existence: God *is*. He did not come to be. He does not say "I was." He is. He exists of Himself without prior cause or present dependence: He always is. We might understand it as signifying: "I am simply because I am," or "I am being that I am being."

2. The name speaks of God's unlimited duration: He is the eternal "I Am." The repetition of the verb ("I am/ I am" in "I am that I am") emphasizes uninterrupted continuance and boundless duration. When biblical characters give their names, they generally relate themselves to their father who gave them being (e.g., Hag. 1:1; Zech. 1:7; Matt. 4:21). The Bible is filled with genealogies (e.g., Gen. 5; 10; 1 Chron.; Matt. 1). But God always is, and of Himself. He has no beginning. As we pointed out previously, there are two levels of reality: the eternal God and temporal creation.

3. The name speaks of His sovereign self-determination. God determines from within His own being. "I am that I am." As the Absolute One, He operates with unfettered liberty. He is not moved by outward circumstances nor resisted by countervailing forces. Consequently, this name speaks of God's absolute and unchangeable constancy. He is not subject to change in character or determination, because He is not subject to change in Himself as the Absolute One. Elsewhere we read: "I am the Lord, I change not" (cf. Mal. 3:6; James 1:17).

The Christian worldview is established on a sure and unchallengeable foundation. It is established on the eternal God of Scripture.

2 Timothy 3:16–17 and 2 Peter 1:20–21

Two important biblical passages speak of the *fact* and the *method* of inspiration. Since we know God most clearly and precisely through Scripture, and because biblical apologetics posits Scripture itself as one of its foundations, you should be acquainted with these passages.

Second Timothy 3:16–17 reads: "All Scripture is inspired by God and profitable for teaching, for reproof, for correction, for training in righteousness; that the man of God may be adequate, equipped for every good work."

This is universally recognized as the key passage establishing the *fact* of the divine inspiration of Scripture. It states forthrightly: "All Scripture is inspired by God." The English word "inspiration" is technically unfortunate in dealing with the origin of Scripture. This English word has an active import that means "to breathe in." It implies that the Scriptures were first written by men, then were "breathed into" by God and given their divine authority as an addition. Although the implication is erroneous, due to the popular and widespread acceptance of the term we will continue to use it in our study.

The Greek word underlying "inspired by God" is *theopneustos*. It is a passive word meaning "breathed of God." The word does not speak of *in*spiration, but of *spiration*. Not God breathing in, but God breathing out. The Scripture here is spoken of as a final product breathed out by the creative breath of God—without reference as to how man received it (whether personally written by God as in Exodus 31:18 or given through the agency of a prophet).

This verse informs us that *all* Scripture is the product of divine "spiration." The Bible does not suggest differing levels of trustworthiness in God's Word: "All Scripture is inspired by God." And because of that, all Scripture "is profitable . . . that the man of God may be adequate, equipped for every good work." The Scriptures adequately equip us for every good endeavor in which we engage. Indeed, it establishes the floor of our worldviews upon which our lives are built.

Now let us consider the *method* of inspiration. Second Peter 1:20–21 reads: "Knowing this first, that no prophecy of Scripture is of any private interpretation, for prophecy never came by the will of man, but holy men of God spoke as they were moved by the Holy Spirit."

Before we begin, we must recognize that the word "prophecy" refers to the entire message of Scripture, not just formal prophecies which foretell the future, such as those found in Isaiah or Daniel. The word "prophesy" means "to speak forth," "to forth tell," not simply "to foretell, predict." In this passage Peter speaks both negatively and positively. Let's see what he denies and affirms.

When you read the phrase "private interpretation" you might think Peter is speaking of our efforts in *interpreting* Scripture today. But he is really speaking of the prophet's original *receiving* of Scripture. For he goes on to declare that "no prophecy was ever made by an act of human will" and "men moved by the Holy Spirit spoke." These statements demand that Peter is speaking of the prophet's original reception of Scripture rather than our current understanding of it.

So then, Peter points negatively to the fact that the Scriptures did not originate as the result of any individual's contemplating matters and declaring his own thoughts. He expands on this by stating that "prophecy never came by the will of man." This means that no divine revelation had its origin in man's will or human effort. Peter is emphatic: Not even one revelation in Scripture originated by human activity. This "never" occurred.

Then he focuses on the positive reality. The phrase "holy men of God spoke as they were moved by the Holy Spirit" asserts the origin and the manner by which Scripture came to man. The importance of "moved" is not that of "directed, guided, or lead," as if God helps the prophet find the truth; rather, it speaks of his being "taken up and carried along" by God's power throughout the process of speaking (or writing) the Scripture. The Scripture was written by men "borne along" (controlled, dominated) by God. They "spoke from God."

This passage emphasizes God's controlling activity in imparting revelation. The Old Testament often condemns false prophets as creating their own (alleged) revelations: "They speak a vision of their own imagination, not from the mouth of the Lord" (Jer. 23:16b; cf. 27:14–17; Deut. 18:20–22; Matt. 7:15).

When reading the Scriptures we find clear evidences of a peculiar and supernatural involvement of God in revealing His will to specially chosen, providentially prepared, and sovereignly governed agents. Consider the following examples.

1. In 372 cases in the Old Testament, we find the phrase, "Thus says the Lord" (e.g., Ex. 4:22; Josh. 24:2; Judges 6:8; Isa. 7:7; Jer. 2:2). In 92 instances we find: "The word of the Lord came" (e.g., Gen. 15:1; 1 Sam. 15:10; Isa. 38:4; Jer. 14; Eze. 1:3).

2. In numerous places in the New Testament, the writers cite the Old Testament as the words of God or of the Holy Spirit. For example: Matthew 15:4: "For God commanded, saying, 'Honor your father and your mother'; and, 'He who curses father or mother, let him be put to death.'" Hebrews 1:5 "For to which of the angels did He ever say: 'You are My Son, today I have begotten You'? And again: 'I will be to Him a Father, and He shall be to Me a Son'?"

3. Paul claims his words are from the Holy Spirit: "These things we also speak, not in words which man's wisdom teaches but which the Holy Spirit teaches, comparing spiritual things with spiritual" (1 Cor. 2:13); "You seek a proof of Christ speaking in me, who is not weak toward you, but mighty in you" (2 Cor. 13:3); "For this reason we also thank God without ceasing, because when you received the word of God which you heard from us, you welcomed it not as the word of men, but as it is in truth, the word of God, which also effectively works in you who believe" (1 Thess. 2:13).

4. Peter places New Testament words on a par with Old Testament words: "Account that the longsuffering of our Lord is salvation; as also our beloved brother Paul, according to the wisdom given to him, has written to you, as also in all his epistles, speaking in them of these things, in which are some things hard to understand, which those who are untaught and unstable twist to their own destruction, as they do also the rest of the Scriptures" (2 Pet. 3:15–16).

Your proper understanding of the divine character of Scripture is absolutely essential for giving you confidence in your faith and in establishing a proper Christian worldview—and for challenging the unbeliever's vain efforts. Any doubt you have about the trustworthiness of Scripture undermines your entire Christian outlook.

3. Questions Raised

Attempt to answer the following questions on your own before looking at the text or consulting the **Answer Key**.

1. What are the three leading issues for any worldview to answer?

2. From what do we derive the word "metaphysics"? What is metaphysics?

3. What are some key metaphysical questions?

4. Do all people have a metaphysical program? Explain your answer.

5. What is the difference between "neutral ground" and "common ground"?

6. In the Christian view, what are the two levels of reality?

7. What do we mean when we say that God is "self-contained"? How is that significant for our apologetic?

8. From what do we derive the word "epistemology"? What is epistemology?

9. What are some key epistemological questions?

10. Why do we say that all the Universe reveals God?

11. What are the three forms of revelation in the Christian epistemology? Briefly explain each one.

12. What are some key ethical questions?

13. Discuss Exodus 3:14 regarding its insight into God's being.

14. What are the two principal Bible passages that clearly assert the Bible is "inspired" revelation from God?

4. Practical Applications

1. Presuppositional apologetics is holistic, worldview apologetics. With some Christian friends discuss ways in which the Christian outlook on any given issue is fundamentally different *at the level of basic principles* from the non-Christian outlook.

2. Carefully read Genesis 1 and Psalm 8 and discuss what it means to exist in the image of God and how man differs from animals in that regard.

3. Write a brief paper on the significance of metaphysics from a Christian perspective.

4. Write a brief paper on the significance of epistemology from a Christian perspective. You might want to consult an article such as found in *Evangelical Dictionary of Theology*.

5. Read and then outline in detail the first chapter of the Westminster Confession of Faith "On Scriptures."

6. Read the "Humanist Manifesto II" and list the metaphysical, epistemological, and ethical differences with your Christian worldview.

5. Recommended Reading

Bahnsen, Greg, "The Importance of Canonicity": www.apologeticspress.
    org/articles/2466

Butler, Michael R. "A Truly Christian Epistemology": http://solagratia.
    org/Articles/A_Truly_Reformed_Epistemology.aspx

"The Chicago Statement on Inerrancy": www.reformed.org/bible/index.
    html

"Humanist Manifesto II": www.americanhumanist.org/3/
    HumandItsAspirations.htm

Thompson, Bert, "In Defense of the Bible's Inspiration": www.
    apologeticspress.org/articles/2466"Humanist Manifesto II": www.
    americanhumanist.org/3/HumandItsAspirations.htm

5

Alternative Worldviews

*Behold, I have found only this, that God made men
upright, but they have sought out many devices.*
(Eccl. 7:29)

O NCE AGAIN WE must understand that a proper apologetic requires that we engage unbelief as an entire worldview and seek
to expose it at the foundations. We have already noted that worldviews necessarily involve three fundamental issues: A theory of
reality (metaphysics), a theory of knowledge (epistemology), and a
theory of ethics (morality). Consequently, worldviews must answer
three leading questions: What is real? How do I know? How should
I live?

1. Central Concerns

We will focus on two central issues: (1) Examples of several worldview options, and then (2) The presuppositional cores sustaining
those worldviews.

As we have noted before, one of the beauties of Presuppositional
Apologetics is that it does not require you to be an expert in the
entirety of human knowledge so that you can be ready to respond
to unbelief. Rather, it digs down to the basic presuppositions men
hold, showing that their most basic assumptions cannot support
their worldview whatever its extraneous details may be.

Particular Worldviews

Let's look at four worldview options that compete against Christianity in the world today. As Christians you should desire to understand the culture around you, for you are to witness to that world (Acts 1:8) striving to "make disciples of all the nations" (Matt. 28:19). As apologists, you have seen that you are obliged to "always be ready to make a defense of *everyone* who asks you to give an account for the hope that is in you" (1 Pet. 3:15). Let us briefly introduce the sample worldview options presented.

Hinduism. Hinduism arose in India somewhere between 2500 B.C. and 2000 B.C. To get our historical bearings, Abraham lived around 2000 B.C., and Moses led the exodus from Egypt about 1450 B.C. Though Hinduism is an indigenous religion to the East, and may be largely unfamiliar to you, it has 900 million devotees placing it third among world religions, with Christianity being the largest (2.1 billion) and Islam second (1.3 billion).[1] This makes Hinduism an important worldview—this, as well as other reasons which we will mention below.

Hinduism is actually a family of merged religions arising out of a thoroughly pagan backdrop. This is very much opposed to Christianity which is exclusivistic (claiming to be the singular truth and offering the only way of salvation). Historically, Hinduism developed its worldview from the forces of nature (seen in storms and fires) and ancient heroes which serve as gods, whereas Christianity's proclaims one God who controls the forces of nature. The Hindu adherent worships his own chosen deity among the millions available, while Christians believe in the only one living and true God.

More developed Hinduism holds that Brahman is the one, ultimate spiritual reality which is the formless, indescribable, unknowable and impersonal Divine. Since Brahman is the sum total of realty, all else is illusion (*maya*). Creation has no beginning or

---

[1]"Major World Religions": http://en.wikipedia.org/wiki/Religions

end, and the history we "experience" is an endless cycle of creation and destruction. Man is but the spark of the divine Brahman who is imprisoned in the physical body and who undergoes a series of reincarnations (the transmigration of the soul through *samsara*) until absorbed into Brahman. We are ultimately not separate individuals, for all is one.

In several important respects, Hinduism comports well with several leading Western perspectives, and especially the New Age movement. It has no problem with evolution in that the Hindu religion itself involves an ongoing adaptation of other religions and an upward spiritual evolution. Much of modern psychology affirms the inherent goodness of man, while Hinduism speaks of man's basic divinity. Relativity of all truth claims, so widespread in our culture, fits comfortably with the Hindu view of illusion, god being a part of everything (both good and bad), as well as its practice of absorbing various beliefs (all other religions are *yoga*, "paths"). Its hyperspirituality (elevating the spiritual to the exclusion of the material) is alluring to many who are disenchanted with the materialism in Western culture.

Behaviorism. Behaviorism is a psychological school particularly associated with the name of Harvard psychology professor B. F. Skinner (1904–1990). It has exercised a powerful influence in modern thinking, spilling over into sociology, politics, criminology, and many other fields.

Skinner argued that people behave as they do through a process known as "operant conditioning." Our individual behavior is a response to certain environmental factors, especially consequences we experienced in the past. Simply put, experience reinforces behavior. In a purely naturalistic way, if a certain action produces pleasant experiences, it will become a conditioned behavior. The material world is the ultimate reality in which man is passively shaped. Some worldview behaviorists speak of "mental processlessness" which teaches that man can be understood totally by external events without reference to any rational processes in the mind. Consequently, free will is a myth, an illusion.

Man's behavior is so thoroughly subject to external conditioning that pure behaviorism teaches that man's thoughts and feelings do not determine his actions. We are biological machines that simply react to stimuli so that we are conditioned by our environment.[2] This removes all responsibility for his actions from the individual.

This view of man leads to efforts to control man's environment in order to manipulate desired behaviors from us. It has significant influences on political theory and practice, as well as jurisprudence and criminology.

Marxism. Marxism is based on the philosophy developed by Karl Marx (1818–1883), a Jewish philosopher and social critic who lived in Germany. It is an inherently atheistic, socio-political scheme holding that the material world is the ultimate reality and that religion is an illusion.

This worldview affirms a process known as **dialectical materialism**, wherein social conflicts between opposing forces and ideas gradually merge into a new synthesis.[3] History is controlled by ideas, by the struggle of thesis against antithesis until a new and better synthesis arises. The *American Heritage Dictionary* defines dialectical materialism this way: "The Marxian interpretation of reality that views matter as the sole subject of change and all change as the product of a constant conflict between opposites arising from the internal contradictions inherent in all events, ideas, and movements."

Marxism is fundamentally utopian[4] in its historical outlook, seeking to root out religious faith as the "opiate of the masses." In

---

[2]David Cohen, "Behaviorism," in *The Oxford Companion to the Mind*, ed. Richard L. Gregory (New York: Oxford University Press, 1987), 71.

[3]**Dialectic** (from the Greek *dialogo*, "to discourse") is the philosophical process (the "dialogue") whereby truth is arrived at by the exchange of ideas between opposing viewpoints.

[4]The word "utopia" is based on the Greek *ou* ("not, no") and *topos* ("place"). It

the materialistic worldview of Marx, human love and faith are inconsequential, whereas competitive exploitation controls man's conduct and societies. Marxists, therefore, believe that history is the story of the struggle between men, classes, societies, and nations moving through revolution from one socio-economic arrangement to another. This will progress through the "dictatorship of the **proletariat**"[5] (the arising of the oppressed classes to overthrow the privileged ruling class), ultimately arriving at the stage of scientific socialism. At this final stage, the State will no longer be needed and will wither away as we move into a classless society of harmony and peace.

The Marxist does not understand man in terms of any individual dignity as the image of God. He is a social creature bound up and defined by various external relations with others. "Adam Schaff relates the Marxist view of man: "Man is a product of society . . . it is society that makes him what he is."[6]

Existentialism. Although existential thought existed prior to these men, it arose to a position of enormous influence as a formal secular and atheistic philosophy in the writings of Martin Heidegger (1889–1976) and Jean Paul Sartre (1905–1980). **Existentialism** is concerned above all else with freedom and self-expression. It exalts the experience of living over against knowing, willing over thinking, action over contemplation, love over law, personality over principle, the individual over society. The religious existentialist seeks the "personal encounter" with God over "propositional understanding" of God. The secular existentialist eliminates God altogether:

- "To kill God is to become god oneself: it is to realize on this earth the eternal life of which the gospel speaks" (Albert Camus).

---

literally means "no place" reflecting only an ideal place rather than reality.

[5]**Proletariat** derives from the Latin *proles* ("offspring"). In ancient Rome this signified the lower class poor in society.

[6]Adam Schaff, *Marxist and the Human Individual*, trans. Olgierd Wojtasiewicz (New York: McGraw-Hill, 1970), 64.

- "If God exists man cannot be free. But man is free, therefore God cannot exist. Since God does not exist all things are morally permissible" (Jean Paul-Sartre).

Existentialism in its various forms prefers viewing man in terms of his will and feelings rather than his mind. It can be, therefore, so subjective as to border on mysticism. The subtle impact of existentialism on our common outlook today is such that where we used to ask others "What do you *think* about that?" We now tend to ask "How do you *feel* about that?" This has also lead to the current relativistic conception of truth as expressed in the popular response: "That's true for you, but not for me."

These are four of the popular schemes impacting our society both directly and indirectly. Let's consider five underlying principles supporting the fuller worldviews in their various forms.

Worldview Cores

You have undoubtedly heard of the particular worldviews highlighted: Hinduism, Behaviorism, Marxism, and Existentialism. But now we dig further down to their more basic worldview cores: Monism, Dualism, Atomism, Pragmatism, and Skepticism. The first three are less familiar to those who haven't studied philosophy. Since we are engaging in system analysis (whole worldviews) by focusing on their philosophical foundations (key presuppositions), we must give these some thought as well.

When you first hear about some of these issues, you may scratch your head and wonder why in the world would philosophers ponder such things?[7] To answer this, you should recognize two important truths: (1) God created man in His image, which includes rational thought, so that man has an innate desire from his creation to know;

---

[7]According to Ambrose Bierce's amusing *Devil's Dictionary*, "philosophy" is defined: "A route of many roads leading from nowhere to nothing."

(2) God specifically calls man to seek and to learn, so that man has an moral obligation from his Creator to discover.

First, God created man to reflect Him. We see this at the very creation of man: "Then God said, 'Let Us make man in Our image, according to Our likeness; let them have dominion over the fish of the sea, over the birds of the air, and over the cattle, over all the earth and over every creeping thing that creeps on the earth'" (Gen. 1:26).

As God exercises absolute dominion over all things, so man was created to exercise derivative dominion on a creaturely level: "The heavens are the heavens of the Lord; but the earth He has given to the sons of men" (Ps. 115:16). "When I consider Thy heavens, the work of Thy fingers, the moon and the stars, which Thou hast ordained; what is man, that Thou dost take thought of him? And the son of man, that Thou dost care for him? Yet Thou hast made him a little lower than God, and dost crown him with glory and majesty! Thou dost make him to rule over the works of Thy hands; Thou hast put all things under his feet, all sheep and oxen, and also the beasts of the field" (Ps. 8:3–7).

Second, man is obligated to search out truth. We could bring forward a great number of Scriptures, but two will suffice to illustrate this call:

- You shall inquire, search out, and ask diligently. And if it is indeed true and certain that such an abomination was committed among you (Deut. 13:14).
- If it is told you, and you hear of it, then you shall inquire diligently. And if it is indeed true and certain that such an abomination has been committed in Israel (Deut. 17:4).

In the matters of judicial inquiry mentioned in these texts, man must search for truth: he must do research to establish his understanding of a situation. He does not instinctively know all things. The same is true in any area of life: we learn through diligent inquiry. Man's philosophical and scientific understanding comes **discursively**[8] by involvement in God's world and under His rule.

Elsewhere we read that "it is the glory of God to conceal a matter, but the glory of kings is to search out a matter" (Prov. 25:2). Even our Lord urges us to "Seek, and you will find; knock, and it will be opened to you" (Matt. 7:7b).

Seeking understanding is a virtue. Solomon returns to this theme often enough in his wisdom literature:

- A scoffer seeks wisdom and does not find it, but knowledge is easy to him who understands. Go from the presence of a foolish man, when you do not perceive in him the lips of knowledge (Prov. 14:6–7).
- Whatever your hand finds to do, do it with your might; for there is no work or device or knowledge or wisdom in the grave where you are going (Eccl. 9:10).

Legitimate, careful research and contemplation seek to uncover knowledge and promote understanding. Philosophical inquiry opens new vistas of comprehension and service to God, Who is the source of all wisdom.

Now then, what of the five worldview cores? The first three issues are directly related to the perennial metaphysical problem facing philosophers all the way back to antiquity: the relationship of the one and the many, or universals and particulars. The problem is resolved in the Christian system. But what is this problem? And how does Christian doctrine resolve it?

Philosophers see in the world certain particulars as well as a basic underlying unity. For instance, many particular dog breeds exist: dachshunds, Dobermans, terriers, pit bulls, etc. Yet all of these have

---

[8]**Discursive reasoning** is analytical reasoning that proceeds by moving from fact to fact, point by point, in a logical fashion, rather than by intuition.

a basic unity, which we might call "dogness." They are all members of the one biological family known as Canidae. The *many* dogs are related by their *one* dogness.

In the world, we see cats, pigs, horses, and humans. Each of these diverse, particular creatures is also a living organism related in some ways to dogs. In fact, they are warm-blooded vertebrates of the unified class Mammalia. Everywhere we look in the Universe we see an array of particulars; yet we see underlying unities tying these together and ultimately being related into an overall unified system of reality. You must have basic unity in order to organize and understand the various particulars of experience. So the philosopher wonders: Which is more basic: The one,[9] or the many?

Yet, the problem of the one and the many is resolved in the biblical doctrine of God. God is both One (the Trinity) and Many (Father, Son, and Holy Spirit). Christianity holds to the equal ultimacy of Oneness and Manyness in that the Trinity is equally as important as each of its individual members, and vice versa. Van Til speaks of the one and the many, resolving the matter in the Trinity:

> If we wish to know the facts of this world, we must relate these facts to laws. That is, in every knowledge transaction, we must bring the particulars of our experience into relation with universals . . . . As Christians, we hold that in this universe we deal with a derivative one and many, which can be brought into fruitful relation with one another because, back of both, we have in God the original One and the Many. If we are to have coherence in our experience, there must be a correspondence of our experience with the eternally coherent experience of God. Human knowledge ultimately rests upon the internal coherence within the Godhead; our knowledge

---

[9]The "one" may be expressed as universals, ideas, general concepts, laws, essences, categories, classes, and so forth.

rests upon the **ontological Trinity**[10] as its presupposition.
. . .

> In paradise Adam had a true conception of the relation of the particulars to the universals of knowledge with respect to the created universe. He named the animals 'according to their nature,' that is, in accordance with the place God had given them in His universe. Then, too, Adam could converse truly about the meaning of the universe in general and about their own life in particular with Eve. . . . In paradise man's knowledge was self-consciously [to think God's thoughts after him]; man wanted to know the facts of the universe in order to fulfill his task as a covenant-keeper.[11]

Now let us survey the five worldview cores set before us. You will note how the first three relate directly to the problem of the one and the many.

Monism. The word **monism** is rooted in the Greek word *mono,* "single." Monism is a metaphysical system asserting only one ultimate substance or principle in the Universe. This view derives from antiquity: Thales[12] (*c.* 635–543 B.C.) held that one substance to be water, Anaximenes (*c.* 585–525 B.C.) air, Heraclitus (*c.* 535–475 B.C.) fire.

Monism denies the multiplicity of things, holding that those many things we deem real are simply phases of a one and are somehow il-

---

[10]Ontology is the study of the nature of being. The **ontological Trinity** is God's triune being in itself, the one being of God the Father, Son and Holy Spirit. The **economic Trinity** looks at the Trinity in terms of the scheme of salvation, the plan of redemption: The Father elects us and sends the Son, the Son becomes incarnate and dies for us, the Spirit calls and sanctifies us. The notion of the economic Trinity focuses on the *roles* of each member of the Trinity. Neither the Father nor the Spirit died on the cross, only the Son.

[11]Cornelius Van Til, *An Introduction to Systematic Theology,* 22, 23, 25. Cited in Greg L. Bahnsen, *Van Til's Apologetic: Readings and Analysis* (Phillipsburg, NJ: Presbyterian and Reformed, 1998), 239.

[12]Aristotle considered Thales the Miletian to be the first philosopher. He is considered the father of science, in that he attempted naturalistic explanations of the world that avoided any reference to the gods.

lusions. Through Hinduism and the modern West's fascination with Eastern mysticism, monism is making its impression upon us in various forms, such as the New Age movement, Christian Science, and Hare Krishna.

Dualism. Contrary to Monism, **Dualism** holds that there are two ultimate realities, usually designated as mind and matter. The Greek philosopher Plato (428–348 B.C.) was a Dualist in dividing reality into the ideal world of eternal "Forms" and the perceptual world of temporal sense experience. In the eternal world beyond the spatio-temporal world exist ideal Forms in perfection as unchanging realities. The world of experience is populated with dim, imperfect particular copies of those ideal forms (which are known to us only through intuition).

Many Dualists hold to an intuitionist epistemology. We can only know truth through intuition of the rational forms that are innate in us. In such a system, ethics is also intuited rather than rationally argued and justified.

Atomism. Atomists are materialists who hold that the material universe is composed of indestructible particles. In fact, the word "atom" is from the Greek *a* ("no") and *temnein* ("cut"), which speaks of the smallest material particle that can be cut down no smaller. In antiquity the Greek philosophers Democritus (460–370 B.C.) and Epicurus (341–270 B.C.) held that reality was composed of an infinite number of atoms. **Atomism** necessarily denies Monism in that it affirms infinite atomic differentiation in reality.

Generally speaking, Atomism is materialistic. The material order composed of atoms is all that exists. Atomists do not accept ideals, forms, or gods.

However, there are two basic types of Atomism: deterministic and non-deterministic. Deterministic atomism denies free will, as in Behaviorism and Marxism. We have already reflected on the denial of free will in Behaviorism. Marxism ultimately crushes free will through its concept of historical determinism which results in predictable (i.e., unavoidable) outcomes.

Non-deterministic atomism endorses man's free will. Even some materialists believed in free will. For example, Epicurus believed that though man was controlled by an infinite number of atoms, he should live for pleasure.

There are also three forms of free will of which we need to be aware. **Egoism** (not "egotism" which is conceit) holds that self-interest is the proper motive for human conduct. This philosophy is strongly individualistic. Libertarianism is egoistic in that it is committed to freedom in human action. **Utilitarianism** holds that men must seek the greatest happiness for the greatest number. This entails living for the group, which leads to socialism. Existentialism holds that man defines what he will be. Freedom gives meaning to life, providing self-essence and character.

Pragmatism and Skepticism. **Pragmatism** holds that the meaning of an idea or proposition lies in its observable practical consequences. Pragmatists argue that we must live to solve our problems, even though we do not need to theoretically account for explanations. We must be able to adapt to the environment, solve our problems and get ahead in life. Pragmatism shuns the traditional problems of philosophy: We do not need certainty, but utility. Pragmatism can be heard saying, "Whatever works for you!"

Skepticism says we do not know anything for certain at all. All human knowledge is so deficient that at best it can only be probably true. Because of this, knowledge is deemed to be simply opinion. These last two worldview cores are generally quite familiar to us today, though not always as formal schools of philosophical thought.

Conclusion

As a Christian desiring to defend the faith, you must remember that the presuppositional apologetic is a *worldview* approach. The basic worldviews summarized above, and the general core features, should be mastered in order to get at the heart of the issue and avoid extraneous rabbit trails. Our worldview presuppositions should be able to account for the structure of reality (since it is God's creation). They should also be aware of and able to challenge the core presuppositions that lie beneath other worldviews.

2. Exegetical Considerations

A classic illustration of the presuppositional method of arguing is found in Acts 17:16–34 where Paul addresses the Athenian philosophers at the famed Areopagus. Luke records Paul's facing a crowd with varying philosophical positions. Several of the differing perspectives in Athens correspond with the worldview cores highlighted above: Luke mentions the Epicurean and Stoic philosophers.

Remember that you must *always* engage *whole worldviews* in apologetics. "The currently popular tendency of distinguishing witness from defense, or theology from apologetics, would have been preposterous to the apostles. The two require each other and have a common principle and source: Christ's authority."[13] That is, apologetics is not a separate, philosophical meeting of the minds in a neutral, theology-free zone. It is the rational pressing of the *theological outlook of Scripture*, the biblical worldview, in opposition to antagonistic worldviews.

In Acts 17:16 Paul is burdened by the city's indulgence in idolatry, which represents a worldview at odds across-the-board with the Christian faith. This leads him to philosophically engage the idolaters: "So he was *reasoning* . . . in the market place every day with those who happened to be present." The word "reasoning" is the same word found in Plato's "dialogues" in which Plato presents Socrates' philosophical discussions. Paul openly declares his view-

---

[13]Greg L. Bahnsen, *Always Ready: Directions for Defending the Faith* (Powder Springs, GA: American Vision, 1996), 237.

point and provides a reasoned, philosophical defense for it. This is apologetics in action. And again, he *includes* theology in his philosophical argumentation because his is a worldview critique and challenge.

It is important to note that Paul did not approach the Athenians from a position of neutrality. This is evident in many ways, including his audience's response to him. Rather than "agreeing up to a point" with an attempted neutrality, they outright decry him as a "babbler." They further complain that he was proclaiming "strange deities" (17:18c), a "new teaching" (17:19), and "strange things," demanding "we want to know therefore what these things mean" (17:20). They see no points of agreement with him. They respond threateningly: "They took him and brought him to the Areopagus" (17:19). Not only does this taking-hold language speak often of arresting Paul (16:9; 18:17; 21:30), but they actually drag him before the judicial Council (which met at the Areopagus). And all of this was due to his "preaching Jesus and the resurrection" (17:18d)—a most definite declaration of the Christian system and its truth claims.

We see that he is not presenting an *argument for* the resurrection here, as do neutralist apologists.[14] He does not present alternative explanations for Christ's resurrection, then counter them by various evidences. He is not giving an *argument for* the resurrection, but declaring the *fact of* the resurrection as an element of his wider Christian worldview (which feeds into his "reasoning"), as presuppositionalists do. He confronts their *worldview* which discounted resurrections altogether. The Greek mind was unalterably opposed to any idea of a physical resurrection. Both Ancient Greeks and Romans had a conception of the afterlife, but these were Platonic, denying the resurrection and calling for the immortality of the soul only: "Why is it considered incredible among you people if God

---

[14]The evidentialist method of apologetics presents "neutral" arguments for the historicity of the resurrection in attempting to prove by human reason the probability of the Christian system. If Christ is resurrected from the dead, how can you explain it? This shows the real probability (but not the certainty) of Christianity.

does raise the dead?" (Acts 26:8).[15] This perspective is well exhibited by the Greek playwright, Aeschylus (525–456 B.C.) "When the dust drinks up a man's blood, once he has died, there is no resurrection." Had Paul wanted to establish *neutral* ground, he would have spoken of the immortality of the soul, which many Greek philosophies allowed. Paul is using the resurrection to set up his whole Christian worldview which does allow for resurrection.

Thus, we see in Paul's method that he is counterposing two complete worldviews. He did not believe the Athenians needed just a little more evidence to correct their thinking and to nudge them over the line into the Christian faith. Instead he presents the Christian truth claim and calls them to wholesale repentance on that basis (26:30–31). You should recall from an earlier lesson that Paul's view of the unbeliever is that he is overcome with vain thinking, ignorance, and hardened hearts (Eph. 4:17–24), that his worldly wisdom is foolish (1 Cor. 1:17–25; 3:18–20), and that his unbelieving ignorance is morally culpable, not simply embarrassingly deficient (Rom. 1:19–20; 2:1). Paul holds that only in Christ do we find "treasures of wisdom and knowledge" (Col. 2:3). Clearly, Paul does not stand in "neutrality" but contrasts worldviews.

Paul is presenting the God of Scripture as the answer to their culpable ignorance and their need of a Savior (later he calls on them to repent, Acts 17:30). Though they mock him as a babbling charlatan, he points out their own admission of "ignorance": they even provide an altar "To An Unknown God" (17:23b). As a worldview presuppositionalist, he appears before them to "proclaim" that very God (17:23d), and not simply the bare philosophical possibility of God's existence, as in evidential apologetics. He even charges that their own philosophers merely "grope" for the truth in darkness (17:27). Note that he "proclaims" God; to "proclaim" speaks of an

---

[15]For example: Socrates' *Phaedrus* and Marcus Aurelius' *Meditations* 10; Pliny, *Natural History* 1:7; cf. Tertullian, *Apology* 48 and *Against Marcion* 5:9; Origen, *Against Celsus* 5:14; Julian *Against the Christians* (known only through Cyril, *Contra Julian* 1:7).

authoritative declaration. Paul is arguing presuppositionally on the basis of God's absolute authority, not on a shared neutrality about questions of authority.

When engaging in worldview apologetics, an important feature of your challenge will be to demonstrate the internal contradictions in the unbeliever's worldview. Consequently, presuppositional apologetics always engages in an "internal critique" of the unbeliever's worldview to show its inherent, destructive self-contradiction. Paul does so here: The Athenians have a God-created knowledge of their Creator in their heart-of-hearts, which is evidenced in their altar "To an Unknown God," their own religiosity ("I observe that you are very religious in all respects," 17:22), and their poets' musings about God ("even some of your own poets have said, 'For we also are His offspring,'" 17:28).[16]

Thus, the unbelieving worldview is schizophrenic, and necessarily so: It has to presuppose the real world implications of the biblical worldview in order rationally to operate in life. But it denies the reality of the God, Who alone can account for those worldview presuppositions.

Now Paul warns them that their ignorance and resistance to the truth would no longer be tolerated by God: "Therefore having overlooked the times of ignorance, God *is now declaring* to men that all everywhere should repent" (17:30).

In his desire to "proclaim" God, Paul highlights the unbeliever's admitted ignorance (17:23). And from there he forcefully declares the absolute authority of the true God of Scripture. "Their *ignorance* was made to stand over against his unique *authority* and ability to expound the truth. Paul set forth Christianity as *alone* reasonable and true, and his *ultimate starting point* was the authority of Christ's revelation. . . . This antithesis was fundamental to Paul's

---

[16]Elsewhere, Paul directly emphasizes the universal of God in the sinner (Rom. 1:19–20).

thought, and it was clearly elaborated at Athens."[17] As noted previously, Paul's "proclaiming" solemnly presents the truth with authority. God is now authoritatively "declaring to men that all everywhere should repent" (17:30). The word "repent" is the Greek word *metanoeo*, which speaks of a "change of mind" (*nous* being the Greek word for "mind"). They must change their whole way of thinking, their whole worldview. Paul is using general revelation in opposing the worldview of the philosophically-minded Athenians and in demonstrating their mishandling of the truth.

Paul challenges the Athenians by setting before them various aspects of the Christian worldview. We see this in his speaking of God as the Creator of all things and providential Governor of history: "He made from one, every nation of mankind to live on all the face of the earth, having determined their appointed times, and the boundaries of their habitation" (17:26; cf. also 14:17). To hold that all men sprang from one
original man (Adam) was an affront to the Athenians whose pride was such that they considered all other men "barbarians."[18]

Returning to the charge that the Athenians grope in darkness (17:27), we note that Paul points out the remarkable nature of their ignorant groping: Men "should seek God, if perhaps they might grope for Him and find Him, though He is not far from each one of us" (17:27). God is not far away and hard to find. Paul magnifies their error by quoting two of their own poets who recognize that God is near them, which underscores the truth that men inherently know God and cannot escape from that knowledge. His statement that "in Him we live and move and have our being" (17:28a) is taken from Epimenides the Cretan (sixth century B.C.) in an address to Zeus. Then he quotes (17:28b) Aratus (*c.* 315–245 B.C.) who wrote:

---

[17] Bahnsen, *Always Ready*, 256–257.

[18] See Paul's culturally-relevant, derogatory reference to barbarians in his epistle to the Greek city of Corinth (1 Cor. 14:11), as well as his setting "Greeks" over against "barbarians" in Romans 1:14.

"for we are also His offspring" in his poem on "Natural Phenomena," which is also reflected in Cleanthes' (*c.* 330–232) "Hymn to Zeus." Even the pagans' abuse of the truth does not shield them from the reality of God.

In Acts 17:24–31, Paul reflects on the Old Testament, which he employs as God's authoritative word. In verses 24 and 25 we read: "The God who made the world and all things in it, since He is Lord of heaven and earth, does not dwell in temples made with hands; neither is He served by human hands, as though He needed anything, since He Himself gives to all life and breath and all things." This clearly is based on Isaiah 42:5: "Thus says God the Lord, who created the heavens and stretched them out, who spread out the earth and its offspring, who gives breath to the people on it, and spirit to those who walk in it." When he speaks of men groping as in darkness (17:27), he is alluding to Isaiah's context which speaks of men in a dark "dungeon" (Isa. 42:7). When he dismisses idols (17:29), he alludes to Isaiah's reference to "graven images" (Isa. 42:8). We can see that Paul's methodology presupposes the authority of God:

> Those who have been trained to think that the apologist must adjust his epistemological authority or method in terms of the mindset of his hearers as he finds them will find the Areopagus address quite surprising in this respect. Although Paul is addressing an audience which is not committed or even predisposed to the revealed Scriptures, namely educated Gentiles, his speech is nevertheless a *typically Jewish* polemic regarding God, idolatry, and judgment! Using Old Testament language and concepts, Paul declared that God is the Creator, a Spirit who does not reside in man-made houses (Acts 17:24). God is self-sufficient, and all men are dependent upon Him (v. 25). He created all men from a common ancestor and is the Lord of history (v. 26). Paul continued to teach God's disapprobation for idolatry (v. 29), His demand for repentance (v. 3), and His appointment of a

final day of judgment (v. 31). In these respects Paul did not say anything that an Old Testament prophet could not have addressed to the Jews.

* * * * *

Consistent with his teaching in the epistles, then, Paul remained on solid Christian ground when he disputed with the philosophers. He reasoned from the Scripture, thereby refuting any supposed dichotomy in his apologetic method between his approach to the Jews and his approach to the Gentiles.[19]

Now let us note how he challenged the various worldview cores among the differing views of the Athenians. When Paul proclaims "The God who made the world and all things in it" (Acts 17:24a), he confronts the monism of the philosophers, the materialism of the Epicureans, and the pantheism of the Stoics. This overt supernaturalism also confronts the naturalism inherent in many philosophies of the day.

By declaring God "made from one, every nation of mankind to live on all the face of the earth, having determined their appointed times, and the boundaries of their habitation" (17:26), Paul effectively dismisses the pagan view of fate, replacing it with the infinite personal God as providential Governor. His asserting that God is not far from anyone (17:27d) overthrows the Stoics' elitist claim to knowledge.

The Athenians must hear Paul's proclamation, for it comes from the absolutely self-sufficient God: "Neither is He served by human hands, as though He needed anything, since He Himself gives to all life and breath and all things" (17:25). They must hear his doctrine of salvation in Christ, for Christ's resurrection assures the future day of judgment wherein God will judge the world: "He has fixed a day in which He will judge the world in righteousness through a Man whom

---

[19]Bahnsen, *Always Ready*, 264, 265.

He has appointed, having furnished proof to all men by raising Him from the dead. Now when they heard of the resurrection of the dead, some began to sneer" (17:31–32).

The Greeks (and virtually all ancient cultures) held to a cyclical view of history. Aristotle wrote: "For indeed time itself seems to be a sort of circle" (*Physics* 4:14). The Roman historian Cornelius Tacitus (A.D. 56–117) wrote that "not only the seasons but everything else, social history included, moves in cycles" (*Annals* 3:55). Marcus Aurelius Antoninus (A.D. 121–180), the Stoic philosopher and Roman emperor, clearly expressed the cyclical view: "Future generations will have nothing new to witness, even as our forefathers beheld nothing more than we of today, but that if a man comes to his fortieth year, and has any understanding at all, he has virtually seen—thanks to their similarity—all possible happenings, both past and to come" (*Meditations* 11:1). Over against this Paul asserts both a creational beginning (Acts 17:24, 26) and a consummating ending (17:31, cf. 24:15) of history.

In all of this Paul is calling men to repent of their way of reasoning which resists God (17:30). Throughout his defense he unashamedly and forthrightly contrasts the Christian worldview over against the non-Christian. His appeal was not built up from neutralist, autonomous philosophical agreements, but from the foundational authority of God's Son who will judge the world (17:31). He challenged the very core presuppositions of their various worldviews.

3. Questions Raised

Attempt to answer the following questions on your own before looking at the text or consulting the **Answer Key**.

1. What are some key issues you must understand in dealing with Hindus? What aspects of Hinduism comport with several contemporary Western views?

2. What are some key issues you must understand in dealing with those influenced by Behaviorism?

3. What is Marxism's view of the progress of history? What is "dialectical materialism"?

4. What is the key idea involved in Existentialism?

5. Discuss two biblical reasons justifying philosophical reasoning.

6. Name the five core worldview presuppositions surveyed.

7. What is the central principle of Monism?

8. What is the central principle of Dualism?

9. What is the central principle of Atomism?

10. What is the central principle of Pragmatism?

11. What is the central principle of Skepticism?

4. Practical Applications

1. Read two brief encyclopedia or Internet articles on Hinduism, with one of them being from a Christian apologetic perspective and the other from a general secular or even Hindu perspective. Summarize the areas of conflict between Hinduism and Christianity.

2. Go to a New Age website and summarize their areas of agreement with Hinduism.

3. Read two brief encyclopedia or Internet articles on Behaviorism, with one of them being from a Christian perspective and the other from a general secular perspective. Summarize the areas of conflict with the Christian view of man.

4. Discuss the principles of Behaviorism with a friend who is sympathetic to the view. Show him how this psychological outlook destroys human freedom.

5. Think about movies you have seen. Name two or three movies that operate on Behaviorist assumptions. Explain how the movie does so.

6. Visit an Existentialist website and summarize distinctive elements of the view which conflict with Christianity.

7. Think about and jot down popular phrases that reflect Existentialism.

8. With a Christian friend watch one of the following existentialist movies: *Forrest Gump, The Weatherman,* or *The Truman Show.* Be alert to its existentialistic perspective. Jot down existential elements and discuss them after viewing the movie. (For help with this, see Brian Godawa, *Hollywood Worldviews* (Downers Grove, Ill.: InterVarsity Press, 2002 and check his webblogs at www.godawa.com.)

9. Watch either of these two movies reflecting a Monistic worldview: *Phenomenon* or *I (Heart) Huckabees.* Be alert to its Monistic perspective. Jot down Monistic elements and discuss them after viewing the movie.

5. Recommended Reading

Bahnsen, Greg, "Prolegomena to Apologetics": www.cmfnow.com/
   articles/PA002.htm

"Hinduism": www.4truth.net/site/apps/nl/content3.asp?c=hiKXLbPNLr
   F&b=784491&ct=932107

6

Worldviews in Collision

What partnership have righteousness and lawlessness,
or what fellowship has light with darkness? Or what
harmony has Christ with Belial, or what has a believer
in common with an unbeliever?
(2 Cor. 6:14b–15)

IN THE LAST few chapters we have studied worldviews fairly care-fully. We are now familiar with what worldviews are, who has them, why they are important in themselves, and their function in apologetics:

- Worldviews may be defined as a network of beliefs and com-mitments which help us intellectually understand and prac-tically and morally operate in the world.
- Worldviews are universally held throughout the human race. Every sane person has a worldview; they are not just narrowly religious constructs.
- Worldviews are based on foundational philosophical pre-suppositions that are essential to maintaining them.
- Worldviews attempt to resolve issues regarding the big three philosophical questions: What is the nature of reality (meta-physics)? How do we know (epistemology)? How should we behave (ethics)?
- Biblical apologetics must operate at the worldview level, challenging unbelief with the totality of the Christian sys-tem. Apologetics should never succumb to piecemeal analy-

sis, allowing the unbeliever to maintain his worldview assumptions.

We will now focus on the conflicts that occur between believing and unbelieving worldviews. Worldviews do not simply offer interesting options as personal preferences for understanding life, several of which can be held simultaneously. Worldviews are all-or-nothing propositions.

1. Central Concerns

Believers recognize the unavoidable, unrelenting, unqualified conflict between Christianity and the worldview of unbelief.[1] The Christian worldview does not simply differ with the unbelieving worldview at some points, but absolutely conflicts with it across the board on all points. The unbelievers' "'epistemology is informed by their ethical hostility to God,' as Van Til said. Thus, Van Til held that there are no main points, systematically basic principles, or central truths in philosophy where the disagreement between the believer and the unbeliever will not be seen. . . . [T]he antithesis between the thinking of the believer and the thinking of the unbeliever must be systematic and total."[2]

Therefore, Presuppositional Apologetics requires that you recognize the antithesis between Christianity and all variations of the non-Christian worldview, whether religious or secular. The neutralist perspective plays down the antithesis, and in the process ends up arguing only the probability of the existence of a god—a far cry from Presuppositionalism's argument for the necessary existence of the God of Scripture.

---

[1] You should be aware that in the final analysis, when all things are considered, "there are only two fundamental outlooks: the Christian and the non-Christian." Greg L. Bahnsen, *Van Til's Apologetic: Readings and Analysis* (Phillipsburg, NJ: Presbyterian and Reformed, 1998), 277.

[2] Bahnsen, *Van Til's Apologetic*, 273, 274.

As we will discuss more fully in the remaining chapters, the antithesis is such that "faith is thus prerequisite for a genuinely rational understanding of anything" and "faith is the necessary foundation or framework for rationality and understanding."[3] That is a bold claim—a claim you must understand if you truly want to challenge the unbeliever's worldview. Unresolvable conflicts exist between the two outlooks on reality, knowledge, and ethics. Consequently, "presuppositional apologetics calls for believers to be steadfast about the antithesis if they would defend the uniqueness, exclusivity, and indispensability of the Christian faith."[4] Hence, our emphasis on the conflict between Christian and non-Christian worldviews.

Redemptive History and the Antithesis

In order to understand the philosophical antithesis necessary for biblical apologetics, you must consider the story of Scripture itself. The antithesis is traced throughout the biblical record as an unrelenting theme of man's rebellion against his Creator.

Adam in Eden. The historical narrative of Adam and Eve in the Garden is the foundational, defining story of the human race and its current predicament. After outlining the creation of all things by Elohim the powerful Creator in Genesis 1, Moses emphasizes the covenantal relation between God and man in Genesis 2. He does this using God's covenant name (*Jehovah*) in the context of the intimate creative formation of man: Adam's body is lovingly created by the hand of God and life is intimately breathed into him by the Spirit of God (Gen. 2:7), whereas animals were "massed produced" (1:20, 24).

Genesis 2 shows the Lord's joyful preparation of a tranquil environment (2:8) with abundant provisions of water (2:6, 10, 13–14), food (2:9 16), peaceful animals (2:19–20)—and a bride for Adam

---

[3]Bahnsen, *Van Til's Apologetic*, 272, 273.
[4]Bahnsen, *Van Til's Apologetic*, 276

(2:21–24). In all of this beautiful environment there was no shame (2:25)—indeed, all was "very good" (1:31).

In that glorious, peaceable, loving context described in Genesis 2, man rebels against his covenantal Creator. Rather than walking with God as he once had (Gen. 3:8), he hides from Him in fear (Gen. 3:10) so that God must call him out of his hiding (Gen. 3:9). Spiritual death had now overcome him. In rebelling against God he immediately senses enmity where amicability once existed. In running from God Adam expresses his alienation. "Adam wanted to be like God but without God, before God, and not in accordance with God" (Maximus the Confessor, 580–662). Peter Kreeft has commented that "the national anthem of hell is, 'I Did it My Way.'"

God's holy response to man's disobedience is to curse the rebel and his environment. Genesis 3:15 establishes the theme of antithesis that will continue throughout Scripture and history:

> And I will put enmity
>
> Between you and the woman,
>
> And between your seed and her seed;
>
> He shall bruise you on the head,
>
> And you shall bruise him on the heel.

Rather than peace and harmony, man's history becomes characterized by conflict and struggle. The "seed of the woman" points to the lineage of the saved which eventually issues forth in Christ the Redeemer; the "seed of the Serpent" speaks of the lineage of the lost who are controlled by Satan (cf. 1 John 3:10).

Cain and Abel. This antithesis expresses itself immediately in the affairs of the human race; brother arises against brother when Cain slays Abel (Gen. 4:8). In Genesis 4:25, though, we learn of the line of the redeemed issuing from Seth, another son of Adam: "And to Seth, to him also a son was born; and he called his name Enosh. *Then men began to call upon the name of the Lord*" (Gen. 4:26).

The Days of Noah. Despite righteous Seth's offspring, the enmity and the antithesis persist among men. The redeemed seed (believers) intermarry with the unredeemed (unbelievers) blurring the antithesis and putting the progress of redemption in history at risk. The "sons of God" (those who "call upon the name of the Lord," Gen. 4:26) begin marrying the daughters of (unbelieving) men (Gen. 6:2) leading to the breakdown of righteousness even within the believing community: "Then the Lord saw that the wickedness of man was great on the earth, and that every intent of the thoughts of his heart was only evil continually" (Gen. 6:5).

God intervenes to save Noah's family, the last remaining family of believers, as He destroys the earth with the Flood: "And the Lord was sorry that He had made man on the earth, and He was grieved in His heart. And the Lord said, 'I will blot out man whom I have created from the face of the land, from man to animals to creeping things and to birds of the sky; for I am sorry that I have made them.' But Noah found favor in the eyes of the Lord" (Gen. 6:6–8). Peter summarizes this event which demonstrates the antithesis: God "did not spare the ancient world, but preserved Noah, a preacher of righteousness, with seven others, when He brought a flood upon the world of the ungodly" (2 Pet. 2:5, cf. 1 Pet. 3:20; Eze. 14:14, 20).

Israel's Exodus. We see this antithesis in Israel's exodus from Egypt. When Israel enters the Promised Land she is commanded to destroy those who dwell in it and to make no covenant with them (Deut. 7:1–6). By this holy war God pre-empts the washing out of the antithesis as occurred in Noah's day, securing the believing lineage and community of Israel:

> Furthermore, you shall not intermarry with them; you shall not give your daughters to their sons, nor shall you take their daughters for your sons. For they will turn your sons away from following Me to serve other gods; then the anger of the Lord will be kindled against you, and He will quickly destroy

you. . . . For you are a holy people to the Lord your God; the Lord your God has chosen you to be a people for His own possession out of all the peoples who are on the face of the earth (Deut. 7:3–4, 6).

Satan v. Christ and Christians. Skipping ahead, we see this antithesis in Christ's incarnational coming as the ultimate Seed of the Woman (Luke 3:38; Gal. 4:4). Satan attempts to destroy Jesus as a young Child by the hand of Herod,[5] causing His family to flee to Egypt (Matt. 2:13–14). We see the antithesis in Satan's demonic opposition to Christ throughout His ministry (Matt. 4:1–11; 12:24–28). We see it in Christ's opposition from the religious leaders who are of their father the devil (John 8:31–44). We see it in Christ's crucifixion which was inspired by Satan (John 13:2). We see it in the assault upon the Christian church in the remainder of the New Testament (e.g., Acts 8:1; 11:19; 2 Cor. 12:10; 1 Thess. 2:16–17), as Satan walks about seeking whom he may devour (1 Pet. 5:8).

Jesus views the world as in two camps. He designates these camps in antithesis as either sheep or goats (Matt. 25:32–33), righteous or unrighteous (John 5:28–29), wheat or tares (Matt. 13:29–30). He warns that your commitment to Christ sets you in opposition to the world (Matt. 10:22; John 15:18–19; 17:14).

Paul teaches us of the antithesis, reminding us of our past alienation and enmity with God in our minds: "You were formerly alienated and hostile in mind, engaged in evil deeds" (Col. 1:21). He vividly emphasizes the antithesis in 2 Corinthians 6:14b–15, warning us to

---

[5]As an aside, Christ was probably between one and two years old (not a newborn) when Herod attempted to destroy him, as the following evidence suggests: (1) It would have taken the Magi some time to travel from the East (Matt. 2:1); (2) Herod inquires about the time they originally saw the star announcing his birth (Matt. 2:7), then has his men seek for a "child," not an "infant" (Matt. 2:8); (3) Herod sends out a decree to kill the children up to two years old (Matt. 2:16); (4) When the Magi found Christ, they saw a "child," not an "infant" (Matt. 2:11); (5) The Magi found Christ in a "house," not in a "stable" (Matt. 2:11); (6) Joseph and Mary gave the temple sacrifice associated with poverty (Luke 2:24; Lev. 12:8), though after the Magi came they would have had gold and other valuables (Matt. 2:11).

"not be bound together with unbelievers; for what partnership have righteousness and lawlessness, or what fellowship has light with darkness? Or what harmony has Christ with Belial, or what has a believer in common with an unbeliever?" Ultimately, he deems men either in Adam or in Christ (1 Cor. 15:22).

James therefore warns us that "friendship with the world is hostility toward God" (James 4:4). For this reason he directs you to "not love the world, nor the things in the world. If anyone loves the world, the love of the Father is not in him" (1 Jn. 2:15).

John divides mankind into two opposing groups: "By this the children of God and the children of the devil are obvious: anyone who does not practice righteousness is not of God, nor the one who does not love his brother" (1 Jn. 3:10). He warns that because of this the world will hate us (1 Jn. 3:13).

Hell as the Final Antithesis. The antithesis is exhibited in its starkest form in ultimate separation from God in eternal Hell. At the Day of Judgment, called the "Great Day of Antithesis," the lost enter into an existence that becomes absolutely and utterly meaningless in Hell.[6] The ungodly enter final Hell at the Second Coming of Christ which issues forth in the Day of Judgment (Matt. 25:41–46).

At Christ's Second Coming the unbelievers' condition is characterized as "destruction" because of the absolute ruin that befalls them as they are separated from God forever: "When the Lord Jesus shall be revealed from heaven with His mighty angels in flaming fire, dealing out retribution to those who do not know God and to those who do not obey the gospel of our Lord Jesus. And these will pay the penalty of *eternal destruction, away from the presence of the Lord* and from the glory of His power" (2 Thess. 1:7–9).

---

[6]The doctrine of Hell is under assault today, even from among evangelicals. This is another evidence of an attempt to blur the antithesis, an attempt found even among God's own people. For a defense of eternal Hell, see Robert A. Peterson, *Hell on Trial: The Case for Eternal Hell* (Phillipsburg, NJ: Presbyterian and Reformed, 1995).

Biblical Apologetics and the Antithesis

To be a good, faithful, and effective apologist you must be aware, be diligent, and be observant.

Be aware of the antithesis. The biblical record exhibits the antithesis as basic to the outworking of redemption; your biblical worldview demands it as the application of your view of God and sin. "The mind set on the flesh is *hostile* toward God; for it does not subject itself to the law of God, for it is *not even able to do so*" (Rom. 8:7). You must understand the Bible in order to understand both the Christian and the non-Christian worldviews.

In that the Presuppositional Apologetic is biblically-based and worldview-oriented, the biblical aspects of your worldview are essential. The biblical angle is generally downplayed in non-presuppositional apologetic systems, but presuppositional apologetic writings contain frequent reference to Scripture. And this is not just to baptize the approach with a mere tipping of the hat to the Bible. The presuppositional apologetic method is rooted firmly in Scripture and requires the Bible in order to flesh it out. The survey of the antithesis in redemptive history is crucial, not only for your understanding of the message of Scripture but for the method in apologetics.

Be diligent in pressing the antithesis. Do not blur the antithesis or overlook it. This is your main apologetic tool. This confronts the unbeliever with his dire condition before God. Press the Christian faith very particularly (not simply by means of a generic, vague theism or morality-in-general) when challenging the unbeliever. The unbeliever must be made to realize the stark difference between his worldview and the Christian faith so that he can be made to see the utter meaninglessness in his own outlook.

The Bible presents the unbeliever as *dead*, not simply wounded or ill. Speaking to Christian converts, Paul reminds them: "you were *dead* in your trespasses and sins" (Eph. 2:1; cf. 2:5; Col. 2:13). This is why salvation is often viewed as a passing from death into life: "Even when we were dead in our transgressions, [He] made us alive together with Christ (by grace you have been saved)" (Eph. 2:5; cf. John 5:24–25; Rom. 6:4; 1 John 3:14). Other images speak of your salvation in terms of a radical new life wherein you are born all over again (John 3:3; 1 Pet. 1:3, 23) and your being re-created as an all new creation (2 Cor. 5:17; Gal. 6:15).

You must prod the unbeliever to understand that he cannot explain being good, helping a stranger, having meaning, and so forth, in his worldview. He must understand that ultimately he has no law governing reasoning, no predictability in his system. He lacks meaning, purpose, and value on his worldview foundations.

The unbeliever does not acknowledge the foundational antithesis; nor does he admit his own prejudice. He will profess neutrality, reason, and innocence. He will charge that you are simply making a leap of faith. You must show him the error in his reasoning.

Be observant in noting inconsistencies. You must challenge the unbeliever to recognize the inherent contradictions in the outworking of his life, in the very foundation of his worldview. The previous chapters on worldviews will be crucial to your being able to do this.

You must show him that he proclaims one thing, such as materialism, but then lives in a way that contradicts materialism. For instance, ask him why the unbelieving materialist scientist kisses his wife good-bye in the morning. Why does the "free love" advocate or the homosexual rights crowd decry right and wrong obligations being imposed upon sexual relations, but then complain in utter moral indignation about the war in Iraq, or America's unfair balance of wealth, or the indebtedness of Third World nations to the West? How can they argue for a relativist view of sexual ethics but an absolutist view of war ethics? C. S. Lewis noted that "the moment you say that one set of moral ideas can be better than another, you are, in fact, measuring them both by a standard, saying that one of them conforms to that standard more nearly than the other."

Dr. Gary North once noticed a blatant and ultimately amusing contradiction in a left-wing public protest. He saw a person carrying a two-sided sign. On one side it read: "Down with capital punishment." On the other side, it stated: "Up with abortion rights." Thus, one side of the protester's placard called for prohibiting putting a person (the murderer) to death, while the other called for allowing putting a judicially innocent person (the unborn) to death. Dr. North realized there was a unifying principle in this protester's worldview, a unity he didn't realize and would be loathe to admit. His unifying principle was: "Condemn the innocent and free the guilty." That is, condemn the murder victim (by not effecting true justice) and the unborn child (by not protecting him), but free the murderer and the aborting mother.

You will want to show the unbeliever that to a certain extent he really wants to see the world around him just as you do, but that he doesn't want to accept your Christian foundations which are necessary to that end. As Van Til argues, the unbeliever lives on borrowed capital; that is, he knows the truth deep down and even secretly assumes it, but he has no right to believe it on his own presuppositions—he must borrow from the Christian worldview.

In philosophically arguing against God, the unbeliever must depend upon a worldview that supports logic—which only the Christian worldview can account for. Therefore, according to Van Til, the unbeliever is like the child who has to crawl up into his father's lap to slap him.

2. Exegetical Observations

Romans 1 contains a key insight for building up and understanding Presuppositional Apologetics. In this passage we see that unbelievers are *self-deceived* in their denial of God so that their very real accomplishments contradict their professed belief system. Let us reflect briefly on the meaning of Romans 1:18–20.

When arguing presuppositionally for the existence of God, you *must press the antithesis* between your own worldview and the unbeliever's. You must show him that only on the basis of your Christian worldview can anyone make sense of reality, logic, and morality, and that the unbeliever himself must, therefore, operate on the principles of the Christian system even when he doesn't realize it.

Paul teaches us that the unbeliever does actually "suppress the truth in unrighteousness" (Rom. 1:18). That is, he actively must hold down, constrain, and resist his own internal awareness of God. The word "suppress" in the original Greek is the present active participle *katechonton*. The word itself indicates forceful effort. The stress of the present active participle emphasizes a *constant, active* suppression. In fact, the context repeatedly states that the ungodly are unsuccessful in holding down this glorious truth (vv. 19, 20, 21), which also proves that ongoing effort is constantly being put forth.

Paul continues, declaring that the unbeliever knows God exists in that the evidence comes to him in two basic forms: "Because that which is known about God is evident *within* them; for God made it evident *to* them. For since the creation of the world His invisible attributes, His eternal power and divine nature, have been clearly seen, being understood through what has been made, so that they are without excuse" (vv. 19–20). He knows God both internally and externally.

The unbeliever knows God *internally*, deep down inside in his heart-of-hearts, for Paul says God is evident "*within* him" in that they are the image of God (Gen. 1:26). Paul follows up on this line of evidence a little later when he mentions the unbeliever's God-given conscience within (Rom. 2:14–15). On Romans 1:19 John Calvin (1509–1564) comments: "And he said, *in them* rather than *to them*, for the sake of greater emphasis, for . . . he seems here to have intended to indicate a manifestation, by which they might be so closely pressed, that they could not evade; for every one of us undoubtedly finds it to be engraven on his own heart."[7]

And the unbeliever knows God externally from divine revelation in nature all around him, because Paul says God is "evident *to* them." His "invisible attributes . . . have been clearly seen, being understood through what has been made."

In all of this we must understand that it is *God* who makes himself known, not man who seeks God (for "no one seeks after God," Rom. 3:11): "for *God* made it evident to them" (3:19). And God does not fail.

As odd as it may sound, as vehemently as atheists may deny it, Paul insists that they really do *know* God, but that they refuse to honor him by suppressing the truth: "For even though they *knew God*, they did not honor Him as God, or give thanks; but they became futile in their speculations, and their foolish heart was darkened" (Rom. 1:21). Truly, as Jeremiah lamented: "The heart is more deceitful than all else" (Jer. 17:9).

This truth is vitally important in the presuppositional method. Presuppositionalism involves whole worldviews, including metaphysics and epistemology simultaneously. Dr. Van Til writes: "There can be no more fundamental question in epistemology than the question whether or not facts can be known without reference to God . . . [and consequently] whether or not God exists."[8] Therefore, God's existence (a metaphysical issue) directly impacts man's ability to know (an epistemological issue). This is significant because it explains how the unbeliever can accomplish so much while denying God: deep down within, without even self-consciously realizing it, he actually is depending upon the world as God created and sustains it.

---

[7]John Calvin, *Commentary upon the Acts of the Apostles* (Grand Rapids: Baker, [2003]), 69–70.

[8]Cornelius Van Til, *A Survey of Christian Epistemology* (den Dulk Christian Foundation, 1969), 4.

It is your duty as a Christian apologist to show the unbeliever that even in his denying God he is actually presupposing him. As Van Til succinctly expresses it: "Anti-theism presupposes theism."[9] Unbelievers cannot be true to their professed disbelief in God, for if they did so and acted consistent with that profession they could not make sense out of the world; they would have no reason for reason. Consequently, Paul finds his point of contact with the unbeliever, not in neutrality but in reality. Even though he denies it, the unbeliever knows God exists.

3. Questions Raised

Attempt to answer the following questions on your own before looking at the text or consulting the **Answer Key**.

1. What is the concept of "antithesis" in apologetics?

2. Where do we see the problem of antithesis begin in Scripture? What is the key verse that sets the pattern of antithesis throughout Scripture?

3. How does Genesis 2 set up the character of Adam's Fall in Genesis 3?

4. Where do we see the ultimate antithesis?

5. Why is it important to understand the Bible in order to bring a *philosophical* challenge against the unbeliever?

6. Give some samples of evidence of contradiction within the unbeliever's worldview as it plays out in his life.

7. What is the basic image of sin which the Bible employs of the catastrophic nature of sin?

8. What biblical passage shows that unbelievers does know God but that he actively suppress that knowledge?

---

[9]Van Til, *A Survey of Christian Epistemology*, xii.

4. Practical Applications

1. With your Bible, jot down some additional stories that point out the antithesis at work in history.

2. Using your notes from the first practical application above, draw up a one lesson Bible study on biblical antithesis and teach it to Christian friends. Invite their discussion and interaction. Challenge them in realizing the significance of this Bible-structuring concept.

3. Choose one biblical sample of the antithesis and look it up in Scripture. Read the whole story in its context and explain the antithesis more fully in your own words.

4. Consider the samples of contradictions at work among unbelievers. For instance, he notes that though a scientist may be a materialist, he treats his wife affectionately by kissing her good-bye in the morning. Think of some other common contradictions in unbelieving worldviews.

5. Read Romans 1:28–2:12 and jot down a detailed outline of Paul's argument. Study the flow of argument and note how suppressing the knowledge of God leads naturally to immorality—when consistently followed out.

6. Discuss with some Christian friends whether they believe that atheists truly exist. That is, ask them their views about the reality of absolute unbelief in God. Have a brief study on Romans 1 prepared so that you can show them the biblical view.

7. Go to the American Atheist website and read Robin Murray O'Hair's "Wedding the Atheist Way" (http://www.atheists.org/comingout/weddings/atheistweddings.html). Draw out of this article several internal contradictions.

8. Search on the web for ex-atheists who have become evangelical Christians. Read their testimonies, then copy them into a file for future reference.

9. Read the article "Atheist Becomes Theist" about famed atheist Antony Flew becoming a theist (http://www.biola.edu/antony-flew/). Note deficiencies in his new worldview.

5. Recommended Reading

Bahnsen, Greg L., *Van Til's Apologetic: Readings and Analysis* (Phillipsburg, N.J.: Presbyterian and Reformed, 1998), 272–287.

Bahnsen, Greg L., "Apologetics In Practice": www.reformed.org/apologetics/index.html?mainframe=/apologetics/index_apol.html

Bumbulis, Michael, "Christianity and the Birth of Science," (http://www.ldolphin.org/bumbulis/)

Gerstner, John H., "Does God Love the Sinner and Hate Only His Sin?": www.the-highway.com/lovesinnner_Gerstner.html

Grigg, Russell, "What's In a Name?": www.answersingenesis.org/creation/v23/i4/name.asp

Jordan, G. Zeineldé, "Birth and Death of an Atheist": www.theism.net/authors/zjordan/docs_files/birth_files/o2birth.htm

Rhodes, Ron, "Strategies for Dialoguing with Atheists": (http://home.earthlink.net/~ronrhodes/Atheism.html)

Schwertley, Brian, "The Biblical Doctrine of Hell Examined": www.reformed.com/pub/hell.htm

7

Overcoming Metaphysical Bias

*For the wrath of God is revealed from heaven against
all ungodliness and unrighteousness of men, who
suppress the truth in unrighteousness.*

(Rom. 1:18)

WE HAVE ALREADY discussed the argument regarding the antithesis separating the believing and non-believing worldviews
and showed its importance by highlighting it as the relentless under-
tow running throughout Scripture. God's Word traces the antithesis
from the fall of Adam in the Garden at the beginning of history to
the judgment of the reprobate in Hell at the end of history. The antithesis is so important God had to send His Son to die on the cross
in order to rectify it in our redemption (John 3:16; Rom. 4:24–5:1,
10–11; 2 Cor. 5:15–21), which effects our new birth (1 Pet. 1:3), our
arising from spiritual death to spiritual life (Rom. 6:3–9), and our
becoming a new creation (2 Cor. 5:14–21).

It has become established both philosophically *and* biblically
that we may *not* assume any neutrality in thought. This denial of
neutrality frustrates the unbeliever who will not recognize the radical nature of the antithesis. He refuses to acknowledge it because of
his inner awareness of God which leads to his own moral culpability
before his Maker. This is Paul's message in the first two chapters of
Romans: Even though "that which is known about God is evident"
(Rom. 1:19), being "clearly seen" (Rom. 1:20b), the unbeliever "sup-

123

presses the truth in unrighteousness" (Rom. 1:18). Consequently, he stands exposed before God "without excuse" in God's world (Rom. 1:20d; 2:1).

The unbeliever professes neutrality and claims innocence before God. He charges that the Christian is engaged in a leap of faith in his commitment to God because there is no evidence for the God in whom he believes. But the unbeliever's thinking is vain and futile *in principle.* You must challenge him at the worldview level by exposing his lack of foundation assumptions capable of supporting his outlook on life. You must understand that the unbeliever's thinking is vain—*in principle.* He has many successes *in practice,* but these are due to his inconsistencies: he could not support his worldview on assumptions that deny God who alone can provide order, purpose, and meaning for human thought and experience. As Dr. Van Til expressed it: "Non-Christian science has worked with the borrowed capital of Christian theism, and for that reason alone has been able to bring to light much truth."[1] That is, the unbeliever is living on the strength of presuppositions which can be justified only on the basis of the Christian worldview.

The proper approach to apologetics is by means of *worldview* analysis. Consequently, you *must* know the *Scriptures.* Your philosophical arguments have no meaning or justification apart from the worldview established in the Bible. And that worldview includes the Bible itself as the revelation of God. Richard Pratt well emphasizes this necessity for apologetics, noting that since your response to the unbeliever must always be according to biblical revelation,

> it is imperative that the defender of the faith be well-studied and familiar with the Bible. One can hardly argue by truth if he is ignorant of truth. Every aspect of biblical revelation is able to be used in apologetics, and the effectiveness of the

---

[1]Cornelius Van Til, *Christian Theistic Evidences* (Phillipsburg, NJ: Presbyterian and Reformed, 1975), 64. Cited in Greg L. Bahnsen, *Van Til's Apologetic: Readings and Analysis* (Phillipsburg, NJ: Presbyterian and Reformed, 1998), 377.

apologist will depend to a great extent on his ability to handle accurately 'the Word of truth' (II Tim. 2:15). In the Word of God lies the truth of the Spirit which will convince the unbeliever of his need of the Savior and the sufficiency of Christ's death and resurrection for salvation.[2]

Let us now look at apologetics in action and the anti-metaphysical bias in contemporary thought so that you may know how to respond to it.

1. Central Concerns

As previously discussed, worldviews involve three fundamental issues: (1) metaphysics (which deals with the nature of reality), (2) epistemology (which deals with the nature of knowledge), and (3) ethics (which deals with the nature of morality). But how can you intelligibly *establish* your view of reality, knowledge, or ethics? This is an important question that you must answer in order to apologetically engage the unbeliever. Biblical apologetics engages *worldview analysis*.

Metaphysics Today

Though metaphysics is a central component in any worldview, as you look around you will discover that much of the modern world discounts the value of metaphysics and resists metaphysical inquiry. Since the Enlightenment of the seventeenth and eighteenth centuries—especially since the work of the famed philosopher and skeptic David Hume (1711–1776)—the modern scientific mind has developed a general hostility toward metaphysics. And the Christian apologist must understand this.

The article on "metaphysics" in *The Oxford Companion to Philosophy* comments that "the exact nature of [metaphysics] has been

---

[2]Richard L. Pratt, *Every Though Captive: A Study Manual for the Defense of Christian Truth* (Phillipsburg, NJ: Presbyterian and Reformed, 1979), 87.

constantly disputed, *as indeed has its validity and usefulness.*"[3] In fact, the next article in this authoritative dictionary is titled: "metaphysics, opposition to," which points out that "the anti-metaphysical theory of the Logical Positivists . . . argued that metaphysical statements were nonsensical, [and] *put metaphysics out of fashion, where on many popular views it remains.*"[4] The article continues by noting that:

> Opposition to metaphysics has come from both within philosophy and outside it. . . . The deference to empirical science displayed by the Logical Positivists is still a feature of much Anglo-American analytic philosophy, creating an intellectual climate inimical to the pursuit of speculative metaphysics. . . .
>
> More recent hostility to metaphysics comes from the postmodernists and deconstructionists, who wish to proclaim that philosophy—and certainly metaphysics —is dead. These writers represent metaphysics as a temporary aberration of the Western intellect.[5]

In an article titled "Beyond Experience: Pragmatism and Nature's God," Professor Robert S. Corrington of Drew University speaks of the "current and fashionable bias against metaphysics."[6]

The popular and influential astronomer Carl Sagan (1934–1996) maintained a strong anti-metaphysical bias. In one review of his *The Demon-Haunted World: Science as a Candle in the Dark* (1996), Gary McGath noted: "Sagan's brand of skepticism leads him to the conclusion that there can be no basic principles of reality known beyond the results of scientific experimentation—that is, there can

---

[3]Ted Honderich, ed., *The Oxford Companion to Philosophy* (Oxford: Oxford University Press, 1995) 556. Emphasis added.

[4]Honderich, ed., *Oxford Companion to Philosophy*, 558. Emphasis added.

[5]Honderich, ed., *Oxford Companion to Philosophy*, 559.

[6]Robert S. Corrington, "Beyond Experience: Pragmatism and Nature's God," in *The American Journal of Theology and Philosophy* 14:2 (May 1993), 147.

be no valid metaphysics which is more than just conjecture."[7] Sagan said it best in the introduction to his Cosmos series: "The universe is all that is or ever was or ever will be."[8]

This denigration of metaphysics is important in that "this anti-metaphysical attitude has been one of the crucial ingredients which have molded culture and history over the last two hundred years,"[9] strongly influencing our Western world. But you should also be aware of a more subtle opposition to metaphysics which derives from the relationship of metaphysics and epistemology.

In arguing for animal rights, legal authority Kyle Ash deems it necessary to dis-establish metaphysics (ontology) in order to rid ourselves of our pride in the human species: "Renunciation of speciesism is essential to a modernization of international law, which discards an ontological approach for an approach more scientific, objective, and consensus-based."[10]

Metaphysics and Epistemology

In the unbelieving intellectual circles which do allow a limited role for metaphysics, the bias continues but in a different direction. Where metaphysics is tolerated today, it is assigned a subordinate position to epistemology. Some philosophers argue that to choose between available worldview options you must first establish your epistemology, then apply it to the facts to learn what reality is all about. That is, you should establish your theory of knowledge without encumbering it with metaphysical considerations. In this wide-

---

[7]Gary McGath: www.mcgath.com/demon.html.

[8]Carl Sagan, *Cosmos* (New York: Random House, 1980), 4. Notice his metaphysical assumption that the future will be like the past so that he can claim that the Universe is all there ever will be.

[9]Greg L. Bahnsen, *Always Ready: Directions for Defending the Faith*, ed. Robert R. Booth (Powder Springs, GA: American Vision, 1996), 178.

[10]Kyle Ash, "International Animal Rights: Speciesism and Exclusionary Human Dignity," *Journal of Animal Law*, Michigan State University College of Law (11) 198: www.animallaw.info/journals/jo_pdf/vol11_p195.pdf

spread approach, worldviews are adopted by a two-step procedure known as "philosophical methodism": (1) You establish your method of research and understanding (epistemology); (2) then using that epistemology you determine your metaphysical conclusions. This seems reasonable and is certainly a widespread method.

This bias favoring epistemology over metaphysics is strongly influenced by our modern enamorment with science. The impressive insights made by modern scientific discovery and practical technological achievements have elevated "scientific method" (an epistemological consideration) above metaphysics. This has created something of a "Science said it, I believe it, therefore it's true" mentality. *The Oxford Companion to Philosophy* highlights this bias among scientists: "This hostility [against metaphysics] is paralleled in the popular writings of many scientists, who seem to think that any legitimate issues once embraced by metaphysics now belong exclusively to the province of empirical science."[11] The *Infoplease Encyclopedia* well captures our fascination with science today:

> The technological advances of modern science, which in the public mind are often identified with science itself, have affected virtually every aspect of life. . . . Perhaps the most overwhelming aspect of modern science is not its accomplishments but its magnitude in terms of money, equipment, numbers of workers, scope of activity, and impact on society as a whole. Never before in history has science played such a dominant role in so many areas.[12]

Encarta summarizes the scientific method which has elevated science to this exalted position: "In the 20th century, scientists achieved spectacular advances in the fields of genetics, medicine, social sciences, technology, and physics. . . .Whatever the aim of their work,

---

[11]*Oxford Companion to Philosophy*, 559.
[12]"Revolutions in Modern Science," *Infoplease Encyclopedia*: www.infoplease.com/ce6/sci/A0860979.html

scientists use the same underlying steps to organize their research: (1) They make detailed observations about objects or processes, either as they occur in nature or as they take place during experiments; (2) they collect and analyze the information observed; and (3) they formulate a hypothesis that explains the behavior of the phenomena observed."[13] This elevates epistemology to its dominant position over metaphysics. Consider our current situation:

> Antagonism to metaphysical claims is quite simply the allegation that "pure reason" apart from sense experience cannot itself provide us with factual knowledge. Metaphysical statements speak of a suprasensible reality which is not directly experienced or verified by natural science. . . . Those antagonistic to metaphysics argue that all informative or factual statements about the objective world must be derived empirically (based on experience, observation, sensation), and therefore human knowledge cannot transcend particular, physical experience or the appearance of the senses. . . .
>
> Because metaphysical claims could not be brought to the critical test of sense experience, they were concluded to be senseless.[14]

In such an environment as we have today, method becomes central to both the intellectual and common outlooks. Therefore, since epistemology deals with how we come to know (involving scientific method), it receives priority over metaphysics, producing further modern antagonism against metaphysics:

> Herein lies the offense of metaphysics to the modern mind. Metaphysics presumes to tell us something about the objective world which we do not directly perceive in ordinary ex-

---

[13]"Science," *Encarta* (http://encarta.msn.com/encyclopedia_761557105/Science. html#s2)

[14]Bahnsen, *Always Ready*, 184.

perience and which cannot be verified through the methods of natural science.[15]

* * * * *

Opponents of metaphysics (and thereby of the theology of the Bible) view metaphysical reasoning as conflicting with empirical science as the one and only way to acquire knowledge.[16]

As renowned atheist philosopher Antony Flew expressed the modern scientific antipathy toward metaphysics: "It has been held that the human mind has no means of discovering facts outside the realm of sense experience."[17]

To understand the significance of the anti-metaphysical complaint, we should recall the definition of "worldview" which we previously discussed: "A worldview is a network of presuppositions (which are not verified by the procedures of natural science) regarding reality (metaphysics), knowing (epistemology), and conduct (ethics) in terms of which every element of human experience is related and interpreted." Note that a worldview involves presuppositions "which are not verified by the procedures of natural science." This is taboo in our science-fixated world.

Our Christian Response

In order to strengthen your ability to defend the faith, you should take to task this anti-metaphysical bias. But what should you think

---

[15]Bahnsen, *Always Ready*, 182.

[16]Bahnsen, *Always Ready*, 184.

[17]Antony Flew, "Metaphysics," in *A Dictionary of Philosophy*, 2nd ed. (New York: St. Martin's, 1984), 229. Cited in Bahnsen, *Always Ready*, 191. Interestingly, in late 2004 Flew declared he was no longer an atheist: "A British philosophy professor who has been a leading champion of atheism for more than a half-century has changed his mind. He now believes in God more or less based on scientific evidence, and says so on a video released Thursday." (www.sciencefindsgod.com/famous-atheist-now-believes-in-god.htm). His view, however, is contrary to Christianity, being more deistic.

about this antagonism to metaphysics? And how can you respond to this common objection generated out of the remarkably success-ful, naturalistic scientific world?

Actually, we can levy a devastating response against the critics of metaphysics. Consider the following seven problems with the anti-metaphysical position.

1. Epistemological method is not neutral. Though the anti-metaphysical crowd claims to be concerned with neutrality in their elevating epistemology, you will recall that neutrality in human thought is impossible. There is ample evidence to that end, and here we will focus a little more on the matter as we consider the question of *method* in reasoning.

Dr. Van Til argues that "the question of method is not a neutral something. Our presupposition of God as the absolute, self-con-scious Being, who is the source of all finite being and knowledge, makes it imperative that we distinguish the Christian theistic meth-od from all non-Christian methods."[18] Every method of reasoning, every system of thought presupposes either the truth or falsity of Christian theism. All worldviews are, at base, either one of two foundational options: Christian or non-Christian, believing or non-believing. You need to understand this as a Christian apologist, and the non-Christian needs to be made aware of this as you challenge him. Dr. Van Til explains the situation that exists from the perspec-tive of the Christian system:

> There are two mutually exclusive methodologies. The one of the natural man assumes the ultimacy of the human mind. On this basis man, making himself the ultimate reference point, virtually reduces all reality to one level and denies the counsel of God as determinative of the possible and the im-possible. Instead of the plan of God, it assumes an abstract

---

[18]Cornelius Van Til, *An Introduction to Systematic Theology* (Phillipsburg, NJ: Presbyterian and Reformed, 1974), 9. Cited in Bahnsen, *Van Til's Apologetic*, 62.

notion of possibility or probability, of being and rationality.
. . .

On the other hand there is the Christian position. When
consistently expressed it posits God's self-existence and
plan, as well as self-contained self-knowledge, as the presupposition of all created existence and knowledge. In that case,
all facts show forth and thus prove the existence of God and
His plan. In that case, too, all human knowledge should be
self-consciously subordinated to that plan.[19]

Let us explain what Van Til means. To get at his point you should
recall the record of the temptation and fall in Eden (again, we must
turn to Scripture!). God sovereignly and unambiguously commanded that Adam and Eve *not* eat of the Tree of the Knowledge of Good
and Evil. But Satan challenged God's direct command and told Eve
the decision was hers to make. Eve took it upon herself to weigh the
two options before her: "Shall I follow Satan who sees no wrong in
this? Or shall I follow God who simply declared it wrong without any
justifying reasons?"

This is the same method the unbeliever chooses: He asserts for
himself *the right to determine proper method.* And he does so without reference to God. Or, as Van Til puts it, the "natural man" assumes "the ultimacy of the human mind." His *method* is to operate
in the world in a way that "reduces all reality to one level and denies
the counsel of God as determinative of the possible and the impossible." Van Til was famous for illustrating the Christian view by a
larger circle (representing God) and smaller circle (representing the
Universe). The unbeliever's method does not bow to the absolute
authority of the Creator but claims all authority to reason on his
own terms without reference to God.

---

[19]Van Til, *Introduction to Systematic Theology*, 19. Cited in Bahnsen, *Van Til's
Apologetic*, 63.

The Christian position, however, holds that foundational to all reality is the personal, self-existent, sovereign God who creates and providentially sustains the Universe by His plan thereby making knowledge possible.

> There are only two fundamental outlooks: the Christian and the non-Christian. "Every method, the supposedly neutral one no less than any other, presupposes either the truth or the falsity of Christian theism." One either has "the mind of Christ" (1 Cor. 2:16) or is an "enemy in your mind" (Col. 1:21). . . . One either begins his thinking with the triune God who has clearly revealed Himself as the One who created and providentially controls all things, and Who graciously saves His people by the redemptive work of the incarnate Son applied by the Holy Spirit—or one does not begin one's thinking with this presupposition. Middle ground is excluded. At base, there are only two options. Of course, there are numerous variations and "family squabbles" within the two fundamental positions. . . . Those whose starting point is not the Christian worldview revealed in Scripture, while sharing this attitude with each other, differ from one another on other points. . . . Unbelieving positions are simply a series of illustrations of the same underlying position that rejects Christianity as its presupposition. . . . "He who is not with me is against me" (Matt. 12:30).[20]

The unbeliever's dismissal of our sovereign God is anything but neutral.

2. Metaphysics is necessary to epistemology. Here you should recall a recurring theme: Worldviews are *systems* of *inter-locking* presuppositions. As systems they include metaphysics *and* epistemology *and* ethics all bound up together in a mutually self-supporting system. Worldviews are not one-issue or single-fact constructs.

---

[20]Bahnsen, *Van Til's Apologetic*, 277, 278.

Consequently, you cannot dismiss metaphysics in deference to epistemology.

As Van Til perceptively notes, "Our theory of knowledge is what it is because our theory of being is what it is . . . . We cannot ask *how* we know without at the same time asking *what* we know."[21] How can epistemology be divorced from metaphysics, in that metaphysics "studies such questions or issues as the nature of existence, the sorts of things that exist, the classes of existent things, limits of possibility, the ultimate scheme of things, reality versus appearance, and the comprehensive conceptual framework used to make sense of the world as a whole"[22]? These issues *necessarily* impact epistemology.

Your theory of knowledge is just *one* aspect of your *entire* worldview, one feature of your interpretive outlook on all of human experience and thought. You cannot jerk it out of its inter-locking setting in your worldview and let it stand on its own. It would have nothing to stand on; it would be suspended in air. It is necessarily and unavoidably linked with your theory of reality and your theory of ethics: Having a way of knowing (epistemology) requires certain assumptions about the nature of reality (metaphysics). How can knowledge operate apart from the real world as it exists? It is impossible for it to be otherwise. Our theory of knowing is adopted as one that comports with our view of reality so that we can distinguish the true from the false. As per Van Til, "It appears how intimately one's theory of being and one's theory of method are interrelated."[23]

"We could not think or make sense of anything without some coherent view of the general nature and structure of reality"[24] because "one's convictions about metaphysics (the nature of reality) will influence one's position on epistemology (the proper method

---

[21]Cornelius Van Til, *The Defense of the Faith* (Philadelphia: Presbyterian and Reformed, 1955), 126.

[22]Bahnsen, *Always Ready*, 181.

[23]Van Til, *Systematic Theology*, 18. Cited in Bahnsen, *Van Til's Apologetic*, 63.

[24]Bahnsen, *Always Ready*, 179.

for knowing things), even as one's epistemology will influence one's metaphysical beliefs. A person's metaphysic and epistemology will be coordinated with each other, constituting a specific world-and-life view set over against other world-and-life views (each with its own interdependent views of reality and the method of knowing)."[25]

Thus, you see that *epistemology necessarily presupposes metaphysics*. Remember the epistemological method of science: "Whatever the aim of their work, scientists use the same underlying steps to organize their research: (1) They make detailed observations about objects or processes, either as they occur in nature or as they take place during experiments; (2) they collect and analyze the information observed; and (3) they formulate a hypothesis that explains the behavior of the phenomena observed."[26] Note carefully that scientific method involves "observations about objects" and "the behavior of the phenomena observed." These are metaphysical issues.

Clearly then, your method of knowing depends on the nature of reality (one feature of reality is the question of God). Interestingly, the Bible itself opens with a metaphysical assertion: "In the beginning God." It is naive to think you can choose an epistemology while remaining neutral toward metaphysics.

This point is illustrated by drawing from an agricultural example. Say that you have an apple orchard and that you must separate nice, healthy-sized good apples from deficient, stunted, bad apples before they are shipped off to market. You will need a device that will sort good and bad apples into separate bins. You want to drop apples in the sorter and let it distribute them into the proper good or bad

---

[25]Bahnsen, *Van Til's Apologetic*, 63 note 55. Although this is not our focus at this point, you should note that our theory of knowing has an obligatory (ethical) character in that it is deemed to match with reality so that it becomes the proper way of knowing. Therefore, ethics is also involved in our worldview.

[26]"Science," *Encarta* (http://encarta.msn.com/encyclopedia_761557105/Science. html#s2)

apple bin. The sorter illustrates your epistemology, your method of knowing; the apples illustrate your metaphysics, your reality.

You cannot devise such a sorting machine, however, if you do not *know in advance* what an apple is, and what is the difference between a good apple and a bad apple. Likewise, if you do not know something about the universe to begin with, you cannot devise a method for separating truth and error (good apples and bad apples). Everyone begins with an *integrated worldview* involving metaphysics *and* epistemology. The contemporary anti-metaphysical bias is unreasonable.

3. Anti-metaphysical arguments are uncritical. Whether those who oppose metaphysics like it or not, whether they think about it or not, things exist and are related somehow—*and these are metaphysical realities.* To dismiss metaphysics is a highly naive way of thinking.

Herein lies the irony in all of this: *The unbeliever who discounts metaphysics does so on the basis of his own hidden metaphysical program.* He is operating on naturalistic, materialistic assumptions which he considers to be the final determiners of reality. The unbeliever shoots himself in the foot when he attacks metaphysics, since his entire worldview is based on metaphysical considerations. "What is glaringly obvious, then, is that the unbeliever rests upon and appeals to a metaphysical position in order to prove that there can be no metaphysical position known to be true!"[27] And this is not simply a knee-jerk Christian response to the matter. *The Oxford Companion to Philosophy* notes this problem:

> Opposition to metaphysics has come from both within philosophy and outside it. . . . This hostility is paralleled in the popular writings of many scientists, who seem to think that any legitimate issues once embraced by metaphysics now belong exclusively to the province of empirical science—issues

[27]Bahnsen, *Always Ready*, 190.

such as the nature of space and time, and the mind-body problem. *Such writers are often blithely unaware of the uncritical metaphysical assumptions pervading their works and the philosophical naïveté of many of their arguments.* But it is ironic that the deference shown by many philosophers to the latest scientific theories is not reciprocated by the popularizing scientists, who do not conceal their contempt for philosophy in general as well as metaphysics in particular.[28]

4. Metaphysical presuppositions are necessary to reasoning. Our earlier discussion on presuppositions explained their necessity in human thought and experience. We may view presuppositions metaphorically as a "foundation" and as a "framework." That is, we can say that they are both "foundations" to and a "framework" for worldviews. They both give a sure base to human experience and provide a guiding framework for human reasoning in the world.

Presuppositions are necessary to reasoning. Every system of thought has some starting point, some standard of authority by which truth and error are evaluated, the real and the unreal are recognized, and the possible and impossible are determined. You must challenge a person's basic assumptions supporting his worldview to uncover his ultimate commitment. You must press the unbeliever to provide you with his standard of evaluation for his outlook. When he offers it, you must challenge it by pressing him: "How do you know *that* is the right standard?" The respondent has one of four options available: (1) He can admit that his standard of evaluation in his worldview has no justification (thus rendering his position arbitrary and irrational); (2) he can argue that his standard is established by some standard outside of itself (thus admitting that a new standard becomes more ultimate, thereby destroying his previously determined "ultimate" standard); (3) he can then keep seeking a more ultimate standard, becoming trapped in an **infinite regress**[29]

---

[28]*Oxford Companion to Philosophy*, 559. Emphasis mine.

[29]**Infinite regress** is an argument procedure which occurs when a suggested ex-

argument, thereby rendering his standard unknown and unknowable; or (4) he can point to a truly ultimate, self-verifying standard that explains all else, in that it is the ultimate standard beyond which no appeal can be made, as in the Christian worldview which points to God (Heb. 6:13).

Unbelieving systems should be pressed to show that they must have an ultimate authority upon which to rest if they are to objectively and intelligibly evaluate anything. Evaluation requires a standard. When *any* system gets around to verifying its *ultimate* authority, it will have to *presuppose* that authority. Let us explain how this is so.

We all must begin with some form of authority. The unbeliever begins with his own authority to weigh, evaluate, and determine options. The Christian begins with the Creator's authority. When one's epistemic authority is challenged, he must rationally account for it in some manner. Since we cannot finalize an argument engaged in infinite regress, we must stop at some self-validating, self-attesting authority. The unbeliever has none.

The Christian system has a self-attesting authority. Your epistemology is grounded in the all-interpreting presupposition of the personal, infinite, eternal, self-contained, self-revealing Creator of all facts and laws. By the very nature of the case, God is your ultimate reference point, and He alone is self-validating. How could the absolute, all-creating God of Scripture appeal to some authority greater than His own? Remember that Scripture recognizes this phenomenon when it declares in Hebrews: "For when God made the promise to Abraham, since He could swear by no one greater, He swore by Himself" (Heb. 6:13).

---

planation or purported standard is challenged. The challenge causes the argument to point back further to a more basic commitment that sustains the explanation. Then that commitment is challenged, pointing to an even more basic commitment, on and on *ad infinitum*.

By definition, God must be absolute authority. He needs no "counsel" to guide Him (Isa. 40:13; Rom. 11:34–35; 1 Cor. 2:16; cf. Job 35:11; 41:11). Indeed, Paul declares: "Let God be true, though every man be found a liar" (Rom. 3:4). Later on we will demonstrate how to employ this presuppositional worldview argument effectively.

We see this self-attesting authority in various places in Scripture. In Matthew 7:29 the people were amazed when Jesus taught "as one having authority, and not as their scribes." The scribes appealed to renowned rabbis to validate their teaching: "You have heard that the ancients were told" (Matt. 5:21, 33). But Jesus' authority was self-attesting. He declares that His word is like a rock which provides absolute stability for one's life (Matt. 7:24–27). In fact, He teaches that His word will be the standard of judgment of all men at the Final Judgment (John 12:48).

The believer's authority, then, rests in the eternal foundation of God Almighty speaking in His objective self-revelation to man (the Bible). This provides a sure foundation to reason and experience. The unbeliever's authority is subjective depending upon his own self-assertion. This leads to subjectivism which destroys reason.

Before moving to our next response against the anti-metaphysical bias, you should be aware of a possible response that the unbeliever will bring against you. He will complain that you are engaging in **circular reasoning**[30] or the informal logical fallacy of **begging the question**.[31] That is, since we assert that God is self-verifying, we are assuming God in order to prove God. However, we should note in response to this objection:

---

[30]**Circular reasoning** (technically known by the Latin phrase *circulus in probando*) occurs when one assumes something in order to prove that very thing. Circular reasoning is often very subtle and hard to detect.

[31]**Begging the question** (technically known by the Latin phrase *petitio principii*) is a fallacious manner of reasoning wherein your premise includes the claim that your conclusion is true, that is, your argument assumes the very point to be proven.

(1) We are not engaged in special pleading for the Christian world-view. We are simply asking which system makes human experience intelligible. For sake of argument, we will grant the unbeliever his system with whatever foundations he adopts in order to see if it can justify its truth claims. But then he will have to grant us ours (for sake of argument) to see if we can justify our truth claims. By the very nature of our God as the self-existing, eternal Creator, our worldview self-justifies its starting point. (We will later explain this two-step procedure of worldview critique.)

(2) All systems must ultimately involve some circularity in reasoning. For instance, when you argue for the legitimacy of the laws of logic, you must employ the laws of logic. How else can you justify laws of logic? This is a **transcendental**[32] issue, an issue that lies outside of the temporal, changing realm of sense experience. Laws of logic do not change: they are universal, invariant, abstract principles.

In the Christian worldview, however, the Christian apologetic is *not* engaged in *viciously* circular argument, a circular argument *on the same plane*. We appeal above and beyond the temporal realm. God's self-revelation in nature and in Scripture informs us of the two-level universe: God is not a fact like other facts in the world. He is the Creator and Establisher of all else. His existence alone makes the universe, reason, and human experience possible.

(3) "Circularity" in one's philosophical system is just another name for 'consistency' in outlook throughout one's system. That is,

---

[32]**Transcendental reasoning** "is concerned to discover what general conditions must be fulfilled for any particular instance of knowledge to be possible; it has been central to the philosophies of thinkers such as Aristotle and Kant, and it has become a matter of inquiry in contemporary, analytically minded philosophy. Van Til asks what view of man, mind, truth, language, and the world is necessarily presupposed by our conception of knowledge and our methods of pursuing it. For him, the transcendental answer is supplied at the very first step of man's reasoning—not by autonomous philosophical speculation, but by transcendent revelation from God." (Bahnsen, *Van Til's Apologetic*, 5–6, note 10).

one's starting point and final conclusion cohere with each other."[33] Here it is more fully explained:

> The "circularity" of a transcendental argument is not at all the same as the fallacious 'circularity' of an argument in which the conclusion is a restatement (in one form or another) of one of its premises. Rather, it is the circularity involved in a coherent theory (where all the parts are consistent with or assume each other) and which is required when one reasons about a precondition for reasoning, its "circles" are destructive of human thought—i.e., "vicious" and futile endeavors.[34]

(4) The unbeliever has no defensible standard whereby he can judge the Christian position. His argument either ends up in infinite regress (making it impossible to prove), has no justification (rendering it subjective), or engages in an unjustifiable same-plane circularity (causing it to be fallacious).Without a self-verifying standard, he has no epistemological way out. And only the Christian worldview has such a self-verifying standard.

5. Anti-metaphysical arguments are mistaken. In *Always Ready*, it is established that the arguments against metaphysics ultimately reduce to two complaints: (1) The opponent of metaphysics will not allow inferring from the realm of sense experience anything that lies outside of that realm, and (2) The opponent of metaphysics will not allow any source of knowledge about reality which is non-empirical (non-observational, without sense experience).[35] We will focus on the first objection at this point, the other in Point 6 below.

First, this contradicts the scientific method itself. Remember the implications of the presuppositional (and non-material) features of a worldview (see Chapter 4). These features are absolutely essential to science even though they cannot be shown under the microscope,

---

[33]Bahnsen, *Van Til's Apologetic*, 170 note 42.
[34]Bahnsen, *Van Til's Apologetic*, 518 note 122.
[35]Bahnsen, *Always Ready*, 185.

dissected in the lab, measured by caliper, or demonstrated by the methods of scientific investigation: e.g., the reality of an objective external world in contrast to a world of illusion (which allows for objective scientific investigation, the reliability of memory (so necessary to scientific experimentation), continuing personal identity over time (so that the scientist's experience of past realities can be related to the present and expected in the future), the reality of cause-and-effect relations (the very essence of experimental predictability), and so forth. Remember, metaphysics "studies such questions or issues as the nature of existence, the sorts of things that exist, the classes of existent things, *limits of possibility, the ultimate scheme of things, reality versus appearance,* and the *comprehensive conceptual framework used to make sense of the world as a whole.*"[36]

Second, scientists constantly deal with unseen realities, such as subatomic particles, gravity, magnetism, radiation, barometric pressure, elasticity, radioactivity, natural laws, names, numbers, past events, categories, future contingencies, laws of thought, individual identity over time, causation, and so forth. For instance, the whole theory of evolution which controls modern scientific inquiry is a non-sensory theoretical projection back into time which is held by many to be indisputable fact. Yet no scientist was there to witness it. They have not seen any other Universe created or one kind of life evolve into another of a different kind.

Such a theoretical projection as demanded by evolutionary theory depends upon metaphysical presuppositions regarding reality (but, of course, we believe evolutionists to be *mistaken* in their metaphysical surmises). For instance, the National Academy of Sciences published an authoritative guide for public school science teachers titled *Teaching About Evolution and the Nature of Science.* That guide defined science as "a particular way of looking at the world. In science, explanations are restricted to those that can

---

[36]Bahnsen, *Always Ready,* 181. Emphasis added.

be inferred from [experimental] data that can be substantiated by other scientists," noting that "anything that can be observed or measured is amenable to scientific investigation. Explanations that cannot be based on empirical evidence are not part of science."[37] Yet, some of our greatest discoveries in the Twentieth Century were in the atomic and sub-atomic worlds which were unseen and depend upon unseen metaphysical principles.

Third, the anti-metaphysical complaint is irrelevant to *biblical* metaphysics. Christian metaphysics is not an arbitrary, groping-in-the-dark effort that blindly leaps from sense experience to the supra-sensical world.[38] The Christian metaphysic is God-revealed, being drawn from the divinely inscripturated, objective revelation of the Creator in the Bible. Therefore, any anti-metaphysical argument is established on anti-theistic presuppositions which deny the existence of God. Such an unproved assumption shuts the door on supra-sensical knowledge drawn from God's own self-revelation in Scripture, which is the very point at issue in our debate with the unbeliever. The unbeliever is therefore simply loudly asserting his disbelief in God as his foundational assumption.

Thus, the believing worldview operates on the presupposition of the infallible revelation of the Creator. Knowledge of basic metaphysical realities do not cause problems within the Christian worldview because the personal, eternal, omniscient, omnipotent Creator who governs all things has sovereignly declared them— metaphysical realities such as God's existence, His governing by a

---

[37] *Teaching About Evolution and the Nature of Science* (Washington, D.C.: National Academy Press, 1998), chapter 3 available on-line: http://www.nap.edu/readingroom/books/evolution98/evol3.html.

[38] The stinging (and unbelieving) wit of Ambrose Bierce in his *The Devil's Dictionary* captures this anti-metaphysical bias when he defines "religion": "Religion, n. A daughter of Hope and Fear, explaining to Ignorance the nature of the Unknowable."

rational plan, and His revealing to us the basics of our metaphysical environment.[39]

6. Anti-metaphysical claims are destructive. When you encounter the claim that all knowledge must derive from our senses, you should point out to the anti-metaphysical objector that:

First, the anti-metaphysical claim is self-contradictory. How can we know that "all knowledge must derive from our senses?" This claim is not found in the objective world of sense experience. Have you ever sensed it in the real world? It is a non-material, mental construct. This sort of self-refuting argument illustrates Paul's statement "they became futile in their speculations" (Rom. 1:21).

Second, the anti-metaphysical claim is presuppositional in nature. The claim does not allow for any empirical verification since it deals with the totality of reality because it asserts that "*all* knowledge must derive from our senses" (yet no man can comprehend all of reality) and is *necessarily* so in that it requires that "all knowledge *must* derive from our senses" (therefore it is not a truth dependent on the changing circumstances of the sense experience world of science). In the final analysis, this claim is a dogmatic assertion rather than an empirical conclusion.

Third, the anti-metaphysical claim destroys the very possibility of science. As we will explain in more detail later, science absolutely depends upon the uniformity of nature (so that experiments under controlled conditions can produce predictable results everywhere) and the assurance that the future will be like the past (so that experiments can predict future results). These two *metaphysical* claims allow scientists to generalize and project. Consequently, any anti-metaphysical complaint undermines science itself.

Fourth, the anti-metaphysical claim destroys reason. Empirical learning and reasoning would be impossible without these and other metaphysical assumptions. As we noted earlier, epistemology depends upon metaphysics. To evaluate arguments requires that we

---

[39]Bahnsen, *Always Ready*, 189.

employ propositions, logical relations, and so forth. And these are not discovered through the senses, even though they are necessary to reason itself.[40]

7. Anti-metaphysical bias is anti-Christian. As a Christian you instinctively recognize that by the very nature of the anti-metaphysics position, the Christian worldview is *precluded* at the outset. Christianity is built upon the supra-sensical, invisible, eternal, self-contained Triune Creator of the Universe (Col. 1:15; 1 Tim. 1:17). Those opposed to metaphysical inquiry are necessarily set against the Christian worldview.

Obviously the Christian cannot adopt the anti-metaphysic for himself and still be a Christian, nor can the scientist who professes faith in Christ. Later, we will show how you *can* stand on the unbeliever's assumptions and adopt an anti-metaphysical worldview *for sake of argument in order to show its impossibility.*

8. Anti-metaphysical bias is sinfully motivated. In the final analysis and given *your* worldview, you must understand that lurking below this anti-metaphysic is sinful rebellion against God. Spiritual insights into this rejection of metaphysics (and therefore the very possibility of God) reveals: "Men will, as it were, build a roof over their heads in hopes of keeping out any distressing revelation from a transcendent God. The anti-metaphysical perspective of the modern age functions as just such a protective ideological roof for the unbeliever."[41]

We have already noted in our introduction to this lesson that this is precisely what Paul teaches in Romans 1: The unbeliever "suppresses the truth *in unrighteousness*" (Rom. 1:18b) so that they become "futile in their speculations" (Rom. 1:21b). Though man is created in the image of God to know and serve the Lord, he actively suppresses the truth to shield himself from the ensuing guilt before his Maker and Judge, just as Adam attempted to hide his nakedness

---

[40]Bahnsen, *Always Ready*, 188.
[41]Bahnsen, *Always Ready*, 188.

and himself from God when he sinned against Him (Gen. 3:7, 10; cf. Job 31:33).

Opposition to metaphysics is often associated with anti-religious sentiment. For instance, consider the following secularist and his views:

> Chauncey Wright [1830–1875] was an American philosopher of science in the second half of the nineteenth century and an early proponent of Darwinism in the United States. Sometimes cited as a founder of pragmatism, he is more appropriately remembered as an incisive and original philosophical thinker in the tradition of British empiricism. Because of his empiricism and positivist spirit, he exercised a great influence at a crucial time in American cultural life— in the 1860s and 70s, when the influence of religious piety and Transcendentalism was waning. Wright was a tireless critic of metaphysics and the natural theology he believed it served.[42]

* * * * *

> Even non-believing philosophers suspect improper motives in the outright rejection of metaphysics. Philosopher W. H. Walsh wrote: "It must be allowed that the reaction against [metaphysics] has been . . . so violent indeed as to suggest that the issues involved in the controversy must be something more than academic."[43]

Conclusion

The modern bias against metaphysics is to be expected, given your Christian worldview. The doctrine of sin anticipates it; the express revelation of God asserts it. You must be prepared to respond to the

---

[42]"Chauncey Wright," *Stanford Encyclopedia of Philosophy* (http://plato.stanford.edu/entries/wright).

[43]W. H. Walsh, *Metaphysics* (New York: Harcourt, Brace and World, 1963), 12. Cited in *Always Ready*, 182.

anti-metaphysical outlook, showing its self-destructive character. This book is equipping you for just such an endeavor.

2. Exegetical Observations

The problem we are confronting at this stage is the modern bias against metaphysics. In our last point analyzing the bias, we noted that ultimately this attitude is a sinful effort to escape God's judgment. In Psalm 139 we see a poetic portrayal of David's attempt to escape the all-seeing eye of God. If this characterizes the believer (i.e., David) in his relationship to God, how much more does it portray the unbeliever's stronger motivation to avoid accountability before God? A quick survey of Psalm 139 highlights the matter for us.

The metaphysical reality of the one True God known to man in both general and special revelation confronts man at all times and in every place (Ps. 19:1, 4). Man knows the all-seeing, all-evaluating eye of the all-creating, everywhere-present God is always watching him (Rom. 1:19–21). David poetically considers various means of escape from God's penetrating analysis, all of which are futile in that God is his Creator and perfectly knows him.

David opens with a statement regarding God's omniscience. He admits that "thou has searched me and known me" (Ps. 139:1). The verb tense "has searched" in Hebrew really expresses a *continual* searching. The Hebrew word itself literally means "to dig," as in digging for gold (Job 28:3). But here it is used metaphorically to express deep moral contemplation and evaluation by means of a full investigation. This is the same God of whom another psalmist asks: "Would not God find this out? For He knows the secrets of the heart" (Ps. 44:21; cf. Job 13:9; Jer. 12:3; 17:10; Acts 15:8; 1 Jn. 3:20). The result of such a penetrating analysis is that God knows him fully.

The Psalmist illustrates this from several angles, each of which reflects the omniscience of God. Though the Lord created the entire enormous universe (Gen. 1:1; Ex. 20:11), though He calls all the innumerable stars by their names (Isa. 40:26), He knows even this one puny man's action in life: "Thou dost know when I sit down and when I rise up" (Ps. 139:2a; 2 Kings 19:27). That is, every time David is at rest, and every time he is in motion, God knows it full well. God knows him in every circumstance of his human experience. This is just as we would expect in our presuppositional metaphysic wherein God is the necessary foundation to human experience.

What is more, "thou dost understand my thoughts from afar" (v. 2b; cf. Ps. 94:11). This does not mean simply that God knows each successive thought that David has, but that he knows everything about his every thought: its origin, motivation, moral character, and tendency. God knows absolutely *everything* about David's every thought. Though men can only know things about you when near to you, by hearing you speak, or watching you act, God knows your very internal thoughts "from afar." This is remarkable in that "God [is] in the height of heaven, look also at the distant stars, how high they are!" (Job 22:12).

David returns to God's full knowledge of his motion in the earth: "Thou dost scrutinize my path and my lying down, and art intimately acquainted with all my ways" (Ps. 139:3; cf. Job 31:4; 28:24; 34:21; Prov. 5:21). Once again, God knows when he is in motion (on the "path") and at rest ("lying down"). He knows both the active and passive situations of life for He is "intimately acquainted with all my ways."

He returns once again to God's knowledge of his inner-most thoughts: "Even before there is a word on my tongue, behold, O Lord, Thou dost know it all" (Ps. 139:4). As noted in verse 2, God knows his very thoughts, so He knows what word is about to come out of his mouth at any moment.

Now David transitions from God's omniscience to His omnipresence: "Thou hast enclosed me behind and before, and laid Thy hand upon me" (Ps. 139:5; cf. 34:7; 125:2). God surrounds him on all sides, in front and behind. The idea of God's surrounding him from *above* is hinted at in the fact that God's hand is "upon" me.

With all of this awareness of God's omniscience and omnipresence, David is overwhelmed: "Such knowledge is too wonderful for me; it is too high, I cannot attain to it" (Ps. 139:6). This signifies his understanding that God's knowledge is beyond comprehension. As a creature he knows he cannot attain such knowledge himself. He is acknowledging the Creator/creature distinction so essential to the believing worldview: two levels of reality exist, God and all else. As such, God's knowledge is beyond attainment for the creature. The finite creature cannot fully comprehend the knowledge of the infinite, eternal Creator (Job 11:7–8; Isa. 55:9; Rom. 11:33).

What is the creature to do then? He knows he is a sinner. But there is nothing he can do, for he cannot escape the all-seeing, everywhere-present God: "Where can I go from Thy Spirit? Or where can I flee from Thy presence? If I ascend to heaven, Thou art there; If I make my bed in Sheol, behold, Thou art there" (Ps. 139:7–8; cf. 1 Kings 8:27; 2 Chron. 2:6; Jer. 23:24). This presents us with a *desire* to escape judgment, and reminds us of God's declaration through his prophet Amos where he warns sinful nations that they cannot hide from God: "Though they dig into Sheol, from there shall My hand take them; and though they ascend to heaven, from there will I bring them down" (Amos 9:2–4; cf. Job 26:6; Prov. 15:11).

He cannot escape by fleeing to the place where the sun dawns or the where it sets over the sea, for God is there also: "If I take the wings of the dawn, if I dwell in the remotest part of the sea, even there Thy hand will lead me, and Thy right hand will lay hold of me" (Ps. 139:9–10). Nor does darkness hide David from God, for to God darkness is as the brightest day: all is easily visible to Him: "If I say, 'Surely the darkness will overwhelm me, and the light around me will be night,' even the darkness is not dark to Thee, and the night is as bright as the day. Darkness and light are alike to Thee" (139:11–12; cf. Job 22:13).

Not only does God know all because He is omniscient and omnipresent, but because He also created David. God formed his "inward parts" and "didst weave" him in his "mother's womb" (Ps. 139:13); He structured David's skeletal "form" (139:15; cf. Job 10:8–10; Eccl 11:5) even creating him as an embryo ("unformed substance") (139:16). This comports well with the fact that man has an inner awareness of God (Rom. 1:19a); in that God intimately created him from the inside out. David has even poetically thought that he might perhaps flee back to his mother's womb, hoping to hide from God there. But God was involved in the very formation of his body and spirit therein.

As a true believer, David must ultimately give praise to God for all of this: "I will give thanks to Thee, for I am fearfully and wonderfully made; wonderful are Thy works, and my soul knows it very well" (Ps. 139:14). God's metaphysical reality is such that He controls all the days of David's life—from even before he was born: "Thine eyes have seen my unformed substance; and in Thy book they were all written, the days that were ordained for me, when as yet there was not one of them" (139:16).

In the final analysis, the true believer realizes the glory and necessity of God's almighty being, for it gives meaning, significance, and value to his entire life and experience: "How precious also are Thy thoughts to me, O God! How vast is the sum of them! If I should count them, they would outnumber the sand. When I awake, I am still with Thee" (Ps. 139:17–18; cf. 40:5). Though the believer may be "anxious" at God's searching, he knows it is for his ethical good: "Search me, O God, and know my heart; try me and know my anxious thoughts; and see if there be any hurtful way in me, and lead me in the everlasting way" (vv. 23–24).

Rather than the unbeliever actually having **autonomy**[44](being a law unto himself), he is fully known and governed by God. The

---

[44]**Autonomy** derives from two Greek words: *auto* ("self") and *nomos* ("law"). It effectively means "self law," or "self rule." Human autonomy asserts that man's

believer ultimately finds comfort in this; the unbeliever suppresses this truth because he, too, knows God's ethical evaluation. He seeks to flee it, since he has no Redeemer to shield him from God's wrath: "For the wrath of God is revealed from heaven against all ungodliness and unrighteousness of men, who suppress the truth in unrighteousness" (Rom 1:18).

3. Questions Raised

Attempt to answer the following questions on your own before looking at the text or consulting the **Answer Key**.

1. What is the modern mind's pre-disposition toward metaphysics? When did this begin?

2. Among those who tolerate metaphysics, which do they deem more basic, metaphysics or epistemology? Why?

3. State five of the seven responses that are provided against the anti-metaphysical bias of today.

4. Explain why epistemology is not neutral. What are the two basic epistemological methodologies available to man?

5. How does the record of Adam and Eve help us see that epistemology is non-neutral?

6. In the Christian worldview, what are the two levels of reality? Explain why the "two levels of reality" are important.

7. Why is metaphysics necessary to epistemology so that our scientific method itself must involve a basic metaphysic?

8. In what way is anti-metaphysical hostility considered to be "uncritical" and naive?

9. Given the Christian's starting point with God, explain how we can avoid the charge of circular reasoning.

---

reasoning is the ultimate criterion of knowledge.

4. Practical Application

1. Survey the letters to the editor and editorials in your daily paper and cut out those that give evidence of an anti-metaphysical bias. Read them at a Christian Bible study and lead a discussion regarding the anti-metaphysical mind set hidden in our thought patterns today.

2. Go on-line or consult a science text book and read about ten pages of the opening material. Jot down evidences of anti-metaphysical bias. Analyze the offending statements in their contexts to see if you can discern the "uncritical" nature of the evidence therein.

3. Discuss with a Christian friend as to whether or not setting aside the question of metaphysics is sinful.

4. Read and discuss with a non-Christian friend the news article on the problem of teaching "Intelligent Design" in the public schools. Discuss the metaphysical implications of this contemporary debate. (www.csmonitor.com/2004/1123/p11s02-legn.html)

5. Search the Internet and compile a list of Christian apologetics sites that discuss the issue of metaphysics and science. Save these in a file for your future research.

6. Write a paper for a college science class on the necessity of metaphysics to science.

7. Read and study Psalm 139, using the brief study above. Lead a Bible study where you bring out some of the apologetical implications of the passage.

5. Recommended Reading

Alston, William P., "What is Naturalism, that we Should be Mindful of It?":www.leaderu.com/aip/docs/alston-naturalism.html

"Are Evolutionists the One's with Closed Minds?": www.answersingenesis.org/docs/506.asp

Bahnsen, Greg L. *Always Ready*, chapter 31.

"How Can You Believe in Creation When There is No God?": www. answersingenesis.org/creation/v9/i4/atheists.asp

Jones, Doug, "The Futility of Non-Christian Thought": www.reformed. org/apologetics/martin-jones/jones_martin1.html

Sarfarti, Jonathan, "If God Created the Universe, then Who Created God?": www.answersingenesis.org/tj/v12/i1/universe.asp

Scott, Ian, "Anti-God Philosophies of Science": www.answersingenesis. org/creation/v3/i4/anti_god.asp

"So You're Doing a Report on Creation vs. Evolution?": www. answersingenesis.org/cec/docs/CvE_report.asp

Unfred, David, "Evolution as Philosophy": www.answersingenesis.org/ creation/v4/i3/philosophy.asp

8

Approaching the Unbeliever

Do not answer a fool according to his folly,
Lest you also be like him.
Answer a fool as his folly deserves,
Lest he be wise in his own eyes.

(Prov. 26:4–5)

Y OU ARE FINALLY ready to learn specifically *how* to engage apologetics with the unbeliever. All of the groundwork laid to this point should now make more philosophical sense for understanding your Christian worldview. It should also begin making *practical* sense for presenting your apologetic challenge to the non-Christian.

In our last lesson we noted that as a Christian you are standing against the cold winds of impersonalism which blow over our cultural landscape today. Because of the great success of modern scientific and technological achievement, Western civilization has tended to discount metaphysical questions. Instead, our mind-set is more toward the sense-oriented, empirical scientific method. You must recognize this default bias of modern man because you need to respond to it.

You have been learning a lot about worldviews. You are now seeing that to justify logical reasoning and to validate human experience, you will have to operate self-consciously in terms of a complete worldview—including not only epistemology (how we know),

155

but metaphysics (what is the nature of reality) and ethics (how we should behave). Despite modern naïveté, you cannot have an epistemology without a metaphysic, for your theory of knowing must be compatible with your theory of reality. This will be the unbeliever's downfall, as we will see.

In this chapter we are ready to outline the general procedure for defending the faith. Although the prior studies may have raised the uneasy concern that apologetics is too philosophical and sophisticated, you will learn that it is actually quite simple. And apologetics is especially simple when employing the presuppositional method because you are not required to learn every fact of human experience "just in case."

Nor may the unbeliever skirt the issue by declaring, "We are working on it." The presuppositional method deals with issues that must exist *prior* to the facts, for the facts to be known and used. Therefore, you will have the apologetic tools to answer all forms of objections from all types of people at all times. Van Til expresses this remarkable nature of the apologetic method:

> When we approach the question in this way we should be willing to start anywhere and with any fact that any person we meet is interested in. The very conviction that there is not a single fact that can really be known unless it is interpreted theistically [i.e., with reference to God] gives us this liberty to start anywhere, as far as a proximate starting point is concerned. . . . We can start with any fact at all and challenge "our friends the enemy," to give us an intelligible interpretation of it.[1]

All facts speak of God's existence, for Acts 14:17 declares that God "did not leave Himself without a witness."

Should you not expect this since Peter commands you to "sanctify Christ as Lord in your hearts, *always being ready* to make a

---

[1] Cornelius Van Til, *A Survey of Christian Epistemology* (Phillipsburg, NJ: Presbyterian and Reformed, 1969), 205.

defense to *everyone* who asks you to give an account for the hope
that is in you" (1 Pet. 3:15)? Consider this more in-depth explanation:

> Despite the variety of criticism and the many modes in
> which they are expressed, there is a common, basic set of
> circumstances and principles that are embodied in each and
> every apologetic encounter. . . . Due to God's inescapable
> revelation every unbeliever nevertheless knows God and
> thereby (contrary to his espoused principles) knows himself
> and the world in some measure; knowing God, all men are
> then without an apologetic for their rebellion against His
> truth. The whole created realm constantly reveals the living
> and true God, thus providing abundant common ground be-
> tween the believer and unbeliever. Since the latter is always
> the image of God, and since he possesses the truth of God
> (though suppressed), the apologist always has a point of con-
> tact with him. . . . The very possibility of knowledge outside
> of God's revelation (savingly presented in Christ) must be
> undermined.[2]

In the last chapter you learned that generally the unbeliever attempts to avoid metaphysical considerations. You also learned that
his system cannot justify his foundational assumptions for logical
reasoning and human experience. You saw that by the very nature of
the situation, worldview presuppositions *must be verified by some
ultimate authority*, if they are to carry any weight and be anything
more than subjective assertions. Unfortunately for the unbeliever,
he has no self-verifying authority. This is where the presuppositional method renders the unbelieving worldview subjective and
irrational.

But now the question arises: How can I get through to the unbeliever in such a situation? If worldviews are self-contained and

---

[2]Bahnsen, *Always Ready*, 104, 105.

self-attesting, how can I reason with the unbeliever in his own self-contained worldview? Are the unbeliever and I at an impasse where we can only call each other "heretic" and then go home?

Rudyard Kipling once wrote of the worldview problems distinguishing the Islamic world from the Christian world: "Oh, East is East, and West is West, and never the twain shall meet" (*The Ballad of East and West*, 1889). Does this sort of problem characterize the confrontation between belief and unbelief? Was the famed Reformed apologist, theologian, and statesman, Abraham Kuyper (1837–1920), correct when he stated of the worldview conflict with the unbeliever: "It will be impossible to settle the difference of insight. No polemic between these two kinds of science . . . can ever serve any purpose. This is the reason why apologetics has always failed to reach results."[3]

We are not left in an irresolvable deadlock. Presuppositional Apologetics is "nuclear strength apologetics."[4] And when nuclear weapons go off, you don't just walk away muttering and complaining. The unbeliever's world is catastrophically impacted, to say the least.

1. Exegetical Observations

We will break with our normal order of approach by *beginning* with "Exegetical Observations," since this portion of the chapter specifically presents the biblical foundation for the apologetic procedure. Then we will return to "Central Concerns," which elucidate and apply the biblically warranted method.

In Proverbs 26:4–5 we discover what becomes an effective procedural outline for biblical apologetics. Upon your first reading

---

[3] Abraham Kuyper, *Principles of Sacred Theology*, trans. J. Hendrik De Vries (Grand Rapids, MI: Eerdmans, [1898] 1968), 160.

[4] A helpful study in apologetics is Bahnsen's ten-lecture "Transcendental Arguments: Nuclear Strength Apologetics." It is available from Covenant Media Foundation (Set # ASV7).

of this passage it might appear contradictory and confusing. But once you analyze it carefully you will discern a beautiful procedural method. Although we know Solomon was not teaching a course in apologetics, it nevertheless is true that he lays down wise principles by means of proverbial maxim, many of which are useful in apologetics.[5]

Solomon's directive reads as follows: "Do not answer a fool according to his folly, or you will be like him yourself. Answer a fool according to his folly, or he will be wise in his own eyes" (Prov. 26:4–5).[6] What in the world is he saying? And how is it helpful for apologetics?

Recognizing the fool

Before we get start unpacking his specific meaning here, we must first understand what he means by "fool." In that we are dealing with worldviews as systems, we should expect that we must look to Scripture (the epistemological foundation to our worldview) to determine the true nature of the fool. In the Bible a fool is not necessarily one who is a mentally deficient, shallow-minded ignoramus. He is not one whom we might pejoratively call an "idiot."[7] In fact, oftentimes

---

[5]Bahnsen frequently lamented that Christian apologists did not use Proverbs more often. As we mentioned in an earlier lesson, Ecclesiastes powerfully confronts the worldview of unbelief by demonstrating the glorious superiority of God's perspective on life over against a view of life approached only "under heaven" or "under the sun." A helpful commentary to this is H. C. Leupold, *Exposition of Ecclesiastes* (Grand Rapids: Baker, 1966).

[6]Here we depart from our use of the New American Standard, in that it is somewhat deficient. The New International Version translates the matter well, as do the King James Version, New King James Version, and the New Revised Standard Version translations.

[7]Nevertheless, the word "idiot" derives from the Greek *idiotes* which itself is based on *idios*. This is most appropriate for our understanding of the biblical notion of a fool, for *idios* means "one's own, private." Etymologically then, we may say the fool does things like an "idiot": he does them his own way without reference to a law outside of himself.

he is bright and respectable before the eyes of the world (Rom. 1:22; 1 Cor. 1:20, 26, 27; 3:18–19).

For apologetic purposes a fool is one who does what "is right in his own eyes" (Prov. 12:15; Judges 17:6)—much like Adam and Eve when they evaluated God's command and dismissed it on their own authority. Thus, the fool is one who "trusts in his heart" (Prov. 28:26; cf. Jer. 9:23), whereas the wise man hears a different call: "Trust in the Lord with all thine heart; and lean not unto thine own understanding" (Prov. 3:5; cf. 22:19; Ps. 37:5).

A fool is someone who rejects God, the ultimate source of wisdom and truth: "The fool has said in his heart, 'There is no God'" (Ps. 14:1; 53:1). He is a fool because "the fear of the Lord is the *beginning*" of "knowledge" (Prov. 1:7; 2:4–6) and of "wisdom" (Prov. 9:10; cf. Job 28:28; Psa. 111:10; Prov. 15:33). Rather than building his life on the sure, rock-bottom foundation of God and His word, the fool builds his house upon shifting sand (Matt. 7:26) for he "does not know the way of the Lord" (Jer. 5:4; cf. Eph. 5:17).

In rejecting God, the unbeliever necessarily becomes "futile in his speculations" (Rom. 1:21) so that he ends up worshiping and serving the creation rather than the Creator (Rom. 1:22–23, 25). Evolutionary scientific theory sees the universe as its own creator and, therefore, the source of all else. With this self-sustaining creative power, the universe effectively becomes god.

World-renowned physicist Stephen Hawking writes that in his cosmological model "there would be no singularities at which the laws of science broke down and no edge of space-time at which one would have to appeal to God or some new law to set the boundary conditions for space-time . . . The universe would be completely self-contained and not affected by anything outside itself. It would neither be created nor destroyed. It would just BE. . . . What place, then, for a creator?"[8]

---

[8]Stephen Hawking, *A Brief History of Time* (New York: Bantam, 1988), 136, 141.

Presuppositional Apologetics shows the foolishness of unbelief. As you now realize, unbelievers actively suppress the truth of God though they know Him deep down in their heart-of-hearts (Rom. 1:18–20). And as you are beginning to see, they have to live against reality, denying God Who alone provides the pre-conditions of intelligibility necessary for human reason and experience. The remaining lessons will bring this problem into bold relief. The unbeliever is very literally "without an apologetic," according to Paul in Romans 1:20. In the Greek the phrase "they are without excuse" is: *einai autous anapologetous.* You can see our English word "apologetics" in the Greek *anapologetous*, which derives from *a* ("no") and *apologeomai* ("defend").

Now then, what does Solomon mean in Proverbs 26? Why does he direct us on the one hand *not* to "answer a fool according to his folly" (v. 4), while on the other, he urges us to "answer a fool according to his folly" (v. 5)? This seems contradictory. But it is not; and it precisely outlines the Presuppositional Apologetic's two-step procedure: Positively, you must present the truth and, negatively, you must warn of folly. Be aware: Though biblical apologetics involves these two steps, you do *not* have to use them *in this order.* The apologetic situation might require that the order be reversed. Nevertheless, *both* steps are necessary, even if not in any particular order.

Presenting the truth

In Proverbs 26:4 Solomon directs the wise man *not* to answer a fool according to his folly. He is warning you against reasoning with a fool *on his own terms.* Applying this to the apologetics enterprise, we can say that you should not reason with the unbeliever according to the assumptions of *his* worldview. That is, you must avoid the neutrality principle as being a vain attempt at meeting the unbeliever on allegedly neutral territory, accepting his worldview and its procedures as valid. You must not surrender the foundational assumptions of your Christian worldview and try to build an apologetic bridge on the foundations of, and by the tools of, unbelief.

Jesus provides a parable, which substantiates Solomon's two-step procedure and illustrates the difference between a wise man and a fool. The Lord's parable confirms the wisdom of building one's life and position on the solid rock of God's Word, on the biblical worldview:

> Therefore everyone who hears these words of Mine, and acts upon them, may be compared to a wise man, who built his house upon the rock. And the rain descended, and the floods came, and the winds blew, and burst against that house; and yet it did not fall, for it had been founded upon the rock (Matt. 7:24–25).

You must build your apologetic upon God's revelation. The unbeliever must see the beauty, integrity, coherence, and necessity of God's Word as the only foundation for interpreting reality and establishing knowledge.

As a Christian you should love God's Word; as a rational creature you should recognize the necessity of God's Word; as an apologist you should admit to the unbeliever your commitment to God's Word. You don't want to hide your commitment to the Bible; you are not playing games with the unbeliever. His eternal destiny is on the line, and your faithfulness is on display. You must "be diligent to present yourself approved to God as a workman who does not need to be ashamed, handling accurately the word of truth" (2 Tim. 2:15).

Remember, *worldviews are in collision.* Worldviews are complex, inter-locking systems of belief. The unbeliever's whole worldview must be challenged by the integrity of the full Christian worldview as revealed in Scripture—with its metaphysic *and* epistemology intact. You must set before him the full-orbed intellectual challenge of the holistic Christian worldview. You must not adopt portions of and procedures from *his* worldview and allow him to think his assumptions about the world are valid. For if you do, Solomon warns, "you will be like him yourself" (Prov. 26:4b).

Warning of Folly

But in Proverbs 26:5, Solomon turns around and immediately recommends that you *do* "answer a fool according to his folly"! Why would he do that? What's going on here?

Here he is instructing you to temporarily stand on the presuppositions of the unbeliever, not as a matter of neutrality and compromise, not as endorsing his worldview procedures. Rather, he does so in order for you to show the unbeliever the vanity of attempting to explain the world and life from his own perspective. You must let him know that you are taking his position *only momentarily*, just "for sake of argument."

In this step you will be showing the unbeliever that on *his* own autonomous presuppositions he cannot justify reality, knowledge, logic, morality, value, meaning, purpose—or anything. You want to show him the *outcome* of his worldview *when his principles are fully followed out*. Thus, Solomon allows that you may "answer a fool according to his folly"—*so that* the fool will see the error of his being "wise in his own eyes" (Prov. 26:5b). If you adopt the unbeliever's procedures as your actual apologetic, he will suppose himself to have the correct position. Whereas, if you only theoretically adopt his presuppositions in order to demonstrate his error, then you are being faithful to the biblical model of apologetics.

Again, Jesus' parable of the two builders helps to illustrate the value of the two-step apologetic methodology embodied in Proverbs 26:4–5. In the first step, where you are encouraged to *avoid* answering the fool according to *his folly*, you saw a parallel with the wise man who built his house on a rock. In this second step, you can *temporar-*

ily adopt, for the sake of argument, the error of the foolish who reject the Word of God. You must show them that they end up building their worldview on sinking sand:

> And everyone who hears these words of Mine, and does not act upon them, will be like a foolish man, who built his house upon the sand. And the rain descended, and the floods came, and the winds blew, and burst against that house; and it fell, and great was its fall (Matt. 7:26–27).

2. Central Concerns

The central concern of this chapter is *procedural* or methodological. It is important that you follow the *biblical pattern* for apologetics as illustrated in Proverbs 26. You must now consider *how* to employ the simple two-step method in order to engage in *practical* apologetics.

As a believer you should follow a dual-track procedure: (1) Positively, you must stand firmly on your own presuppositions to present the truth claims of Christianity to the unbeliever. You must respond from within your own worldview, refusing to accept the unbeliever's assumptions and method. (2) Negatively, you should temporarily adopt the unbeliever's presuppositions to do an internal critique of his worldview in order to show him its futility. You must show the unbeliever where his presuppositions lead: to epistemological futility.

Having carefully analyzed worldviews and their presuppositions, you should now realize the bold nature of the Christian claim that must be made to the unbeliever. That claim is: *Christianity is the only rational worldview to hold.* You heard correctly! Your holy faith is the *only reasonably defensible position* that a person can adopt. You must have this clearly in mind when confronting the unbeliever.

To put this another way: You should not argue that Christianity is the *best* worldview. This suggests other competing philosophies of life have some rational merit and might even be almost as good.

It adopts Satan's method of suggesting that men are to evaluate and choose worldviews based on their own fallen assumptions. Dr. Van Til comments in this regard: "This whole Christian theistic position must be presented not as something just a little or a great deal better than other positions, but must be presented as the only system of thought that does not destroy human experience to a meaningless something. . . . Any other way of defense reduces the uniqueness of Christianity at once. The question is one of 'this or nothing.'"[9]

Given all that has been presented thus far, you must understand that the Christian outlook is the *only* reasonable worldview. It is the only worldview that makes human experience understandable and whose principles do not annihilate human understanding. On the unbeliever's own principles "autonomous man can never give an intelligible, coherent, or meaningful *account* of how he is able to know anything or accomplish anything culturally. The unbeliever's failure is a rational or philosophical failure to make sense out of knowledge, morality, beauty, etc."[10]

Consequently, your twin apologetic strategy boils down to this: *You are challenging the unbeliever in one form or another to answer the question as to which worldview makes human experience intelligible.* This is crucial for biblical apologetics. You are requiring the unbeliever to think about and declare the final reference point in his system which makes all facts and laws intelligible. Dr. Van Til discusses the goal of our apologetic engagement with the unbeliever: "What we shall have to do then is to try to reduce our opponent's position to an absurdity. Nothing less will do. Without God, man is completely lost in every respect, epistemologically as well as morally and religiously."[11]

Because of the worldview nature of biblical apologetics, it does not focus on particular facts. It is not a *direct* argument dealing with

---

[9]Van Til, *A Survey of Christian Epistemology*, 222.
[10]Bahnsen, *Van Til's Apologetic*, 113.
[11]Van Til, *A Survey of Christian Epistemology*, 205.

individual facts, but an *indirect* one dealing with the *nature* of facts. It does not defensively construct atomistic answers to an endless variety of criticisms. An "indirect argument" is an argument

> from the impossibility of the contrary. . . . A direct argument is possible between two people who share relevant assumptions. Within the context of that interpretive agreement, they can directly appeal to observed facts, personal values and standards, or lines of reasoning that should 'carry weight' with the other person; no entrenched "interpretive" disagreement would be expected. . . . However, when the argument involves disagreement over one's ultimate assumptions (e.g., the existence of God, man's nature and place in the cosmos, or the standards of right and wrong), there is nothing to which direct appeal can be made which is not itself weighted or interpreted in terms of the very standards or values that are being debated.[12]

This method digs down beneath the facts to the foundation, to uncover more basic and broader questions regarding the *fundamental character* that give meaning to the facts. To put it another way, you do not want to trim the unbeliever's tree; you want to dig it up by its roots:

> Factual argumentation may become necessary, but it is never sufficient. What one takes to *be* factual, as well as the *interpretation* of accepted facts, will be *governed* by his underlying *philosophy of fact*—that is, by more basic, all-pervasive, value-oriented, categorizing, possibility-determining, probability-rating, supra-experiential, religiously-motivated *presuppositions.* It is at this presuppositional level that the crucial work in defending the faith must thus be done.[13]

---

[12]Bahnsen, *Van Til's Apologetic,* 485.
[13]Bahnsen, *Always Ready,* 71.

Ultimately then, apologetics must ask whether facts are random events in a chance universe, as per the unbeliever's worldview, or are they elements of the all-organizing, rational plan of God who created, governs, and gives meaning, value, and purpose to the universe and all of its facts? For you see, once God is denied, the only explanation possible for the original creation of the universe is by chance. Consequently, the unbeliever's worldview is ultimately rooted in chance.

Facts in themselves can't settle anything because they need a worldview to provide their interpretation.[14] But in the unbelieving worldview, facts are random, chance events. They have no meaning because, ultimately considered, they sustain no necessary connection to any other facts, in that chance is the opposite of law (which organizes and relates facts). You should not attempt to settle issues by a direct discussion of particular facts. This could last forever (think of all the facts in the universe!) and would never get at the undergirding philosophy of fact that flows from and reveals the mind of God. Remember, that "although the Christian does not know all the facts . . . he does know the pattern . . . in which alone they make sense (are connected)."[15]

This is why we take so much time and expend so much energy in explaining worldviews as a network of beliefs established upon presuppositional foundations. Now you should begin seeing more clearly that to reason by presuppositions you must understand your *own* metaphysical and epistemological program, *and* make the unbeliever understand *his*—because this is where the battle lies.

---

[14]Remember our earlier denial of "brute," uninterpreted, free-standing facts. All facts require interpretive context. For instance, if I mention the word "shoe," what does it mean? To understand the word "shoe," you must know the English language, understand something of the human foot, realize the human method of erect, bi-pedal locomotion, be aware of the hard character of the rock-studded surface of the earth, know something of the nature of pain, appreciate the advantage of comfort, grasp the usefulness of leather, nails, and string, and much, much more.

[15]Bahnsen, *Van Til's Apologetic*, 174 n 51.

As we are about to see, in the final analysis the presuppositional argument may be put very simply, profoundly, and boldly: *The proof of Christianity is the impossibility of the contrary.*[16] That is, the validation of the Christian worldview is that without it you cannot prove anything. This phrase encapsulates the biblical proof of God. Dr. Van Til expresses it this way: "The only 'proof' of the Christian position is that unless its truth is presupposed there is no possibility of 'proving' anything at all."[17] As C. S. Lewis (1898–1963) put it: "There is a difficulty about disagreeing with God. He is the source from which all your reasoning power comes."

In the two-step Presuppositional Apologetic, you must challenge the unbeliever to provide the *preconditions of intelligibility*, that is, the necessary conditions that must exist in order to provide for the possibility of rational thought and meaningful discourse. And you must show him that only Christianity can do so. He must see that if he doesn't hold to the Christian worldview he cannot make sense of anything. Only Christianity makes sense of human experience. Thus, "by his foolish presuppositions the unbeliever actually works against himself. He suppresses the clear truth about God which is foundational to an understanding of the world and of oneself, and he affirms a position which is contrary to his better knowledge. He is intellectually schizophrenic. This must be made clear to him."[18]

This is effectively what Paul teaches in 1 Corinthians 1:20: "Where is the wise man? Where is the scribe? Where is the debater of this age? Has not God made foolish the wisdom of the world?" This is the theme of apologetics: God made foolish the wisdom of

---

[16]This is a familiar phrase to the readers of Van Til and Bahnsen. Cornelius Van Til, *A Survey of Christian Epistemology* (Phillipsburg, NJ: Presbyterian and Reformed, 1969), 205. Bahnsen, *Van Til's Apologetic*, 6, 485. *Always Ready*, 74, 121, 152, 253.

[17]Cornelius Van Til, "My Credo," in E. R. Geehan, ed., *Jerusalem and Athens* (Phillipsburg, NJ: Presbyterian and Reformed, 1971), 21.

[18]Bahnsen, *Always Ready*, 65.

the world. Your challenge to the unbeliever is: "Where is he who can make sense out of human dignity, science, morality, and so forth?"

In the methodological challenge of Presuppositional Apologetics, this is precisely what you are doing. You are standing on your own worldview presuppositions to show that they account for both reality and reason. Then you stand upon the unbeliever's assumptions to show that he cannot account for rationality, human experience, ethics—or anything else. As Van Til explains it:

> Since on the **Reformed**[19] basis there is no area of neutrality between the believer and the unbeliever, the argument between them must be *indirect*. Christians cannot allow the legitimacy of the assumptions that underlie the non-Christian *methodology*. But they can place themselves upon the position of those whom they are seeking to win to a belief in Christianity for the sake of argument. And the non-Christian, though not granting the presuppositions from which the Christian works, can nevertheless place himself upon the position of the Christian for the sake of the argument.[20]

Consider the biblical view of the self-sufficient unbeliever. If you are to be a confident, faithful, and effective apologist, you must realize the non-Christian's predicament and point it out to him:

> The philosophy of the unbeliever has been afflicted with vanity (Rom. 1:21) so that his "knowledge" is (in terms of his own assumptions) falsely so-called (1 Tim. 6:20),

---

[19]By **Reformed**, Van Til means the strongly Calvinistic, covenantal theological branch of evangelicalism. A good summary of the Reformed view of theology may be found in the famed doctrinal formulation known as the Westminster Confession of Faith (drawn up in the mid 1640s in England). Both Van Til and Bahnsen adhered to the Westminster Standards (the Confession of Faith plus the Larger and Shorter Catechisms).

[20]Cornelius Van Til, *The Christian Theory of Knowledge* (Nutley, NJ: Presbyterian and Reformed, 1969), 18.

and he opposes himself by it (2 Tim. 2:25). By pitting his foolish thinking (in the name of "wisdom") against the wisdom of the gospel (which he labels "foolish"), the unbeliever must be unmasked of his pretensions (1 Cor. 1:18–21) and shown that he has no apologetic for his viewpoint (Rom. 1:20) but has been left with a vain, darkened, ignorant mind which needs renewal (Eph. 4:17–24).[21]

Let us now briefly illustrate a few approaches which you can effectively use in this two-step worldview challenge to the unbeliever. Even something as mundane as the very act of sitting down to talk about God with an unbeliever or going to a concert can be used to prove God's existence.

Human experience. As you learned earlier, in the Christian worldview all facts are revelatory of God because He created them all and for His glory: "All facts show forth and thus prove the existence of God and His plan."[22] *All* facts. Even the fact of human experience itself, such as the fact of your discussing the existence of God with an unbeliever. How is this so? What does this mean? And how can you use this in apologetics?

The unbeliever can run from God, but he cannot hide. As you begin discussing God and His existence, ask the unbeliever if he thinks your mutual discussion about God is meaningful. Point out to him the fact his talking with you assumes his own self-awareness whereby he knows himself, recognizes that he lives in an environment involving other self-aware humans, and sees value in communication, conversation, and debate between equally self-aware beings. If he did not, he would be admitting that conversing on the existence of God—*or any subject whatsoever*—would be meaningless.

---

[21]Bahnsen, *Always Ready*, 69.

[22]Van Til, *Introduction to Systematic Theology*, 19. Cited in Bahnsen, *Van Til's Apologetic*, 63.

Now ask him how he accounts for human self-awareness as a fundamental factor of life. Where does it come from? How is it that man is self-aware? Put yourself in his worldview, that is, "answer a fool according to his folly." Point out to him that his system is ultimately committed to chance (in that no God or personality governs the universe). Remind him that from the perspective of evolution the universe was self-created by chance (the Big Bang[23]) and is self-diversifying by chance (exploding stars, galactic collisions, planetary accretions, mutating life forms, and so forth).

The *Humanist Manifesto III* creedalizes this non-Christian view: "Humans are an integral part of nature, the result of unguided evolutionary change. Humanists recognize nature as self-existing. We accept our life as all and enough, distinguishing things as they are from things as we might wish or imagine them to be. We welcome the challenges of the future, and are drawn to and undaunted by the yet to be known." The American Humanist Association declares the philosophy of humanism to be "a nontheistic world view that rejects all forms of supernaturalism and is in accord with the spirit and discoveries of science." The chance-oriented, cold, impersonal universe is the ultimate reality in the humanist's worldview. Again, as Carl Sagan put it: "The Cosmos is all there is, all there was, and all there ever will be."

Now note that in such a naturalistic, materialistic conception of the universe, all must be accounted for in terms of the material interaction of atoms. Point out that this forces us to view ourselves as

---

[23]"About ten billion years ago, the Universe began in a gigantic explosion—the Hot Big Bang! Its subsequent evolution from one hundredth of a second up to the present day can be reliably described by the Big Bang model. This includes the expansion of the Universe, the origin of light elements and the relic radiation from the initial fireball, as well as a framework for understanding the formation of galaxies and other large-scale structures. In fact, the Big Bang model is now so well-attested that it is known as the standard cosmology." (Paul Shellard, ed., "The Hot Big Bang," University of Cambridge website [1996]: www.damtp.cam.ac.uk/user/gr/public/bb_home.html).

simply matter-in-motion. Ask him how matter can be self-aware. Are rocks self-aware? Trees? Hammers? In fact, what view of the world makes self-awareness intelligible? Slime is certainly not self-aware. Ask the unbeliever to explain where inert matter comes from, then how it becomes living matter, which eventually becomes self-aware, which eventually becomes rational, which eventually becomes moral—and all by the evolutionary mechanism of time plus chance.

Then point out that in your worldview (whereby you are determined to "answer not a fool according to his folly"), the personal, sovereign God of Scripture created all things and gave them their properties. And that He created man in His image, thereby establishing personality and self-awareness in us. At the very beginning God communicated with man, speaking intelligently to His rational, self-aware creature (Gen. 1:28–29) and giving him commands (Gen. 1:28; 2:16–17). Consequently, self-awareness and personality are not problems in the Christian worldview.

So then, the very self-awareness of the unbeliever is evidence for the existence of God. This is due to "the impossibility of the contrary."

Rationality. As you continue speaking further about your faith with your unbelieving friend, you will want to discuss the question of rationality itself. After all, you are engaged in rational discussion, seeking *reasons* for believing in God or for not believing in God.

But standing on the unbeliever's worldview quickly demonstrates internal problems. Because of his opposition to the absolute God of Scripture, he must account for reality in some other way than by a personal, rational, sovereign Creator. In discounting an absolute mind creating and controlling the universe, in the final analysis he is committed to chance. In his view of origins, the material universe sprang into being from nothing and under no rational oversight. The rational, then, is built upon the irrational.

This view of origins produces insurmountable rational problems, for such a chance-based worldview can have no laws, no necessity, no logical principles, but only randomness. According to cosmic evolutionary theory all is ultimately subject to random change and is in a constant state of flux. But our very rationality requires laws so that things may be distinguished, classified, organized, and explained. Rational comprehension and explanation demand principles of order and unity in order to relate truths and events to one another. Consequently, on the basis of the non-believer's worldview rationality itself has no foundation.

The unbeliever may attempt to account for rationality by asserting that man's mind *imposes* order so that rationality results. If he does so, then his view of reality becomes subjective rather than objective. But even this attempt is impossible, for how can the mind impose order on a chaotic universe?

And what if your friend denounces your Christian worldview for its being governed by "faith" as over against "reason"? What if he argues that you are naive in not employing the scientific method?

Point out to him the futility in his argument. The scientific method proceeds on the basis of observation through the senses. As the *Humanist Manifesto III* (1993) expressed it: "Knowledge of the world is derived by observation, experimentation, and rational analysis. Humanists find that science is the best method for determining this knowledge as well as for solving problems and developing beneficial technologies."

This method holds, then, that knowledge must be limited to observation and sense perception. Once your unbelieving friend has committed to this procedure, demonstrate his epistemological self-contradiction: If all knowledge is governed by observation, then how did he come to know *that*? That is, how did he come to know that "all knowledge is governed by observation"? Did he *observe* that in the lab? Did he measure, weigh, or count it? Did he detect *that* conceptual limitation by exploring nature? And furthermore, does he observe that this principle is a *universal* limitation on knowledge in all places and at all times so that he can confidently trust it?

If he attempts to use the laws of logic in reasoning with you, ask him where in nature he has seen the laws of logic? Show him that you can't use the scientific method to prove the laws of logic, for you can't observe, taste, or feel them since they are not material entities extended in space. How then can he justify logic? Or the scientific method of empiricism?

But with the believer's worldview, a personal, absolute Creator God accounts for the rational, coherent, law-ordered reality that you and the unbeliever both experience and depend upon. In God's sovereign revelation to man (Scripture) we learn that He spoke, "and it was so" (Gen. 1:7, 9; Ps. 33:6; 2 Cor. 4:6; Heb. 11:3). Not only do we discover order and harmony throughout the narrative of creation (days 1 through 6 following logically one after the other[24]), but the very idea of God's *speaking* reality into existence itself requires rationality. The universe is ultimately rational because the rational, law-ordaining God of Scripture created it thus. Man is a rational being because he is created in the image of God, who is the standard of rationality. In Eden, God commands him through verbal communication (Gen. 2:16–17); Adam authoritatively speaks (2:19–20); God reasons with him (3:1–19).

Oftentimes the unbeliever objects to the idea of faith in the Christian worldview. This is due to his basic misunderstanding of the role and function of faith, deeming it essentially a blind leap beyond the limits of reason. Yet, your Christian faith does not discount reason and logic. Rather it *requires* the use of logical reasoning, because in God's mind there is perfect coherence and rationality whereby He upholds (Col. 1:17; Heb. 1:3) and governs (Isa. 46:10–11; Eph. 1:11) all

---

[24]Henry Jackson deals with self-awareness as evidence for a transcendent God in *Science, World, and Faith* (Ferndale, WA: BookSurge, 2005).

things. God is as "wise in heart" as He is "mighty in strength" (Job 9:4; cf. 12:13). The laws of logic reflect the orderly mind of God, so that man as the image of God should reflect God's rationality (see Chapter 11 for more detail). After all, God "put wisdom in the inner-most being" and "has given understanding to the mind" (Job 38:36). And remember: as a Christian you are particularly called to love God with "all your mind" (Mark 12:30).

Empirical (observational, sense-based) scientific investigation is also called for in the Christian worldview because God created an objective, material universe, governs it by predictable laws (Gen. 1:14–19; 8:22; Job 38:31–33; Jer. 33:22, 25), and placed within a think-ing, sensing man to inhabit it (Gen. 1:27–29; Ps. 8:6; 115:16b). Fur-thermore, God created man as a sensate, physical being, for "the hearing ear and the seeing eye, the Lord has made both of them" (Prov. 20:12; cf. Ex. 4:11; Ps. 94:9).

Empirical learning, then, is necessary because of the way the God-created world and God-reflecting man operate. The world is real, not imagined. The law of gravity exists because God's mind made the world this way. God made a world that comports with our minds and calls us to go out and investigate that real, objective, sense-oriented world that He made (Gen. 1:26–28; Ps. 8:4–8; Eccl. 1:13).

The unbeliever's problem only gets worse when he demands that we provide proof for the existence of God. Think about the irony of this position:

> The problem for the unbeliever is that he keeps com-mitting himself to some (quite proper and unavoidable) requirement of "rationality" and insisting upon its be-ing honored, only to find upon analysis that only the Christian worldview coheres with it (makes it intelli-gible). The unbeliever has been borrowing essentially Christian ideas in epistemology, without giving God

the glory and thanks. After all, given the unbeliever's worldview, why should reasons be required for what we believe? Why should logical consistency be demanded? Why should arbitrariness be disreputable? There is no reason for the normativity of rationality.[25]

Ask your friend: "Why do you require that I give you a reason proving God's existence? After all, on your view there is no reason for reason itself." Point out to him that the very fact you are discussing and debating the matter proves the existence of God, for rationality can't be accounted for in the unbeliever's worldview. As Van Til would express it: To slap God's face you must first crawl onto His lap.

Aesthetics. Let's say that you have been debating with a friend the existence of God for a couple of hours over dinner before your planned attendance at a piano concerto. The time now comes that you need to leave for the concert hall together to enjoy the work of Johann Sebastian Bach. After the concert is over and you are leaving the hall, your friend exclaims: "What a marvelous performance of such beautiful musical works!" He has just stepped into the Christian worldview and undermined his own worldview without knowing it.

Ask him the key apologetic question: "What view of life makes the notion of 'beauty' intelligible?" Challenge him to declare what standard he is using whereby he may declare something is "beautiful." Point out that on his materialist, chance, relativistic foundations, he cannot account for beauty. He has no ultimate standard for evaluation so that he may distinguish between that which is beautiful and that which is ugly.[26] Nor does he have any coherent, law-bound sys-

---

[25]Kenneth L. Gentry, Jr. and Michael R. Butler, *Yea, Hath God Said?: The Framework Hypothesis / Six-Day Creation Debate* (Eugene, Ore.: Wipf & Stock, 2002), 52–53.

[26]An amusing notation made by economist Thomas Sowell highlights in a different context the problem we are considering in apologetics. Sowell said you should never ask an economist, "How are you doing?" This is because he will re-

tem that can associate things in such a way that certain "patterns" may be declared "beautiful." As already noted, he cannot even account for human self-awareness so that beauty may be rationally experienced, intelligibly discussed, and aesthetically appreciated. Does a platypus "appreciate" a beautiful sunset?

Furthermore, beauty can only be appreciated in the mind. If there is no objective standard or value for beauty, it becomes simply a subjective, arbitrary, emotive experience. In addition, the prevailing naturalistic worldview cannot account for aesthetic values in man because appreciation of beauty has no survival value as per the demands of evolution.

But on the Christian worldview, the all-creating (Gen. 1; Neh. 9:6; John 1:3), all-ordering (Ps. 115:3; 135:6; Dan. 4:35; Matt. 5:45) God of Scripture is the ultimate standard of evaluation (Prov. 15:3; Eccl. 3:17; 12:14; Isa. 45:5–6, 21; 46:9). He creates a world of order that can exhibit beautiful patterns of facts. Man is created as a rational creature in the image of God so that he can discern those patterns of beauty, distinguishing them from those which lack beauty (Phil. 4:8).

Ethics. Now you and your unbelieving friend are traveling home from the concert. You turn on the radio and hear a distressing news item about a heinous act of child abuse. Your non-Christian friend expresses indignation at this act, complaining that this is a terrible tragedy. Once again he has stumbled into your worldview.

In your whole apologetic endeavor you must insist that the unbeliever be consistent when standing on his position. The fundamental problem with unbelief is that it *cannot* be consistent. As Van Til has argued, the unbeliever's worldview collapses into absurdity and incoherence.

How is it that the things the unbeliever and the believer both hold in common can be true? For example, how can we both agree that

---

spond: "Compared to what?" Evaluations require a standard of measure.

torturing children is wrong? Remember the key apologetic challenge: "Which worldview makes sense out of that? Which network of pre-suppositions?"

When you talk of child abuse with your non-Christian friend, you both agree it is wrong. But he cannot declare that it is absolutely wrong on his chance-based, relativistic worldview. Moral evaluations require an absolute standard, which the unbelieving worldview can't produce from the perspective of his chance universe. Why shouldn't some people take advantage of a child?

Suppose your discussion leads to talking about the problem of oppressing the poor. Perhaps your friend will declare such to be immoral. You know the apologetic challenge by now. Ask him: "What outlook on reality, knowledge and ethics makes this position meaningful?" That is, on the evolutionary worldview (materialistic atheism), we must ask the question: "What is man?" Is he just an advanced animal? Physicist Stephen Hawking has declared: "We are just an advanced breed of monkeys on a minor planet of a very average star" (*Der Speigel*, 1989). Is he the result of primordial slime developing by chance into the complicated, self-aware creature we know as "man"? But how can that view make sense of condemning oppression of the poor? In fact, if evolution is true, then we live in a survival of the fittest, dog-eat-dog world. We got here by clawing our way to the top, overcoming other animals. Oppression is part of our nature, part of our method for development and improvement. It is necessary and, therefore, "good."

Once again though, on your believing worldview, morality makes sense—and is even demanded: "He has told you, O man, what is good; and what does the Lord require of you but to do justice, to love kindness, and to walk humbly with your God?" (Mic. 6:8; Isa. 56:1). In fact, His Word expressly commands: "Thus says the Lord, 'Do justice and righteousness, and deliver the one who has been robbed from the power of his oppressor. Also do not mistreat or do violence to the stranger, the orphan, or the widow; and do not shed innocent blood in this place'" (Jer. 22:3; cf. Ex. 22:21–24).

The righteous and holy God of Scripture is the ultimate, eternal, absolute, perfect standard of morality (Matt. 5:48; Rom. 2:5–6). Man is created in His image so that he himself is a moral creature (Gen. 1:26; 9:6). He trades in moral currency—even as a sinner (Matt. 5:47; 7:11; Rom. 2:14–15; 7:7). The Bible reveals the objective laws of morality (Mic. 6:8a; Heb. 5:14), for example, the Ten Commandments (Ex. 20:1–17; Deut. 5:6–21).

If the unbeliever attempts to defend his rejection of absolute standards of morality while condemning both child abuse and oppression of the poor, he may skirt the issue of objective moral standards. He often will be reduced to declaring, "I just know it is wrong." But then morality becomes subjective, and it can't condemn the child molester who doesn't believe it is wrong or the rich who oppress the poor. It's their view against his.

The Unbeliever's Response

One thing you will hear from the unbeliever is: "I am a scientific, good, rational person." To this your response should be: "Yes, you are, because you live in God's universe and are created in His image." You must show him that he has deceived himself about reality by denying the Creator and Governor of the universe. The goal of unbelief is the attempt of Adam to escape the voice of God.

The unbeliever actually uses the Christian worldview without acknowledging it. You can say: "You know these things are true, otherwise you would not be able to make sense out of anything. You are suppressing the truth in unrighteousness." He will then deceive himself about his own deception. This may harden him more—unless the Holy Spirit intervenes.

You must understand that the unbeliever is not himself a system of thought; he is a person. For that reason, he is not true to his own system of thought. We must challenge his inconsistency with the Christian worldview, showing him the impossibility of the contrary.[27]

Worldviews and Facts

Remembering that we must think holistically in a worldview fashion helps us realize that even mundane experiences create problems for the unbeliever—if he tries to operate consistently with his worldview. Consider the following:

> The beliefs which people hold are always connected to *other* beliefs by relations pertaining to linguistic meaning, logical order, evidential dependence, causal explanation, indexical and self-conceptions, etc. To assert "I see a ladybug on the rose" is to affirm and assume a *number* of things simultaneously—some rather obvious (e.g., about the usage of English words, one's personal identity, a perceptual event, categories of bugs and flowers, physical relations), others more subtle (e.g., about one's linguistic, entomological, and botanical competence, the normalcy of one's eyes and brain-stem, theories of light refraction, shared grammar and semantics, the reality of the external world, laws of logic, etc.)[28]

In taped lectures elsewhere on transcendental arguments, there are helpful examples of how unbelievers look at things differently. With Christ we might demand of the unbeliever: "Consider the lilies" (Luke 12:27). The unbeliever is stymied—in his system. The simple flower shows the explanatory power of Christian theism over against anti-theism.

---

[27]Van Til notes that the unbeliever cannot be consistent with his own worldview assumptions. If he were, his worldview would become absurd as he "integrates downward into the void."

[28]Bahnsen, *Always Ready*, 216.

1. The unbeliever can't explain matter. He can't understand the origin of the flower, making sense of its material composition. Where did it come from? How does the Big Bang explain the flower?

2. He can't explain induction. That is, he is unable to explain the flower's history and development, since his system is materialistic and the process of induction is not.

3. He can't account for logic. He can't explain the flower's conception which requires logic in order to even talk about flowers, in that it requires the universals of "flowerness" and "dirtness." (See Chapter 11 for discussion of universals.)

4. He can't explain values. He can't account for value judgments about flowers. He has no account for aesthetic or ethical values. What do we do about the flower? The Christian sees it reflecting God's glory and reminding him of his moral obligation to praise God. The unbeliever can simply stomp on it as having no value whatsoever—*if* he follows out his own worldview consistently.

5. He can't explain the flower's adaptation to its environment. Why is it related to anything else in the random world? Why can things outside of me be made suitable to my purposes?

6. He can't explain the explanation of "flower". In a chance universe of ultimate randomness, he can't account for unity, differentiation, and classes of things in order to explain what he means by "flower."

7. He has no way to explain our consciousness of flowers. We are self-conscious, the flower is not. How is this so since I am but matter-in-motion?

So then, in your apologetic enterprise, you must demonstrate that Christianity alone is rational. To summarize:

> Differing worldviews can be compared to each other in terms of the important philosophical question about the 'preconditions of intelligibility' for such important assumptions as the universality of logical laws, the uniformity of nature, and

the reality of moral absolutes. We can examine a worldview and ask whether its portrayal of nature, man, knowledge, etc., provide an outlook in terms of which logic, science and ethics can make sense. It does not comport with the practices of natural science to believe that all events are random and unpredictable, for instance. It does not comport with the demand for honesty in scientific research, if no moral principle expresses anything but a personal preference or feeling. Moreover, if there are internal contradictions in a person's worldview, it does not provide the preconditions for making sense out of man's experience. For instance, if one's political dogmas respect the dignity of men to make their own choices, while one's psychological theories reject the free will of men, then there is an internal defect in that person's worldview.[29]

In the final chapters, we will expand on these problems for the unbeliever, providing us much material for contemplation. You must recognize the fundamental idea in all apologetical encounters: You are asking which worldview can resolve foundational questions of how we think and live in the world. You grant the unbeliever the opportunity to respond to the challenge. Then you present to him the Christian foundations which alone can give meaning to human experience.

3. Questions Raised

Attempt to answer the following questions on your own before looking at the text or consulting the **Answer Key**.

1. What specific Bible passage sets up the two-fold structure of the apologetic challenge to the unbeliever?

2. What does the Bible mean when it speaks of a "fool"?

---

[29]Bahnsen *Always Ready*, 121.

3. What are the two particular aspects of the biblical apologetic challenge to unbelief? Briefly explain each of the two steps of apologetics.

4. In what limited circumstances should you adopt the unbeliever's worldview?

5. Why should you avoid arguing that Christianity is the "best" position to hold? What should you argue instead?

6. In the final analysis, what phrase by Dr. Van Til encapsulates the biblical proof of God, displaying the very essence of our argument?

7. What do we mean when we speak of the "preconditions of intelligibility"?

8. How is our very self-awareness an argument for God's existence?

9. Explain how the Christian worldview establishes logic while the non-Christian worldview can't.

10. How would you respond to someone who claims to use the "scientific method," which asserts that all knowledge comes by way of observational analysis through sense experience?

11. How would you show the futility of unbelief by the unbeliever's declaring child abuse or oppressing the poor to be morally wrong?

12. How can a flower be used to show the incoherence of the non-Christian worldview?

4. Practical Applications

1. Search either on the Internet or in a print Encyclopedia for articles on the "Big Bang." Draw out from those articles citations that establish chance as the source of the Big Bang which brought about all of reality. Put them in your apologetics folder.

2. Two sound, evangelical creationist groups are well known in America: The Institute for Creation Research (www.icr.org) and

"Answers in Genesis" (www.answersingenesis.org). Though they both hold to the same understanding of Scripture and creation, they differ in their apologetic methodology. Go on-line to both of their sites and read some of their articles to see if you discover which one is more compatible with the Presuppositional Apologetic.

3. Talk to an unbelieving friend about self-awareness and where he thinks it derives from. Discuss with him the Christian foundations for human self-awareness.

4. Talk with an unbelieving friend about the scientific method. Ask him if he thinks all knowledge comes through empirical evidence. Challenge him with the problems with such a view.

5. Go on the Internet, search for and read some reviews of art. See if you can point out the assumption of a standard of beauty while there are subtle indicators of a denial of the Christian world-view.

6. Read your local newspaper editorials and letters-to-the editor. Watch for an article or letter that tries both to discount Christianity and to affirm a particular moral position. Using the material in our lessons, frame a brief letter exposing the futility of claiming a moral point-of-view while writing off Christianity. Send it to the newspaper.

7. Using this lesson, work up a one lesson Bible study illustrating the biblical apologetic. Ask your pastor if he will look over it with you, then see if you can teach it in a Sunday school class.

8. Consider taking a distance learning course in apologetics from a Presuppositional Apologetics perspective. Several are available through the Southern California Center for Christian Studies.

5. Recommended Reading

Aniol, Scott, "The Believer's Pursuit of Beauty": http://weblog.
karaministries.com/archives/2005/03/29/the_believers_pursuit_of_
beauty_conclusions_from_adler.php

Bahnsen, Greg L., "Origins, Revelation, and Science": www.cmfnow.
com/articles/pa001.htm

Finnamore, David J., "Beauty, Wisdom and Truth": www.elvenminstrel.
com/lontext/beautywisdomtruth.htm

Hodges, John Mason, "Aesthetics and the Place of Beauty in Worship:
www.crichton.edu/iaca/aesthetics_beauty.htm

Sarfati, Jonathan "Loving God with all your mind: logic and creation":
www.answersingenesis.org/tj/v12/i2/logic.asp

"Aesthetic Arguments for the Existence of God": www.quodlibet.net/
williams-aesthetic.shtml

"The Christian Worldview, the Atheist Worldview, and the Laws of
Logic": www.carm.org/atheism/logic.htm

"Presuppositional Apologetics": www.carm.org/apologetics/
presuppositional.htm

9

The Problem of
Moral Absolutes

*For we must all appear before the judgment seat of
Christ, that each one may be recompensed for his deeds
in the body, according to what he has done, whether
good or bad.* (2 Cor. 5:10)

IN THE PREVIOUS chapter we focused on the biblical outline for your
apologetic defense of the Christian faith and your philosophical
challenge to the unbeliever. We noted that Proverbs 26:4–5 establishes the basic method for Christian apologetics. It warned of the
"fool" and the danger of adopting his worldview (the "fool" being
one who does not believe in God). Positively, this passage directs
you to stand on your own Christian assumptions, not giving in to
the lure of the unbelievers methodology. Negatively, it encourages
you to attack the unbeliever's worldview, exposing its futility by momentarily stepping into it for the sake of argument. It directs you
(1) to present your worldview in its fullness and (2) to critique the
non-Christian's in its emptiness.

We also briefly introduced several examples of the indirect, presuppositional method for defending the existence of God. Each one
of these is drawn from rather mundane life situations. Our lesson
quickly surveyed some of the basics for setting up a worldview chal-

lenge by looking at human experience, rationality, aesthetics, and ethics. You saw how any "fact" could be used to demonstrate the existence of God due to "the impossibility of the contrary."

In the remaining chapters, we will expose the fundamental problems in the non-Christian worldview. In that the negative portion of a two-part apologetic involves internally critiquing the unbeliever's worldview, this will be extremely important to understand. The non-believer needs to be challenged to give a rational account for his outlook on life and the moral demands he makes on others. Through persuasion and reasoned argument, you will need to force him to account for the foundation that he claims supports his worldview. In this chapter we are considering the problem of moral absolutes.

1. Central Concerns

We have already discussed the problem of moral absolutes several times. Moral concerns are inescapable in human life. You will find that anytime you forgo beating up your neighbor, he will be grateful for your moral restraint. And what would society be if "every man did what was right in his own eyes" (Judges 17:6; 21:25)? We would all fear going out in public—or even staying at home with morally unpredictable family members. Every waking moment of life involves moral challenges as we choose one action as preferable over another. We are not animals merely reacting to our environment by instinct. We are moral creatures "sovereignly" engaging our social environment according to rational, moral considerations.

The Humanist Influence

You probably are also aware of the many peculiar approaches to morality which are grabbing headlines today. For instance, consider "animal rights." Animal rights activists do not simply protest the perverse torture of pets for amusement or deadly dog fights for sport. Nor are they simply trying to preserve "endangered species" from extinction. Animal rights are now legal and political issues that have generated an "Animal Legal Defense Fund," the "Animal Liberation Front," an *Animal Rights Internet Encyclopedia of Philosophy*, and more. Many even decry "speciesism" (elevating man over animals, of all things), lamenting "human chauvinism," "human supremicism," and "anthropocentrism."[1]

One animal rights website presents an article titled "Freedom is a Basic Right for Animals." It opens with these words: "This article is about the central role that freedom plays in our sense of justice. According to Ruut Veenhoven, a Dutch researcher on happiness, this is the most important factor in seeking happiness. Should that be any different for animals?"[2] In *The Animal Question*, Paola Cavalieri argues regarding the modern moral argument that "its very logic extends to nonhuman animals as beings who are owed basic moral and legal rights and that, as a result, human rights are not human after all."[3]

Many vegetarian groups argue for the immorality of eating animals.[4] Others decry wearing fur coats or leather shoes as involving the destruction of animal life.[5] And, of course, you are quite familiar with extreme environmentalism which can stop the building of dams or drilling for oil. A few years ago an "endangered" four

---

[1]Kyle Ash, "International Animal Rights: Speciesism and Exclusionary Human Dignity," *Journal of Animal Law*, Michigan State University College of Law (11), 195ff. (www.animallaw.info/journals/jo_pdf/vol11_p195.pdf)

[2]"Freedom is a Basic Right of Animals" at the Animal Freedom website: www.animalfreedom.org/english/opinion/freedom/html

[3]Paola Cavalieri, *The Animal Question: Why Non-Human Animals Deserve Human Rights* (Oxford: Oxford University Press, 2005), back cover copy.

[4]The Bible clearly allows eating meat (Gen. 9:3; 12:4; Deut. 12:15; Mark 14:12; 1 Cor. 10:25).

[5]In Eden after the Fall of Adam, God Himself made Adam and Eve "garments of skin" from animals (Gen. 3:21). He also required animal skins for the Tabernacle (25:5; 26:14; 35:7). The greatest prophet of the old covenant era was John the Baptist (Matt. 11:11), who was God's special messenger (Matt. 11:10). He wore camel hair and leather clothing (Matt. 3:4; Mark 1:6).

inch Snail Darter fish stopped the building of the Tellico Dam on the Tennessee River, making international news for months. More recently a debate has raged over whether the federal government should allow drilling for oil on the Arctic National Wildlife Refuge in Alaska.

But the more widely spread and more dangerous problem today is the denial of absolute moral standards, and, as naturally follows, condemning Christians for holding to absolutistic morals. You are well aware that your Christian moral values are everywhere challenged. Just think of your pro-life commitments (Ex. 20:13; 21:22–23) and note the loud uproar over the appointment of conservative judges to the various courts in America. Or your calls for the sanctity of sexual relations in marriage (1 Cor. 6:9; Gal. 5:19; Heb. 13:4) and the mockery you must endure for being "puritanical." Or your condemnation of homosexual conduct (1 Cor. 6:9; 1 Tim. 1:10) and your being written off as one opposed to the right to privacy. These are but a few of the moral challenges Christians face in our relativistic world.

The question of moral values is an important component of the Christian's challenge to the unbeliever. You must *always* remember that your conflict with him is at the *worldview* level. And you were taught in a previous chapter that worldviews necessarily involve three key components: metaphysics, epistemology, and *ethics*.

The Unbeliever's Emphasis

Now let us consider the particulars of the moral relativism that infects our culture today. In each of the quotations below, the emphases are mine and are not found in the original documents. The third point in the *Humanist Manifesto II* (1973) vigorously asserts autonomous, relativistic, God-denying morality:

> We affirm that *moral values derive their source from human experience.* Ethics is *autonomous and situational* needing *no*

theological or ideological sanction. Ethics stems from human need and interest. To deny this distorts the whole basis of life. Human life has meaning because we create and develop our futures. Happiness and the creative realization of human needs and desires, individually and in shared enjoyment, are continuous themes of humanism. We strive for the good life, here and now.

French researcher Emile Durkheim (1858–1917) was a primary figure in developing modern "scientific" sociology. He expressed moral relativism well:

> *It can no longer be maintained nowadays that there is one, single morality which is valid for all men at all times in all places. . . .* The purpose of morality practiced by a people is to enable it to live; hence morality changes with societies. There is not just one morality, but several, and as many as there are social types. And *as our societies change, so will our morality.*

A recent teen publication on sexual mores and sexually transmitted disease is titled "The Quest for Excellence." It reads in part:

> Early on in life, you will be exposed to different value systems from your family, church or synagogue, and friends. . . . *It is up to you to decide upon your own value system to build your own ethical code. . . .* You will have to learn what is right for yourself through experience. . . . *Only you can decide* what is right and comfortable for you.

Pray that no cannibals read this! The Internet encyclopedia *Wikipedia* has an entry on "Moral Relativism." It reads in part:

> In philosophy, moral relativism is the position *that moral or ethical propositions do not reflect absolute and universal moral truths but instead are relative to social, cultural, his-*

torical or personal preferences, and that there is no single standard by which to assess an ethical proposition's truth. Relativistic positions often see moral values as applicable only within certain cultural boundaries or the context of individual preferences.

Aldous Huxley, in his novel *Ends and Means*, presented the following:

> The philosopher who finds no meaning in the world is not concerned exclusively with a problem in pure metaphysics; he is also concerned to prove that *there is no valid reason why he personally should not do as he wants to do.*
>
> For myself, as, no doubt, for most of my contemporaries, the philosophy of meaninglessness was essentially an instrument of liberation. The liberation we desired was simultaneously liberation ... from a certain system of morality. We objected to the morality because it interfered with our sexual freedom; we objected to the political and economic system because it was unjust. The supporters of these systems claimed that in some way they embodied the meaning (a Christian meaning, they insisted) of the world. There was one admirably simple method of confuting these people and at the same time justifying ourselves in our political and erotic revolt: *we could deny that the world had any meaning whatsoever.*[6]

Humanist Max Hocutt says that human beings "may, and do, make up their own rules. . . . Morality is not discovered; it is made."[7] Regarding evolution and ethics, we learn that:

> The position of the modern evolutionist is that . . . *morality is a biological adaptation* no less than are hands and feet

---

[6] Aldous Huxley, *Ends and Means* (London: Chatto & Windus, 1937), 272, 273

[7] Max Hocutt, "Toward an Ethic of Mutual Accommodation," in *Humanist Ethics*, ed. Morris B. Storer (Buffalo: Prometheus, 1980), 137

and teeth. Considered as a rationally justifiable set of claims about an objective something, ethics is illusory. I appreciate that when somebody says 'Love thy neighbor as thyself,' they think they are referring above and beyond themselves. Nevertheless, such reference is truly without foundation. Morality is just an aid to survival and reproduction . . . and *any deeper meaning is* illusory.[8]

Even the field of medicine is susceptible to relativism in the area of morality. One medical ethics text states:

It certainly should give anyone rather *severe doubts* that we have available to us a firmly articulated normative ethical theory that affords us a systematic knowledge of good and evil, right and wrong, such that it could give ethicists confidence that they have a moral expertise that will enable them to chart the way in applied ethics.[9]

In his "Hermeneutics, General Studies, and Teaching," Stanford University Professor of Philosophy Richard Rorty puts it succinctly: "To say that there really are objective values out there, that there is a moral reality to be corresponded with, seems as *pointless* as saying that God is on our side." Existentialist philosopher Jean-Paul Sartre writes:

The existentialist, on the contrary, thinks it very distressing that God does not exist, because all possibility of finding values in a heaven of ideas disappears along with Him; there can no longer be an *a priori* Good, since there is no infinite and perfect consciousness to think it. Nowhere is it written that the Good exists, that we must be honest, that we must

---

[8]Michael Ruse, "Evolutionary Theory and Christian Ethics," in *The Darwinian Paradigm* (London: Routledge, 1989), 262–269.

[9]Kai Neilson, "On Being Skeptical About Applied Ethics," in *Clinical Medical Ethics: Exploration and Assessment*, eds. Terrence F. Ackerman and Glenn C. Graber, et al. (Lanham, MD: University Press of America, 1987), 100.

not lie; because the fact is that we are on a plane where there are only men. Dostoevsky said, "If God didn't exist, everything would be possible." That is the very starting point of existentialism. Indeed, *everything is permissible if God does not exist*, and as a result man is forlorn, because neither within him nor without does he find anything to cling to. He can't start making excuses for himself.[10]

According to agnostic Yale University Law Professor, Arthur Allen Leff, with the rise of an empiricist philosophy of law

most likely conditioning it in fact, the knowledge of good and evil, as an intellectual subject, was being *systematically and effectively destroyed*. The historical fen through which ethical wanderings led was abolished in the early years of this century (not for the first time, but very clearly this time); *normative thought crawled out of the swamp and died in the desert*. There arose a great number of schools of ethics—axiological, materialistic, evolutionary, intuitionist, situational, existential, and so on—but they all suffered the same fate: either they were seen to be ultimately premised on some intuition (buttressed or not by nose counts of those seemingly having the same intuitions), or they were more arbitrary than that, based solely on some "for the sake of the argument" premise. I will put the current situation as sharply as possible: *there is today no way of 'proving' that napalming babies is bad* except by asserting it (in a louder and louder voice), or by defining it as so, early in one's game, and then later slipping it through, in a whisper, as a conclusion. Now this is a fact of modern intellectual life so well and painfully known as to be one of the few which is simultaneously horrifying and banal.[11]

---

[10]Jean-Paul Sartre, "Existentialism," trans. Bernard Frechtman, in *Existentialism and Human Emotions* (New York: Citadel, 1957), 23. Quoted in Ed. L. Miller, *Questions That Matter: An Invitation to Philosophy*, 3rd ed., (New York: McGraw-Hill, 1992), 396.

[11]Arthur Allen Leff, "Economic Analysis of Law: Some Realism About Nomi-

Needless to say, University of Toronto philosopher John Rist notes that there is "widely admitted to be a crisis in contemporary Western debate about ethical foundations."[12] This is greatly impacted by Western scientism's commitment to materialism, which is well expressed by renowned evolutionary bio-ethicist Peter Singer: "We are evolved animals, and we bear the evidence of our inheritance, not only in our anatomy and our DNA, but in our behavior too."[13]

Atheist philosopher Bertrand Russell captures the essence of the materialistic ethic: "Brief and powerless is man's life; on him and all his race the slow, sure doom falls pitiless and dark. *Blind to good and evil, reckless of destruction, omnipotent matter rolls on its relentless way.*"[14]

Even those who deny moral absolutes have at least one moral absolute: "You should not believe there are moral absolutes. You should believe there is no morality." In effect, *they contradictorily have a morality about no morality.* They say you *should* ("should" entails moral obligation or duty) believe there are no moral absolutes. This is illustrated by the ethics professor, committed to moral relativism and denying moral absolutes, who will absolutely demand that his students not cheat on his exams.

This is the moral point of view of fallen man. As you have learned from worldview analysis, worldviews necessarily involve metaphysical, epistemological, and ethical considerations. Therefore, the reason that those who demand no moral absolutes are engaged in self-contradiction is because *moral absolutes are inescapable.*

How does the unbelieving world make sense of moral absolutes? Can it make sense of such? The answer comes back as a resound-

---

nalism," *Virginia Law Review* (1974), 454–455.
    [12]John Rist, *Real Ethics* (Cambridge: Cambridge University Press, 2003), 1.
    [13]Peter Singer, *A Darwinian Left: Politics, Evolution, and Cooperation* (New Haven, CT: Yale University Press, 2000), 11.
    [14]Bertrand Russell, *Why I Am Not a Christian, And Other Essays on Religion and Related Subjects*, ed. Paul Edwards (New York: Simon and Schuster, 1957), 115.

ing, "No!" The non-Christian cannot make sense of moral absolutes, even his own absolutistic (!) relativism. We must challenge the unbeliever: "Which worldview makes sense of our human experience? Which makes human experience intelligible?" We want to demand of the unbeliever how he can make judgments regarding good and evil in the world. Just what are the options for the non-Christian? He does not accept God's Word as the authority for determining moral good, so what defines "good" for him?

The Christian obviously has notions of right and wrong. At the very foundation of your worldview stands the eternal, personal, moral God who clearly and sovereignly reveals Himself in both nature and Scripture thereby showing us the unchanging character of the good. Jesus challenges the rich young ruler with his understanding of the "good," by declaring: "No one is good but God alone" (Mark 10:18).[15] The very character of God is the foundation of our ethical outlook.

The Unbeliever's Problem

The standard response to define "good" follows two outlooks: Good is either what evokes approval, or it is that which achieves certain ends. Let us engage in an internal critique of these two ethical approaches.

Good is What Evokes Approval

In this perspective we find two forms of the evocative approval ethic: (1) Good is what evokes *social* approval; (2) Good is what evokes *personal* approval. That is, good is defined either by society or by the individual. Let us consider the two forms of this approach:

---

[15]When Christ responds to him, "Why do you call me good? No one is good but God," He is not saying that He (Christ) Himself is not good (which would imply that He is not God in the flesh). He is seeking to see if the young man knows what "good" is and who Jesus is. This is a rhetorical question designed to see if the rich man would submit to His authority. Tragically, the young man left Jesus, preferring his wealth to Christ's authority.

1. *Good is what evokes* social *approval.* One Internet article summarizes the social-approval ethic in a way that shows the problem inherent in moral relativism:

> Cultural relativism ascertains that moral standards differ from one culture to the next. It says that good and bad are relative to culture. What is 'good' is what is "socially approved" in a given culture. Cultural relativism holds that "good" means what is "socially approved" by the majority in a given culture. This means that anyone who is born into a particular culture is expected to follow the moral codes of that culture because they were already in existence. In addition, cultural relativism states that there are different ways of applying basic ethical principles from one culture to the next.

In this perspective a difficulty arises: If social approval defines good, we must ask where this leads us. When we look at the history of human culture we will discover many cultures engaged in morally reprehensible practices. If good is society-determined, then we may not condemn such practices as genocide, cannibalism, human sacrifice, infanticide, pederasty, widow immolation, or community suicides, to name but a few problems.

Genocide. Entire societies have gone along with oppressing the Jews, giving rise to what we know as anti-Semitism in general and the German holocaust in particular. The sentence "The entire society went along with oppressing the Jews" is coherent and makes sense. But if good is that which evokes social approval, then by definition it becomes impossible to criticize a society for what it does, even for burning Jews to death in concentration camps. The *Wikipedia* article on genocide notes that "[I]n the past century, sprees of deliberate large-scale killings of entire groups of people have occurred in what is now Ottoman Empire, Namibia, Democratic Republic of the Congo, Soviet Union for example Stalin's forced starvation of Ukrainian farmers, Mao's murder of 20 to 60 million Chinese, Cambodia, Rwanda and Sudan."

Cannibalism. Some societies have practiced cannibalism (also called "anthropophagy"[16]). The literature of ancient Chinese civilizations speaks of widespread cannibalism. European explorers discovered that the Aztec Empire in Mexico was practicing cannibalism. Not all that long ago cannibalism existed among the Aborigines in Arnhem Land, in the far north of Northern Territory of Australia. According to anthropologists, the southeastern Papua Korowai tribe and the New Guinea Fore tribe are cannibalistic cultures even today.

According to recent genetic research from *National Geographic*, "Genetic markers commonly found in modern humans all over the world could be evidence that our earliest ancestors were cannibals, according to new research. Scientists suggest that even today many of us carry a gene that evolved as protection against brain diseases that can be spread by eating human flesh."[17]

Human sacrifice. Human sacrifice is another cultural practice with strong moral implications. According to the *Wikipedia* article: "Human sacrifice was practiced in many ancient cultures. Victims were ritually killed in a manner that was supposed to please or appease gods or spirits. On very rare occasions human sacrifices still occur today." This practice was known among the ancient Phoenicians, Carthaginians, and Chinese, the early mediaeval Celtics, Vikings, and in the Aztec, Mayan, and Inca societies.

Infanticide. The practice of infanticide has been widely experienced in human societies. The *Wikipedia* article on "Infanticide" comments:

---

[16]Anthropophagy is derived from the compounding of two Greek words: *anthropos* ("man, human") and *phagein* ("to eat").

[17]John Roach, "Cannibalism Normal For Early Humans?" *National Geographic News* (4/10/03). (http://news.nationalgeographic.com/news/2003/04/0410_030410_cannibal.html)

Infanticide was common in all well-studied ancient cultures, including those of ancient Greece, Rome, India, China, and Japan. The practice of infanticide has taken many forms. Child sacrifice to supernatural figures or forces, such as that allegedly practiced in ancient Carthage, is one form; however, many societies only practiced simple infanticide and regarded child sacrifice as morally repugnant. The end of the practice of infanticide in the western world coincided with the rise of Christianity as a major religion. The practice was never completely eradicated, however, and even continues today in areas of extremely high poverty and overpopulation, such as parts of China and India. Female infants, then and now, are particularly vulnerable.

The article goes on to speak of the practice in high Roman culture, the darling of modern humanism:

Classic Roman civilization can serve as an example of both aspects. In some periods of Roman history it was traditional practice for a newborn to be brought to the *pater familias*, the family patriarch, who would then decide whether the child was to be kept and raised, or left to death by exposure.

Child molestation. Ancient Greek and Roman society engaged in "pederasty." This encourages practices that most Americans would deem nothing but child molestation and that Christian ethical standards condemn outright. According to *Wikipedia*:

Pederasty, as idealized by the ancient Greeks, was a relationship and bond between an adolescent boy and an adult man outside of his immediate family. In a wider sense it refers to erotic love between adolescents and adult men. The word derives from the combination of *paidi* (Greek for "boy") with *erastis* (Greek for "lover"; cf. *Eros*). In those societies where pederasty is prevalent, it appears as one form of a widely practiced male bisexuality. In antiquity, pederasty as a moral and educational institution was practiced in Ancient

Greece and Rome. Other forms of it were common, and also found among the Celts (as per Aristotle, *Politics*, II 6.6. *Then.* XIII 603a) and among the Persians (as per Herodotus 1.135). More recently, it was widespread in Tuscany and northern Italy during the Renaissance. Outside of Europe, it was common in pre-Modern Japan until the Meiji restoration, in Mughal India until the British colonization, amongst the Aztecs prior to the Spanish conquest of Mexico and in China and Central Asia until the early 20th century. The tradition of pederasty persists to the present day in certain areas of Afghanistan, the Middle East, North Africa, and Melanesia.

Even today in America the "North American Man/Boy Love Association" advocates free love between adults and children. On its website you can find an article that reads: "Pederasty is the main form that male homosexuality has acquired throughout Western civilization—and not only in the West! Pederasty is inseparable from the high points of Western culture—ancient Greece and the Renaissance."[18]

Widow immolation. The practice of *sati* in Hindu culture is widespread. Hinduism is the third largest religion in the world, with 900 million adherents. A Hindu funeral custom today usually involves the practice of *sati*, wherein the widow immolates herself on her husband's funeral pyre. The expectation is so strong that evidence exists for the widespread forcing of widows to burn themselves alive, even if they don't want to. This practice dates back to around 500 A.D. and was very widely practiced in pre-modern times.

Community suicide. The Indian practice of *jauhar* occurred in medieval times. According to *Wikipedia*, "The practice of *jauhar*, only known from Rajasthan, was the collective suicide of a community. It consisted of the mass immolation of women, and sometimes also of

---

[18]David Thorstad, "Pederasty and Homosexuality." (http://216.220.97.17/pederasty. htm)

the children, the elderly and the sick, at the same time that their fighting men died in battle."

But even unbelievers who deny absolute moral standards criticize these and other societies for their moral conduct. They speak of societies that are either humane or inhumane, that are warlike or peaceable, that are puritanical or sexually tolerant of sexual practices. While decrying Christianity's absolute moral standards, unbelievers nevertheless make moral evaluations of societies. Those evaluations, however, are meaningless if good is whatever evokes social approval and if no ultimate moral standard exists.

Furthermore, we ordinarily think of things evoking approval because they are in themselves good. We do not normally think of evoking approval as that which constitutes goodness. Why *did* some particular action evoke society's approval? The non-Christian's own theory of ethics is meaningless, given his philosophical ethical outlook, given his unsustainable worldview.

If unbelievers in this school of ethics argue that good is intuited, then another problem arises: You cannot argue about good—you just intuit what is good. Once again, you cannot have a rational discussion about right and wrong, because you have no way to resolve differences of opinion. This reduces morality to subjective preferences that bind no one, not even the subjectivist who may change his view at any moment. In fact, you have no predictable way to say that a person's intuition about good is good itself. You end up having to intuit that your intuition is right, then intuit that your intuition about your intuition is right. On and on through an infinite regress which results from not having an absolute, self-verifying standard. So then, on this approach to ethics you cannot criticize any society.

2. *Good is what evokes* personal *approval.* The personal approval approach to morality ends up with an emotivist theory of ethics: Good and evil are just expressions of our emotional responses. Good and evil do not really describe anything. This school of ethical thought

claims that moral judgments cannot be deemed either as true or false. This is due to their being expressions of either individual or societal subjective preference.

We all have heard the statement: "It is good to help orphans." Note that this statement is not the same when Ted says it as when Bill says it. When Ted states it, it merely means: "Ted likes helping orphans." When Bill states it, it merely means: "Bill likes helping orphans." Consequently, in this approach we have no objective or public quality, just subjective, emotional expressions. In such an approach, ethics becomes impossible and subjectivistic. So then: "Good is that which evokes personal approval" is not meaningful.

Good is What Achieves Certain Ends

Some ethicists argue that good is **teleological**, that is, it seeks a certain end (*telos*= "end" or "purpose") which defines goodness. In an Internet article on "Teleology and Ethics" we find this view described:

> The idea that the moral worth of an action is determined by the consequences of that action is often labeled consequentialism. Usually, the "correct consequences" are those which are most beneficial to humanity—they may promote human happiness, human pleasure, human satisfaction, human survival or simply the general welfare of all humans. Whatever the consequences are, it is believed that those consequences are intrinsically good and valuable, and that is why actions which lead to those consequences are moral while actions which lead away from them are immoral.[19]

But examine the fallacies in such an ethical system. If good is that which achieves chosen ends, this leads to certain consequences. Utilitarianism teaches that good is that which produces the greatest

---

[19]Austin Cline, "Teleology and Ethics: Actions and Consequences" at the About.Com site (http://atheism.about.com/library/FAQs/phil/blfaq_phileth_teleo.htm).

happiness for the greatest number. Hedonists teach that our own individual happiness and well-being are the goals of good. But either way, if good is conducive to what you have chosen, the question becomes: How is it that good is the end that the "means to the end" is supposed to be toward? When the utilitarian says that the good is for the greatest number, we must ask: "Why is the greatest number determinative of good?" This assumes the end is itself good. But how do you know *that* is good? Furthermore, when whole cultures accept certain ends as "good" (such as eating one's defeated enemy), how could we declare that end to be evil?

We then must ask what we mean by the word "good" in such views. The unbeliever knows in his heart of hearts that good is what matches God's attitude toward things, and evil is that which is contrary to God's attitude. Unbelievers use good and evil language in absolutistic ways and then seek a theory to cover it. Paul exposes the true source of man's moral conscience when he writes of the unbelieving Gentiles that "when Gentiles who do not have the Law do instinctively the things of the Law, these, not having the Law, are a law to themselves, in that they show the work of the Law written in their hearts, their conscience bearing witness, and their thoughts alternately accusing or else defending them" (Rom. 2:14–15).

In our apologetic approach to ethics, we need to follow Paul's example at the Areopagus. At Athens he declares: "I find you are very superstitious. This god you do not understand, I now proclaim to you." This is effectively what we need to do for the unbeliever so that he may find a true foundation for his ethics.

2. Exegetical Observations

The question of an absolute standard for ethics is an important aspect of the Christian worldview. You should now understand the futility of non-believing ethical systems in that they lack an absolute standard. The application of God's law to modern ethics is essential to the Christian's apologetic approach. One important Scripture passage where the

apostle Paul points out the absolute standard of morality and its applicability in the new covenant is 1 Timothy 1:8–11. Here he speaks of
God's Old Testament law:

> We know that the Law is good, if one uses it lawfully, re-
> alizing the fact that law is not made for a righteous man,
> but for those who are lawless and rebellious, for the ungodly
> and sinners, for the unholy and profane, for those who kill
> their fathers or mothers, for murderers and immoral men
> and homosexuals and kidnappers and liars and perjurers,
> and whatever else is contrary to sound teaching, according
> to the glorious gospel of the blessed God, with which I have
> been entrusted.

We must notice several important truths contained in this statement. First, God's law is "good." He states this also in Romans 7:12
where we read: "So then, the Law is holy, and the commandment is
holy and righteous and good." In fact, Paul confesses that he would
not have known "sin" except through the law of God: "I would not
have come to know sin except through the Law; for I would not have
known about coveting if the Law had not said, 'You shall not covet'"
(7:7).

The reason the law is "good" is because it is rooted in God's own
character. When we survey the Scriptural representations of the
character of God's Law, we quickly discover that the same moral
attributes applied to it are also used in referring to God Himself:

- God is good (Mark 10:18; Ps. 143:10)—the Law is good (Deut.
  12:28; Ps. 119:68; Rom. 7:12, 16; 1 Tim. 1:8).
- God is righteous (Deut. 32:4; Ezra 9:15; Ps. 116:5)—the Law is
  righteous (Deut. 4:8; Ps. 19:7; Rom. 2:26; 8:4).
- God is just (Deut. 32:4; Ps. 25:8, 10; Isa. 45:21)—the Law is
  just (Prov. 28:4–5; Zech. 7:9–12; Rom. 7:12).
- God is holy (Isa. 6:3; Rev. 15:4)—the Law is holy (Num. 15:40;
  Rom. 7:12).

- God is perfect (2 Sam. 22:31; Ps. 18:30; Matt. 5:48)—the Law is perfect (Ps. 1:25; James 1:25).

Consequently, God's law reflects God's character which defines "good." The good is not something outside of God to which God Himself must measure up. Nor is it what it is because of God's sovereign determination (for then He could change notions of "good"). Rather, good is that which reflects His own internal character and, therefore, is that which is revealed objectively to us in His Word, particularly in His holy law.

Second, God's law can be abused. "The law is good, if one uses it lawfully." Absolute moral standards can be abused by *sinful* application. The classic example of abusing God's law is found in the New Testament record of the Pharisees, who sought to use God's law to put down others and to elevate themselves (Matt. 6:5; 23:2–4; Luke 18:10–11).

Third, God's law is not oppressive. The modern charge, that Christians who follow God's law are "puritanical," shows the unbeliever's hatred of God's law in that he uses a term that's commendatory (pure) to be derogatory (oppressive). We should strive to be "puritans" (i.e., pure) in our moral values. The law is not a constraint upon those who would act righteously, but only upon those who do evil deeds: "Law is not made for a righteous man, but for those who are lawless and rebellious" (1 Tim. 1:9).

The absolute principles of morality are designed to curb the evil desires of the sinner's heart. God's law condemns the "societal good" of those cultures that practiced genocide, cannibalism, human sacrifice, infanticide, pederasty, widow immolation, or community suicides—and the more mundane evils in our own culture.

Fourth, God's law is intended for the whole world. This is true today even in this New Covenant age. We know that Paul is speaking of God's law as especially expressed in the Mosaic law, because he often commends Moses' law (Rom. 2:13, 23; 7:7, 12; 13:8, 10). In the

Old Testament we see that the Mosaic law is, in fact, *God's* law for it is repeatedly referred to as "His law," "My law," or "God's law."[20] In fact, Paul defines love by the keeping of Moses' law in our relationship to others (Rom. 13:8, 10; Gal. 5:14), as do Jesus (Matt. 22:36–40) and James (James 2:10).

Paul, who is known in the New Testament as the apostle to the Gentiles and to the uncircumcised (Rom. 15:16; Gal. 2:9; Eph. 3:8), nevertheless, upheld the "Jewish" Mosaic Law as an ethical ideal for God's people. When writing to the church at Rome, he was addressing a Gentile church (Rom. 1:13; 15:12; 16:4). Yet he could write: "Therefore the law is holy, and the commandment holy and just and good.... For we know that the law is spiritual" (Rom. 7:12, 14). And this was well into the New Covenant era. He even absolutely declares to these Gentiles the law's continuing relevance:

- Now we know that whatever the Law says, it speaks to those who are under the Law, that every mouth may be closed, and *all the world* may become accountable to God (Rom. 3:19).
- Do we then nullify the Law through faith? May it never be! On the contrary, *we establish the Law* (Rom. 3:31).

Paul expressly declares that promoting God's law is a feature of "sound teaching" and is "according to the glorious gospel of the blessed God" which had been entrusted to him (1 Tim. 1:10–11). We should also remember previously studying Paul's statement on inspiration: "All Scripture is given by inspiration of God, and is profitable for doctrine, for reproof, for correction, for instruction in righteousness, that the man of God may be complete, thoroughly equipped for every good work" (2 Tim. 3:16–17). This necessarily

---

[20]Deuteronomy 30:10; Joshua 24:26; 2 Kings 10:31; 17:13; 21:8; 1 Chronicles 22:12; 2 Chronicles 6:16; 31:21; Ezra 7:6, 12, 14, 21; Nehemiah 8:8, 18; 9:3; 10:28, 29; Psalms 78:1; 81:4; 89:30; 119:34, 77, 92, 97, 109, 174; Isaiah 1:10; Jeremiah 6:19; 9:13; 16:11; 22:26; 26:4; 31:33; 44:10; Daniel 6:5; Hosea 4:6; 8:1.

declares God's law (a large portion of Scripture) to be "profitable" for "instruction in righteousness."

As Christians we have an absolute, unchanging, holy God who has revealed an absolute, unchanging, holy law to provide an absolute, unchanging, holy foundation for our ethical outlook and our moral conduct. The non-Christian can have no abiding moral standards because he has no foundations for them. He can't even declare wrong such atrocities as genocide, cannibalism, human sacrifice, infanticide, pederasty, widow immolation, or community suicides.

3. Questions Raised

Attempt to answer the following questions on your own before looking at the text or consulting the **Answer Key**.

1. Why is morality an important issue in defending the existence of God?

2. List some extreme moral positions in the modern world that are helpful for showing the absurdity of attempting to establish ethics without reference to God.

3. State three moral positions for which modern Christians are denounced, showing the antithesis between the Christian and non-Christian worldviews.

4. Define what we mean by "ethical relativism."

5. What is the contradiction involved in asserting that no one should declare absolute moral values?

6. What is the standard apologetic challenge we make against the unbeliever? Re-phrase that challenge for use in the debate over moral absolutes.

7. What is the absolute standard for good in the Christian worldview?

8. One school of unbelieving ethics asserts that "good" is what evokes approval. Explain this position, being careful to note the two divisions in this approach.

9. State five historical reprehensible practices that have been held in various societies, and which show the absurdity of the view that good is that which evokes social approval.

10. What is the problem with claiming that ethical values are intuited?

11. How would you respond to the claim that good is that which evokes personal approval?

12. How would you respond to the claim that good is that which achieves desired ends?

13. Defend from Scripture the claim that God's law is our revealed standard of absolute good.

4. Practical Applications

1. In our study, we mention seven examples of evils that have been deemed good by whole societies. Try to come up with three more examples.

2. Ask an unbelieving friend if he thinks morality is relative from culture to culture. Ask him how on that basis he would condemn Hitler's slaughter of the Jews.

3. Try to think of common expressions that indicate moral relativism. For instance, we hear people say: "To each, his own"; "Different strokes for different folks"; "You can't impose your morality on me." What other relativistic phrases can you come up with?

4. Look up the word "law" in the New Testament. Make a list of verses that speak of God's law as admirable. Choose one of the verses as your base verse (a verse easy to remember), then in the Bible margin at that verse jot down all the positive affirmations of God's law.

5. Make a list of those passages that speak of God's law in a negative fashion. Explain how these verses can be explained in light of the overarching commendation of God's law in Scripture.

6. Go to the Covenant Media Foundation or American Vision websites and look up articles on God's law. Prepare a 40–45 minute Bible study lesson promoting the modern applicability of God's law and present it at a Bible study.

7. Go on the Internet and look up websites promoting moral relativism. Read a few of the articles defending this view. Write a five page paper responding to two or three of their main arguments.

8. Find the articles in our "Recommended Reading" section below. Print and put them in a three ring notebook. Begin collecting articles that either illustrate the absurdity of moral relativism or assert the value of Christian absolute morals. Keep this notebook for future additions.

9. Read and critique John Corvino's "What's Morally Wrong with Homosexuality?" (http://www.indegayforum.org/authors/corvino/)

5. Recommended Reading

Copan, Paul, "The Moral Argument for God's Existence": www.4truth.net/site/apps/nl/content3.asp?c=hiKXLbPNLrF&b=778665&ct=1264233

DeMar, Gary, "Homosexual Marriage, and the End of the West": www.americanvision.org/bwarchive/homosexual%20marriage%2011-04.pdf

"Ethical Relativism": www.carm.org/relativism/ethical.htm

"Moral Relativism Refuted": www.bringyou.to/apologetics/p17.htm

Gentry, Kenneth L., "Privacy, Tolerance, and Social Morality": https://host186.ipowerweb.com/~kenneth1/homosexuality.htm

Groothius, Douglas, "Confronting the Challenge of Ethical Relativism": www.mustardseed.net/html/tomoralrelativism.html

10

The Uniformity of Nature

While the earth remains, seedtime and harvest, and
cold and heat, and summer and winter, and day and
night shall not cease.
(Gen. 8:22)

CONTINUING IN OUR study of the dynamics of defending the Christian worldview, we must recall the serious problems in four major areas of worldview concern: morality, the uniformity of nature, universals and laws, and human dignity. The complications in these areas reduce the unbelieving worldview to irrational absurdity. Hence, it is important for you to understand these matters so that you can internally critique the non-Christian's worldview, which is one track in the dual-track apologetic of Scripture (see Chapter 8). Remember that the argument for the Christian faith is: "the impossibility of the contrary." This impossibility must be demonstrated to the unbeliever.

In our last chapter we focused on the first point of concern: the problem of moral absolutes. We showed that the unbelieving system is confounded by internal contradictions and an inability to rationally justify moral standards. In that God created us as social creatures (Gen. 2:18) who live in a world crowded with other people, you absolutely depend on a basic shared morality so that "you will know that your tent is secure, for you will visit your abode and fear no loss" (Job 5:24). Otherwise, we would fear the unpredictable social world and would be unable to function in it at all (Prov. 1:16; Ps. 55:1–8; 71:4; 140:1–5; Isa. 57:20–21; 59:7–14).

We saw that the Christian worldview establishes a firm foundation for ethics: the character of the absolute, righteous God of Scripture. God not only provides the foundation for ethics but reveals the standards for them in Scripture. As always, you must recognize the fundamental idea in all apologetic encounters: You are asking which worldview can resolve the foundational questions. You grant the unbeliever the opportunity to respond to the challenge. Then you present to him the Christian foundation which alone can give meaning to human experience.

In this chapter we move to the second consideration: the problem of the uniformity of nature.

1. Central Concerns

The uniformity of nature is a crucial metaphysical issue which provides a world system in which we can practically live out our lives, as well as engage in scientific research. But the non-Christian has a problem explaining the uniformity of nature. Let us see how this is so. Whereas in the previous chapter we dealt with moral issues, in this one we are dealing with the uniformity of nature which involves scientific matters.

Uniformity Defined

As we briefly noted in an earlier chapter, we live in what we call the "universe." The idea of a *uni*-verse encompasses all created things collectively. The word "universe" is derived from *unus,* the Latin word "one" and *versus* is the Latin "to turn," meaning "to turn into one," i.e., from many parts. That we live in a *uni*verse indicates that we exist in a single, unified, orderly system which is composed of many diversified parts. These parts function together as a whole, rational, predictable system. We do not live in a "multiverse." A multiverse would be a dis-unified, totally fragmented, and random assortment of disconnected and unconnectable facts. These unconnectable facts would be meaninglessly scattered about in chaotic disarray and ultimate disorder.

The idea of a universe is necessarily bound up with the scientific principle of the uniformity of nature. The *uni*formity of the *uni*verse predicts that what happens at any given time in the material world will, under sufficiently similar conditions, occur again. That is, the same material causes under the same material conditions will produce the same material results. The uniformity of nature, therefore, entails two important component truths:

1. Uniformity is valid in all places. The character of the material universe is such that it functions according to a discernible regularity. Natural laws that operate in one place of the universe will uniformly operate throughout the universe so that the same physical cause will in a similar circumstance produce the same physical result elsewhere.

2. Uniformity is valid at all times. We may expect the future to be like the past in that natural laws do not change over time. Consequently, even changes in the universe caused by such super-massive events as exploding supernovas, colliding galaxies, and so forth, are predictable, being governed by natural law. These laws hold true at all times, from the past into the future.

The Importance of Uniformity

Science is absolutely dependent upon this uniformity because without it we could not infer from past events what we can expect under like circumstances in the future. Physical science absolutely requires the ability to predict the future action of material entities. Scientific experimentation, theorizing, and prediction would be impossible were nature non-uniform. Scientific investigation is only possible in an orderly, rational coherent, unified system.[1]

If reality were haphazard and disorderly, we would have no basic scientific laws governing and controlling various phenomena. For instance, medical labs do controlled experiments to create procedures and medications that cure and prevent disease, and so forth. Our space program could not use the laws of gravitation to provide boost assists for interplanetary probes.[2] All branches of science learn from past experiences so that that knowledge will help control future experience.

And of course our everyday lives would be inconceivable without uniformity. We would have no unity at all in either experience or thought. This is true at the most mundane levels of daily life, such as walking, riding a bicycle, or driving a car. These common experiences depend upon uniformity. When you successively put one foot in front of the other and lean forward, you expect to move a certain distance over the surface of the earth, not turn into an octopus or become a mathematical formula.

Everyone assumes the uniformity of nature, otherwise we could not know that gravity would hold us to the surface of the earth, that inertia would cause us to remain at rest until a force is applied,

[1]As an aside, we should note that properly conceived, the uniformity of nature and the operations of science do not preclude the possibility of miracles by God. The scientific law of uniformity is a *universalistic* principle, not a particularistic one. Miracles, by definition, are *rare* divine, particular interventions in nature that are appropriately called in Scripture "signs" or "wonders" due to their overriding natural law. That is, even though God may occasionally override natural law through miraculous intervention in limited individual cases, these are rare *exceptions* to the overwhelmingly universal operation of natural law. If there were no uniformity, there could be no miracles in that all would be surprisingly wondrous and unpredictable.

[2]For an intricate, mind-boggling look at the math necessary for guiding the Cassini-Huygens probe through several planetary gravitational boosts in order to reach its destination at Saturn's moon Titan, see: "Gravitational Orbits: Gravitational Assists from Planets" at http://www.go.ednet.ns.ca/~larry/orbits/gravasst.html. These complex calculations employ and adapt Johannes Kepler's (1571–1630) three laws of planetary motion.

that the sun would rise tomorrow, that ingested food would energize our bodies, and so forth. The laws of nature are deemed by scientists to be true (they are never contradicted), universal (they apply throughout the universe), absolute (nothing alters them), and simple (they can be expressed as mathematical formulas).

If we lived in a multiverse each and every single fact would necessarily stand alone, utterly disconnected from other facts, not forming a system as a whole. Consequently, nothing could be organized and related in a mind because no fact would be relatable to any other fact. Thus, science, logic, and experience necessarily require uniformity as a principle of the natural world.

The Problem of Uniformity

Now the problem that arises for the unbeliever is in *accounting* for the uniformity of nature. Since the unbeliever is so enamored with science and the scientific method, this is a good place to demonstrate his worldview crisis. You must present your standard apologetic challenge to the unbeliever: "Which worldview may reasonably expect that causal connections function uniformly throughout the universe or that the future will be like the past?" We are asking, in other words, which worldview makes human experience intelligible and science possible? All sane people assume uniformity, but only the Christian worldview can *account for* it.

Unbelievers claim: "We only know things based on observation and experience. We only know things that are results of sense experience in the material world." But the problem arises: We have no experience of the future, for it has yet to occur. Therefore, on this experience-based scientific method, how can we predict that the future will be like the past so that we may expect scientific experiments to be valid?

The unbeliever will attempt to respond: "We know the future will be like the past because our past experience of the oncoming future has always been thus." But this statement still only tells us about the past, not the approaching future we now must anticipate.

Furthermore, you can't expect the future to be like the past apart from a view of the nature of reality that informs you that events are controlled in a uniform way, as by God in the Christian system. Even the renowned atheist philosopher Bertrand Russell (1872–1970) admitted the principle of induction (that we can take past experiences and project them into the future, that we can know the future by gaining knowledge of the past) has no foundation in observation, in sense experience. Therefore, it has no "scientific" foundation. Yet all formal science and all rational human experience assumes uniformity. Russell's exact statement is as follows:

> It has been argued that we have reason to know that the future will resemble the past, because what was the future has constantly become the past, and has always been found to resemble the past, so that we really have experience of the future, namely of times which were formerly future, which we may call past futures. But such an argument really begs the very question at issue. We have experience of past futures, but not of future futures, and the question is: Will future futures resemble past futures? This question is not to be answered by an argument, which starts from past futures alone. We have therefore still to seek for some principle which shall enable us to know that the future will follow the same laws as the past.

* * * * *

> The general principles of science, such as the belief in the reign of law, and the belief that every event must have a cause, are as completely dependent upon the inductive principle as are the beliefs of daily life. All such general principles are believed because mankind has found innumerable instances of their truth and no instances of their falsehood.

But this affords no evidence for their truth in the future, unless the inductive principle is assumed.

Thus all knowledge which, on a basis of experience tells us something about what is not experienced, is based upon a belief which experience can neither confirm nor confute, yet which, at least in its more concrete applications, appears to be as firmly rooted in us as many of the facts of experience. The existence and justification of such beliefs—for the inductive principle, as we shall see, is not the only example—raises some of the most difficult and most debated problems of philosophy. [3]

Ultimately, Russell ends up falling into subjectivism as he recognizes he cannot account for the objective world as it is:

In **ontology**,[4] I start by accepting the truth of physics. . . . Philosophers may say: What justification have you for accepting the truth of physics? I reply: merely a common-sense basis. . . . I believe (though without good grounds) in the world of physics as well as in the world of psychology. . . . If we are to hold that we know anything of the external world, we must accept the canons of scientific knowledge. Whether . . . an individual decides to accept or reject these canons, is a purely personal affair, not susceptible to argument.[5]

Another philosopher of science speaks of the paradox of induction:

The paradox of induction is the problem that in all scientific reasoning we form conclusions, called laws, that are of a general nature; however, the evidence we have for those laws is based upon particular experiences. For example, we form the conclusion that all rays of light will bend as they pass

---

[3]Bertrand Russell, *The Problems of Philosophy* (Oxford: Oxford University Press, 1998), ch. 6.

[4]**Ontology** is the branch of metaphysics that deals with the nature of being.

[5]Bertrand Russell, *Human Knowledge: Its Scope and Limits* (New York: Clarion Books, Simon and Schuster, 1948), xv–xvi.

from air into glass, but we have only ever observed a finite number of instances of this law. On further reflection we see that there is no necessary connection between something happening on one occasion and the same thing happening in like circumstances on another occasion. We are not directly acquainted with the "power" behind events that ensures the uniformity of nature throughout space and time.

The general law encompasses a potentially infinite number of instances that no amount of observation could possibly affirm. The problem is usually expressed as a problem of inference from past to future, but strictly this is only an instance of the problem; unobserved past events are also subject to the paradox of induction—we can never be sure that any general law has applied uniformly even in the past. No general law can ever be certain.[6]

Furthermore, another complication arises for the non-Christian: How do we know assuredly that the universe is in fact uniform? Has man investigated every single aspect of the universe from each one of its smallest atomic particles to the farthest flung galaxies and all that exists in between, so that he can speak authoritatively? After all, as Kilgore Trout amusingly observes: "The universe is a big place, perhaps the biggest." Does man have totally exhaustive knowledge about every particle of matter, every movement in space, and every moment of time? How does man know uniformity governs the whole world and the entire universe? As "The Paradox of Induction" laments: "We have no way at present of being sure that the universe is uniform. We have only sampled physical nature in our own limited portion of the universe. . . .[W]e are wanting the laws of the universe to be such that we can understand them, but there is no reason offered as to why the universe should be like this."[7]

6“The Paradox of Induction,” *Black's Academy*, 2003: www.blacks.veriovps.co.uk/html/PXQEPJ11.html
    7“The Paradox of Induction,” 2, 7.

In addition, since man claims to have an experience of external things, how do we know our experience is accurate and actually conforms to reality as it is, so that science may function? How do we know that we are not free-floating minds? Or simply one mind? We saw these problems in earlier chapters on metaphysics and alternative worldviews.

Such questions are not commonly asked but are nevertheless vitally important. This point demonstrates that any and every attempt to prove uniformity in nature necessarily requires *circular reasoning*. To prove uniformity one must assume or presuppose uniformity.

If I set out to argue the uniformity of the universe because I can predict cause-and-effect, am I not presupposing the uniformity and validity of my experience? How can I be sure that my experience of cause-and effect is an accurate reflection of what really happens? Furthermore, am I not presupposing the trustworthy, uniform coherence of my own rationality—a rationality that requires uniformity?

The issue boils down to this: Since man cannot know everything he must *assume* or *presuppose* uniformity and then think and act on this very basic assumption. *Consequently the principle of uniformity is not a scientific law but an act of faith which undergirds scientific law.* Thus, adherence to the principle of uniformity— though absolutely essential to science and the scientific method—is an intrinsically religious commitment.

Here the problem of the unbeliever's ultimate view of reality collapses into absurdity. He is committed to the notion that chance explains the universe. For instance, the Big Bang model of the beginning of the universe "represents the instantaneous suspension of physical laws, the sudden, abrupt flash of lawlessness that allowed something to come out of nothing. It represents a true miracle— transcending physical principles."[8] It teaches that

---

[8]Paul Davies, *The Edge of Infinity* (New York: Simon and Schuster, 1981), 161.

[a]ll matter and energy, as well as time, were created in the Big Bang between 10 and 20 billion years ago. In other words, at some point in the distant past, everything in the universe was concentrated into a point-like region of space called a singularity. For some reason, and astronomers are unsure why, this singularity expanded rapidly in an explosion, releasing all the matter-energy and time—this event is what is termed The Big Bang.[9]

The Big Bang view of the origins of the universe dominates the scientific community so much that "today, virtually all financial and experimental resources in cosmology are devoted to Big Bang studies."[10] Elsewhere we read: "Physicist Gregory Benford is even more enthusiastic: 'It is as though prodigious, bountiful Nature for billions of years has tossed off variations on its themes like a careless, prolific Picasso. Now Nature finds that one of its casual creations has come back with a piercing, searching vision, and its own pictures to paint.'"[11]

Nobel Prize-winning French molecular biologist Jacques Monod puts it bluntly: "Pure chance, absolutely free but blind, [lies] at the very root of the stupendous edifice of evolution.... The universe was not pregnant with life nor the biosphere with man. Our number came up in the Monte Carlo game."[12]

---

[9]"What is Cosmology?" at the University of Dublin website (www.csc.tcd.ie/~tass/HTML/Cosmology/cosm.html).

[10]"An Open Letter to the Scientific Community," *New Scientist* (May 22, 2004): www.cosmologystatement.org. We should recognize that the Big Bang model of the universe is not the only one physicists suggest, though it is the most familiar and most widely accepted. Other theoretical models include Quasi-Steady State Cosmology (F. Hoyle, G. Burbidge, J. V. Narlikar, 2000), Plasma Cosmology (E. J. Lerner, 1991), Meta- Model Cosmology (T. Van Flandern, 1999), Variable Mass Cosmology (H. Arp, 1998), universe Cycle Model (A. Gulko, 1980s), and Aetherometric Model (P. Correa and A. Correa, 2002). They all have the same problem though: Without the God of Scripture creating it, chance must prevail.

[11]Dinesh D'Souza, "Staying Human: The Danger of Techno-utopia" *National Review* (January 22, 2001).

[12]Jacques Monod, *Chance and Necessity* (New York: Knopf, 1971), 112.

Evolutionist K. Rohiniprasad comments in his "The Accident of Human Evolution": "As the evolutionary biologist Stephen Jay Gould puts it, humans arose as a fortuitous and contingent outcome of thousands of linked events. We should humbly acknowledge the fact that any one of these events could have occurred differently and sent history on an alternative pathway."[13] Regarding four evolutionary turns, she goes on to state in the same article: "It is important to realize that the above four incidents were totally unrelated and *random*. Like every other phenomenon or catastrophe that changed the course of events on the earth, *biological evolution trundled along without any pre-ordained plan or purpose.*"

Unfortunately for the non-Christian cosmology, chance involves randomness and unpredictability.[14] As the source of all being, it undercuts the uniformity of all material reality, for a "singularity" (such as predicted of black-holes as well as for the beginning of the whole universe) "is a point where physical laws break down, where matter is infinitely dense."[15]

The unbelieving worldview requires faith in miracles, yet without a reason for those miracles. Life arises from non-life. Intelligence from non-intelligence. Morality from that which is a-moral. These are faith claims for explaining our world and how it came to be. The world becomes like Mark Twain's (1835–1910) introductory comment in *The Adventures of Huckleberry Finn*: "Persons attempting to find a motive in this narrative will be prosecuted; persons at-

---

[13]K. Rohiniprasad, "The Accident of Human Evolution": http://sulekha.com/blogs/blogdisplay.aspx?cid=3899

[14]The problems presented by the notion of a chance-created universe are such that many philosophers and physicists are beginning to postulate an infinite number of universes, speaking of multi-verses instead of a singular universe. These other worlds are known as parallel universes, bubble universes, baby universes, and such like terms.

[15]Byron Spice, "Pitt team may detect ripples in space-time caused by cataclysms," *Pittsburgh Post-Gazette* (October 26, 1998): www.post-gazette.com/healthscience/19981026waves.asp.

tempting to find a moral in it will be banished; persons attempting to find a plot in it will be shot."

The uniformity of nature is perfectly compatible, however, with the Christian worldview. The absolute, all-creating, sovereignly-governing God reveals to us in Scripture that we can count on regularities in the natural world. The Bible teaches that the sun will continue to measure time for us on the earth (Gen. 1:14–19; Eccl. 1:5; Jer. 33:20), that seasons will come and go uniformly (Gen. 8:22; Ps. 74:17), that planting and harvest cycles may be expected (Jer. 5:24; Mark 4:26–29), and so forth. Because of this God-governed regularity in nature, the scientific enterprise is possible and even fruitful.

2. Exegetical Observations

Three particularly important texts are immensely helpful for understanding the rationality of the world and coherence of our experience: Ephesians 1:11; Colossians 1:16–17; and Hebrews 1:3. These verses account for the uniformity of nature.

We will begin with the Colossians passage as a very pointed text which opens up the biblical foundations for uniformity. In Colossians 1:16 we learn that "all things were created, both in the heavens and on earth, visible and invisible, . . . all things have been created by Him." The Greek verb form of "created" is the perfect tense, which speaks of a past completed action with a continuing effect. The Lord created the world as it is, and it continues to exist as such.

In this brief statement the word "all" (Gk., *panton*) appears four times, emphasizing the totality of His creative activity. Not only so, but it specifies that things "visible *and* invisible" were created by Him. Paul emphatically declares: *All things without exception—material and spiritual—have been created by the Lord.* That is, the Lord is the source of all creation, not only the material elements but their invisible laws. Every aspect of reality derives from the creative power of God, not from the inherent, self-creating powers of chance. After all, He exists "before all things" as their ultimate source.

In addition, Paul makes a fundamental point that all things have been created not only "by Him" but also *for* Him" (cf. Rom. 11:36; 1 Cor. 8:6). The universe does not exist on its own and without reference to God: it is not self-contained and self-explanatory. It exists as God's own personal possession and ultimately for His singular glory. It has meaning, significance, and purpose as a God-created, God-glorifying reality. It cannot be properly understood apart from Him—hence our apologetic of "the impossibility of the contrary."

As we continue to read, we discover that the created order is *maintained* by Jesus: "In Him all things hold together." The Greek verb *sunistemi* ("hold together") is derived from *histemi* ("to stand") and *sun* ("with"), it literally means "to cause to stand together." In Greek the world is called a *kosmos*, which is the opposite of the Greek word *chaos*: it is a place that is caused to "stand together" in a harmonious whole. "The unity, order, and adaptation evident in all of nature and history can be traced to the Upholder or Sustainer of all."[16] Indeed, "the order and regularity of natural processes and the human power of reasoning resonates with this rationality. In the modern era, Newtonian physics and the scientific investigation of 'the laws of nature' were premised on a similar axiom."[17]

In Ephesians 1:11 we see further evidence of the rational purpose lying back of the universe, for Paul reveals that God "works all things after the counsel of His will." Rather than chance and impersonalism being ultimate in the universe, the rational God of Scripture governs and controls all things after His own deliberate counsel (Gk., *boule*, "plan") arising from His sovereign, willful determination. The universe does not exist as an accident. Nor does God cre-

---

[16]William Hendrikson, *Colossians and Philemon* (NTC) (Grand Rapids, MI: Baker, 1964), 74.

[17]James D. G. Dunn, *The Epistles to the Colossians and to Philemon* (NIGTC) (Grand Rapids, MI: Eerdmans, 1996), 94.

ate it arbitrarily. Rather the magnificent universe results from the deliberate planning of God who embraces "all things."

The clause in Hebrews supplements both the Colossians and Ephesians statements noting that He "upholds all things by the word of His power" (Heb. 1:3b). The verb "upholds" is *hupostasis* which is a compound of *histemi* ("to stand") and *hupo* ("under"): "that which stands under." He upholds the universe not only by raw "power" (*dunameos* from whence we derive "dynamite") but by power governed by His "word." The mention of His "word" not only highlights the effortlessness by which He sustains the universe (given His absolute power), but speaks of its rationality and coherence.

Since God created the rational, coherent universe by His sovereign, willful plan, and since He created man in His image to function in that world, we see clear revelatory evidence for the foundation of that which scientists call "the uniformity of nature."

3. Questions Raised

Attempt to answer the following questions on your own before looking at the text or consulting the **Answer Key**.

1. How is the idea of the "universe" bound up with the notion of "uniformity of nature"?

2. Explain the meaning of the uniformity of nature using the two basic elements involved.

3. Why is the uniformity of nature important to human experience and to science?

4. State the apologetic challenge you should present to the unbeliever regarding nature's uniformity.

5. The unbeliever argues that the scientific method operates on the basis of observation and experience. How does this present a problem for defending his worldview?

6. Respond to the claim that we can know how things will operate in the future because we have seen how they operate in the past.

7. What problem arises in the unbeliever's worldview when he claims he knows the universe is uniform?

8. List some Bible verses that provide a foundation for our knowledge of the uniformity of nature.

9. How would you show that the Christian system easily accounts for the uniformity of nature?

4. Practical Applications

1. Go on the Internet or do research in appropriate books to discover the names of some of the great scientists who were Christians who believed that God created the universe. Choose three of them and read brief biographies on their lives, noting especially their commitment to the Christian faith and how it encouraged their labors.

2. Compose a Bible study on the three verses we highlighted in "Exegetical Observations" above. Present it to a group of Christian friends or in your Sunday school class. Your careful research, personal preparation, and formal presentation of the material will help secure it in your mind.

3. Go to some of the creation science Internet sites and search for articles on uniformity in nature. Download three of the more helpful ones, read them, and put them in a file for future reference.

4. While at the creation science websites, look over their book offerings. Purchase two books that appear helpful for understanding scientific issues from a biblical perspective. Begin building a personal library of helpful apologetic tools.

5. Recommended Reading

Butler, Michael, "TAG v. TANG": www.reformed.org/apologetics/martin/pen896.html

Bumbulis, Michael, "Christianity and the Birth of Science": www.1dolphin.org/bumbulis

Dwiggins, Jeff, "Science, Logic, Rationality, and the Uniformity of Nature": www.forerunner.com/aalarm/X0011_Logic.html

Frame, John, "Science": www.reformed.org/apologetics/martin/frame_contra_martin2.html

Joyce, George Hayward, "The Divine Omnipotence": www.nd.edu/Departments/Maritain/etext/pnt13.htm

"The Light Has Come: Quotations on the History of Christian Contributions to the Progress of Civilization": www.christianciv.com/LightHasCome.htm

Morris, Henry, *Men of Science Men of God: Great Scientists of the Past Who Believed the Bible* (Green Forest, Ariz.: Master, 1988).

"Physics, Cosmology, and the Big Bang": www.nwcreation.net/cosmology.html

Samples, Kenneth Richard, "The Historic Alliance of Christianity and Science": www.reasons.org/resources/apologetics/christianscience.shtml

11

The Problem of Universals

God is not the author of confusion.
(1 Cor. 14:33a)

W E HAVE SEEN the crippling problems inherent in the unbelieving worldview. This is important for you to understand due to the two-fold method of biblical apologetics. Not only must you take the positive step in presenting the Christian worldview's truth claims, but you must also negatively confound the unbeliever by engaging in an internal critique of his worldview. You must show him that it cannot account for reality as it is. In a way, your positive and negative work has the evangelistic effect of telling him of heaven and warning him of hell. You are, as Cornelius Van Til put it, demonstrating "the impossibility of the contrary." You are showing that without the Christian worldview man can't rationally account for anything in human life, experience, or reason.

In our last two chapters we noted two monumental difficulties facing the non-Christian: the problem of moral absolutes and the problem of the uniformity of nature. Without moral principles we would be reduced to living like animals in a fearful world "red with tooth and claw." Without the uniformity of nature we could not enjoy practical living or engage in scientific research. As always, the trouble for the unbeliever is that in denying the existence of God he is asserting chance as the ultimate backdrop of the universe. But in a chance universe man cannot account for principles of morality or laws of nature. Nor, as we shall see, for the laws of logic.

1. Central Concerns

In this lesson we will be considering the related philosophical issues of the laws of logic *and* universals. These are quite important matters in that without logic and universals we could not understand anything at all or engage in coherent reasoning. Not only must nature as a whole operate under the principle of uniformity (as per our last chapter), but we ourselves must be able to reason by means of the laws of logic accessing universals.

Universals and Thought

Let's address the problem of **universals** and the "laws of logic" as related issues causing additional problems for the unbeliever. Though you may not normally contemplate universals, you invariably and necessarily employ them in your everyday life.[1] But what are they? And why are they so significant? And how do they demonstrate the existence of God? *Van Til's Apologetic* defines a "universal" as

> any truth of a general or abstract nature—whether it be a broad concept, law, principle, or categorical statement. Such general truths are used to understand, organize, and interpret particular truths encountered in concrete experience. . . . If one does not begin with some such general truths (universals) with which to understand the particular observations in one's experience, those factual particulars would be unrelated and uninterpretable—i.e., 'brute.' In a chance universe, all particular facts would be random, have no clas-

---

[1]Rather than contemplating universals, Zen Buddhism urges the contemplation of absurd riddles through the exercise of koan. The next time someone asks you what is the sound of one hand clapping, all you have to do to answer that is reach over and slap him in the face. The contemplative riddle will be solved and you can get on about your business in the world of reason rather than contemplating the absurd.

sifiable identity, bear no pre-determined order or relation, and thus be unintelligible to man's mind.[2]

Philosophers note that a universal involves three notions: (1) By definition, "universals" must apply to multiple things (otherwise, they would be particulars); (2) They are abstract rather than concrete (therefore, they do not appear in the material world); (3) They are general truths rather than specific.

To illustrate the function of universals in a simple way, let's look at Huey, Louie, and Dewey, the fictional nephews of the Disney cartoon character Donald Duck.[3] Huey, Louie, and Dewey are "ducks." But consider: "To what does the term 'duck' refer?" The answer, of course, is *all* of them. Huey, Louie, and Dewey are *particular* individuals who are in the *class* of "ducks," which is the general, universal organizing concept. They each share "duckness."

Further note that universals are immaterial realities distinct from material particulars. For instance, when you use the concepts of "horseness" or "duckness," you know these apply to *many* individuals but are *separate* from them. For instance, you can eat Huey as a particular duck, but you cannot eat duckness. "Duckness" is an abstract concept that relates those many individual things we call "ducks."

By the very nature of reasoning you necessarily assume abstract, invariant universals. These are essential to understanding concrete, changing particulars, because you have to be able to associate, classify, and organize in your mind the particular things in your ex-

---

[2] Greg L. Bahnsen, *Van Til's Apologetic: Readings and Analysis* (Phillipsburg, NJ: Presbyterian and Reformed, 1998), 38, note 10.

[3] If you have ever wondered, the three brothers were named after Huey Pierce Long, a politician from Louisiana, Thomas Edmund Dewey, a politician from New York, and animator Louie Schmitt. In "Duck Tales," the boys are teenagers with their names revealed as Huebert, Deuteronomy, and Louis Duck. Don't ask me why. I am only reporting the facts: www.weirdspace.dk/Disney/Huey%20Dewey%20and%20Louie.htm

perience. Your everyday, observational, sensate *experience* always consists of particular, historical, objective things. Yet you *reason* in terms of universal, abstract principles so that you can bring it all together and understand it. For instance, you may speak of the particular rock, which you experience through your senses as hard, rough, cold, and heavy. But when you contemplate or speak of any specific rock, you must generalize by abstracting the universals of hardness, roughness, coldness, and heaviness.

Again, universals are absolutely essential to knowing and communicating. As Van Til puts it: "If we wish to know the facts of this world, we must relate these facts to laws. That is, in every knowledge transaction, we must bring the particulars of our experience into relation with universals."[4]

Laws of Logic

Universals include natures (e.g., human nature), moral values, propositions—and laws. Thus, the laws of logic are universals. They are the most general propositions one can possibly hold. They are used every single time you think or talk about anything whatsoever. They are the abstract, universal, invariant rules that govern human rationality. In fact, they make rationality possible by allowing for coherent meaning, rational thought, and intelligent communication.[5]

Be careful in how you speak of the laws of logic. You should not say that these are "laws of thought," as if they were matters of subjective human psychology informing us how people think. We know, of course, that people actually breach the laws of logic regu-

---

[4]Cornelius Van Til, *Introduction to Systematic Theology* (Phillipsburg, NJ: Presbyterian and Reformed, 1974), 22.

[5]You can see the theological significance of universals, for instance, in the fact that Christ became *truly* human, in that human nature is a classifying universal. "Since then the children share in flesh and blood, He Himself likewise also partook of the same" (Heb. 2:14).

larly. The laws of logic are not laws of thought, but *presuppositions* of (coherent) thinking.

The three basic laws of logic are the Law of Identity, the Law of Contradiction (sometimes called the Law of Non-Contradiction), and the Law of Excluded Middle.

The Law of Identity states that "A is A." This means that if any statement is true, it is true; it cannot be both true and not true simultaneously. That is, anything that exists in reality has a particular identity and is not something else. The thing is what it is. A thing may be a cow but not simultaneously a cat. A dog may be all black, but not simultaneously all white (that is, both black and white in the same way and the same place).

The Law of Contradiction states that "A is not not-A." That is, no statement can be both true and false in the same sense at the same time. A person cannot be both alive and not alive simultaneously and in the same way. An astronaut cannot be on the moon and not on the moon at the same time and in the same manner.

The Law of Excluded Middle states that "A is either A or not-A." That is, every statement must be either true or false exclusively, there is no middle ground.[6] Or to put it differently: if a given statement is not true, then its denial must be true. For instance, we may say that something is either a chair or not a chair, it cannot be *neither* a chair nor not a chair. You are either here or you are not here, you cannot be *neither* here nor not here.[7]

Obviously universals and the laws of logic are fundamentally important to rationality. Without them you could not relate one thing to another, nor reason about the world and life.

---

[6] This law is sometimes facetiously called the Law of Excluded *Muddle*.

[7] This particular law has been debated by philosophers. You must be careful in understanding it. The law of excluded middle does not say there is no middle ground between opposites (such as large and small). Rather it is dealing with the question of middle ground between a statement and its negative.

Problems for the Unbeliever

You should recall that the Presuppositional Apologetic is such that it can take *any* fact to demonstrate the existence of God. This, of course, holds true for even the laws of logic and universals. By this stage of the game, you can reflexively utter the apologetic challenge to the unbeliever: "Which worldview makes sense of universals and the laws of logic?"

The recurring problem for the unbelieving worldview arises once again: He cannot *account* for universals and the laws of logic. Remembering that apologetics deals with *worldviews* and the *principles* inherent in them, we now look at the unbeliever's problem:

> Van Til says the spiritually dead man cannot *in principle* even count and weigh and measure. Van Til says that unbelievers cannot even do math or the simplest operations in science. By that he means *the unbeliever's espoused worldview* or philosophy cannot make counting or measuring *intelligible*. Now why is that? Briefly, because counting involves an abstract concept of law, or universal, or order. If there is no law, if there is no universal, if there is no order, then there is no sequential counting. But the postulation of an abstract universal order contradicts the unbeliever's view of the universe as a random or chance realm of material particulars. Counting calls for abstract entities which are in fact uniform and orderly. The unbeliever says the world is not abstract—but that the world is only material; the universe is not uniform but is a chance realm and random. And so by rejecting God's Word—which accounts for a universal order or law—the unbeliever would not in principle be able to count and measure things. As it is, unbelievers do in fact count and do in fact measure and practice science, but *they cannot give a philosophical explanation of that fact*. Or as Van Til loved to put it: unbelievers can count, but they cannot account for counting.[8]

---

[8]Greg L. Bahnsen, "At War with the Word: The Necessity of Biblical Antithesis" (www.reformed.org/apologetics/At_War_With_the_Word.html). Emphasis mine.

Logic is crucial to any rational thinking: it provides common laws of reasoning, good patterns of inference. "In the generic sense 'reason' simply refers to man's intellectual or mental capacity. Christians believe in reason, and non-Christians believe in reason; they both believe in man's intellectual capacity. However, for each one, his view of reason and his use of reason is controlled by the worldview within which reason operates."[9] But which worldview makes laws of logic intelligible? Can the unbeliever justify the laws of logic in his chance universe? Especially a chance universe conceived naturalistically as involving only material things? Once he tries to justify universals and the laws of logic, he steps out of his worldview and into yours. His presuppositions cannot sustain his worldview and cannot account for universals. Let us see how this is so.

The Non-Christian's Predicament

Why can't the unbeliever's worldview account for universals and the laws of logic?

1. *Empirical Limitations.* When modern man commits exclusively to the scientific method, then he has committed to empiricism. Empiricism is the view that all human knowledge ultimately derives through the senses and through experience. We discover laws of physics, for instance, by observing, measuring, counting, and analyzing the behavior of things around us.

The unbelieving empiricist cannot account for the laws of logic which regulate human reasoning. The laws of logic are not physical objects existing as a part of the sense world. They are not the result of observable behavior of material objects or physical actions. Do the laws of logic exist in the natural world so that they can be empirically examined? If we are materialists, then only that which is objective in the realm of sense experience is real. What sense do

---

[9]Greg L. Bahnsen, "At War with the Word: The Necessity of Biblical Antithesis," in *Antithesis* (1:1), 8.

the laws of logic make for unbelievers? What are the laws of logic? If they are just the firing of nerve endings in the neural synapses, then logic differs from person to person and therefore its laws are not laws at all. The inherent materialism in the modern world cannot account for laws of logic.

Furthermore, since the laws of logic are universal, invariant, abstract, eternal truths, how do they continually apply in our changing world of experience? How do we get those laws from "above" down into the historical process?

The unbelieving world cannot account even for universals beyond the laws of logic. They obviously speak about concepts, but if they are devoted to the scientific, empirical method then they must hold that only things which exist in the material world are real. When unbelievers talk of concepts, they need a worldview to make them meaningful. But they do not have one. With all of their particulars, they can't account for universals. As Dr. Van Til expressed it, they are "trying to put beads on a string with no holes in the beads." They have no universals to hold things together.

2. *Chance Foundations.* Not only does the unbeliever's investment in empirical science destroy the laws of logic and universals in principle, but so does his commitment to a chance universe.

One of the most renowned atheists was also a philosopher—a philosopher of science. Bertrand Russell took chance to its ultimate conclusion, destroying unity: "Academic philosophers, ever since the time of Parmenides, have believed that the world is a unity. . . . The most fundamental of my intellectual beliefs is that this is rubbish. I think the universe is all spots and jumps, without any unity, without continuity, without coherence or orderliness . . . . Indeed, there is little but prejudice and habit to be said for the view that there is a world at all."[10] Oddly enough, at least he was consistent

---

[10]Bertrand Russell, *The Scientific Outlook*, 98.

with his atheism in stating this, though the act-of-stating is evidence against his view! Elsewhere he called upon man "to worship at the shrine that his own hands have built; undismayed by the empire of chance."[11]

Jacques Monod's comment is worth repeating: "Pure chance, absolutely free but blind, [lies] at the very root of the stupendous edifice of evolution. . . . The universe was not pregnant with life nor the biosphere with man. Our number came up in the Monte Carlo game."[12] Evolutionary biologist Julian Huxley (1887–1975) has written:

> The broad outlines of the new evolutionary picture of ultimates are beginning to be clearly visible. Man's destiny is to be the sole agent for the future evolution of this planet. He is the highest dominant type to be produced by over two and a half billion years of the slow biological improvement effected by the *blind opportunistic workings of natural selection*; if he does not destroy himself, he has at least an equal stretch of evolutionary time before him to exercise his agency.[13]

The late Harvard paleontologist Stephen Jay Gould exercised much influence in evolutionary circles. Walter Gilberti's obituary for Gould states that he "concluded that the sudden accelerations of evolutionary change that have certainly manifested themselves throughout the earth's history were the result of events in which chance played the preponderant role. For Gould, the determinism in nature that is contained within the blind process of natural selection was increasingly de-emphasized in his writings, in favor of the purely accidental. Gould's 'radical' contingency even excluded any notion of direction, such as evolution from the simple to the com-

---

[11]"Bertrand Russell, *Why I Am Not a Christian, And Other Essays on Religion and Related Subjects*, ed. Paul Edwards (New York: Simon and Schuster, Clarion, 1957), 116.

[12]Jacques Monod, *Chance and Necessity* (New York: Knopf, 1971), 112.

[13]Julian Huxley, ed., *The Humanist Frame* (New York: Harper, 1961), 17.

plex, for example."[14] Physicists are committed to the notion of chance as the ultimate source of all reality. As astronomer and cosmologist Marcus Chown comments:

> Space and the material world could be created out of nothing but noise. . . . According to [physicists] Reginald Cahill and Christopher Klinger of Flinders University in Adelaide, space and time and all the objects around us are no more than the froth on a deep sea of randomness.
>
> * * * * *
>
> "This is where physics comes in," says Cahill. "The universe is rich enough to be self-referencing. For instance, I'm aware of myself." This suggests that most of the everyday truths of physical reality, like most mathematical truths, have no explanation. According to Cahill and Klinger, that must be because reality is based on randomness. They believe randomness is more fundamental than physical objects.[15]

But chance can't account for law. Universals and the laws of logic are inimical to chance and randomness: "In a chance universe, all particular facts would be random, have no classifiable identity, bear no pre-determined order or relation, and thus be unintelligible to man's mind."[16]

Furthermore, an evolving, chance universe cannot account for absolute, unchanging, universal laws of logic. Indeed, absolute law contradicts the notion of incessant change which necessarily involves relativism.

3. *Dialectical Tension.* But of course the modern scientist does operate in terms of universals and law. It is just that his worldview can't

---

[14]Walter Gilberti, "On the Death of Palaeontologist Stephen Jay Gould," World Socialist Website: www.wsws.org/articles/2002/jul2002/goul-j01.shtml

[15]Marcus Chown, "Random Reality," *New Scientist* (February 26, 2000), 24.

[16]Bahnsen, *Van Til's Apologetic*, 38, note 10.

account for them. This brings dialectical tension (contradiction) into his system:

> On the assumptions of the natural man logic is a timeless impersonal principle, and facts are controlled by chance. It is by means of universal timeless principles of logic that the natural man must, on his assumptions, seek to make intelligible assertions about the world of reality or chance. But this cannot be done without falling into self-contradiction. About chance no manner of assertion can be made. In its very idea it is the irrational. And how are rational assertions to be made about the irrational?[17]

This tension is also seen in the unreflective association of logic and empirical science. For instance, Kyle Ash writes of "logic and empiricism—fundamental aspects of science."[18]

One recurring complaint made against us is that Christianity depends more upon faith than upon reason. In fact, it is as though the whole notion of faith *necessarily* discounts reason. The modern mind is enamored with the rationality of science and pities the naïveté of faith. As Thomas Paine expressed it two centuries ago, since the Enlightenment we are in the "Age of Reason," while Christianity is a part of the primitive, out-moded "Age of Faith." The Harvard Objectivist Club at Harvard University presents on their website arguments for Objectivism (the philosophy developed by Ayn Rand), noting that "reason is the only source of knowledge." This obviously precludes by definition divine revelation as a source of knowledge.

To the modern man who challenges us with Reason, we should ask him what form of reasoning does he follow? Empiricism? Utilitarianism? Pragmatism? Foundationalism? Logical positivism? Ex-

---

[17]Cornelius Van Til, *The Defense of the Faith* (Philadelphia, PA: Presbyterian and Reformed, 1955), 143.

[18]Kyle Ash, "International Animal Rights: Speciesism and Exclusionary Human Dignity," *Journal of Animal Law*, Michigan State University College of Law (11), 198: www.animallaw.info/journals/jo_pdf/vol11_p195.pdf

istentialism? Essentialism? Idealism? Sensationalism? Objectivism? Nihilism? Intuitionism? Instrumentalism? Falliblism? And why are there so many competing and contradictory approaches to knowledge and understanding, if reason stands alone as *the* source of knowledge?

4. *Conventional Subjectivity.* During a worldviews debate, atheist Gordon Stein was once asked to give an account for the laws of logic. Dr. Stein took a common non-absolutist route when he declared that they are "human conventions" agreed upon by man. This was the best he could do in his chance world. In the first place the laws of logic are not agreed upon by all people. Stephan Bevans interacts with Raimon Panikkar on this sort of issue:

> Panikkar maintains that Indians cannot really accept the principle that might be called the backbone of western philosophical thinking: the principle of contradiction. For Indians, Panikkar insists, things can indeed 'be' and 'not be' at the same time....This seems to be close to the Taoist idea of yang and yin, where all things participate in the reality of their opposites: light and darkness, male and female, good and evil, flesh and spirit, and so forth.[19]

William Dyrness also notes this of Eastern thought:

> There are those who argue that these Eastern patterns of thought are inviolable and Christianity must adapt to them completely. Jung Young Lee has argued that in Asia we must get out of the habit of thinking in terms of either/or; we must be able to think of both/and. Change, he believes, may be the key to the universe, and ambiguity and differences merely the reflection of aspects of reality. In traditional Chinese thought, yin and yang are believed to be complementary

---

[19]Stephen B. Bevans, *Models of Contextual Theology* (Maryknoll, NY: Orbis, 1992), 5.

modes of being. . . . He seeks to apply this to his view of God.[20]

This problem arises from the basic monism at work in these systems. Since all is one, obviously there can be no law of contradiction. The renowned Zen Buddhist D. T. Suzuki notes that: "Zen is one thing and logic another. When we fail to make this distinction and expect Zen to give us something logically consistent and intellectually illuminating, we altogether misinterpret the signification of Zen."

If the unbeliever states that the laws of logic are agreed upon conventions, then they are not absolute because they are subject to "vote" and therefore to change. The laws of logic are not dependent upon people: they are true whether or not people exist.

The Christian's Resolution

1. *The Source of Logic.* The Christian holds as a basic presupposition that God is the Creator of the world (Gen. 1) and of the human mind (Gen. 1:26–27), so all intelligibility is due to Him. He is the author of all truth, wisdom, and knowledge (Prov. 1:7; 9:10; Col. 2:3). Christians see the laws of logic as expressions of God's thinking, His own consistent personal nature, not as principles outside of God to which He must measure up. The laws of logic reflect the nature of God, for in Him we find perfect coherence. "The law of contradiction, therefore, as we know it, is but the expression on a created level of the internal coherence of God's nature."[21]

We must be careful here, though. We are not saying God *created* the laws of logic by His volitional self-determination. Were this so, then He could alter or discard them as well. On the Harvard Uni-

[20]William A. Dyrness, *Learning about Theology from the Third World* (Grand Rapids: Zondervan, 1990), 140–141.

[21]Cornelius Van Til, *Introduction to Systematic Theology*, 11. Cited in Bahnsen, *Van Til's Apologetic*, 235.

versity website, the Objectivist Club mistakenly discounts theism on the basis that "the existence of god would imply that there exists a being capable of suspending the laws of nature by sheer act of will. This contradicts two important premises of Objectivism: the primacy of existence and the Law of Identity."

Rather, we are saying that the laws of logic reflect His *nature*, the way He is in Himself. They are, therefore, *eternal* expressions of the *unchanging* character of God (Num. 23:19; Mal. 3:6; James 1:17). God's unchanging character is just that, unchanging. Therefore, the laws of logic (which reflect that character) are unchanging and unchangeable, in that God "cannot deny Himself" (2 Tim. 2:13).

2. *The Coherence of the World.* For our experience to be rationally coherent, a correspondence must exist between our minds and God's, since He is the ultimate source of uniform reality and coherent reason. This is just what we find in the Christian system: Man is created in the image of God to engage the world in a rational way. Not only is man's mind analogical to God's, but it is compatible with the God-created universe because of God's designing us and our environments. In fact, "the gift of logical reason was given by God to man in order that he might order the revelation of God for himself."[22]

Van Til speaks of our "thinking God's thoughts after Him." That is, we must think according to the pattern of God's mind, rationally and realistically. Perfect coherence characterizes the mind of God so that for us to reason we must think with logical consistency.

2. Exegetical Observations

God's own revelation expresses or assumes the primary logical laws. For instance, the law of identity is affirmed by God when He iden-

---

[22]Cornelius Van Til, *An Introduction to Systematic Theology* (Phillipsburg, NJ: Presbyterian and Reformed, 1974), 256.

tifies Himself: "I am that I am" (Ex. 3:14). God is Himself and not something else. Though the pantheists claim God is everything and everything is God, and though monists believe all is one (including god), in Scripture we find a fundamental and unrelenting assertion of the Creator / creature distinction (Rom. 1:25; cf. Gen. 1:1). Here in Exodus 3:14 God defines Himself in such a way as to underscore the law of identity. Consider all of Jesus's "I am" statements, such as "I am the bread of life" (John 6:35, 41, 51; 8:58; 10:7, 11; 14:6; 15:1).

The law of non-contradiction lies beneath the command to "Let your yes, be yes, and your no, no so that you may not fall under judgment" (James 5:12). A "good tree" is different from a "bad tree" (Matt. 12:33). After all, "God is not the author of confusion" (1 Cor. 14:33) and "It is impossible that God should lie" (Heb. 6:18).

The law of excluded middle appears in the notion of antithesis, as when Jesus says: "He who is not with Me is against Me; and he who does not gather with Me scatters" (Matt. 12:30, cf. Mark 9:40). Obviously, one is either "for" Christ or "against" him. There is no middle ground—according to Christ Himself.

We should note that Jesus used logic (Matt. 21:24–27) and Paul "reasoned" with the Greeks (Acts 17:17; 18:4). In fact, as a matter of Christian witness we are called upon to "give an answer" to those who ask of us (1 Pet. 3:15).

3. Questions Raised

Attempt to answer the following questions on your own before looking at the text or consulting the **Answer Key**.

1. What do we mean when we speak of "universals"?

2. Is the concept of universals practical to our everyday lives? Explain.

3. What three notions are involved in universals that define them?

4. Are laws of logic in the category of universals? Explain.

5. Why should the laws of logic not be called "laws of thought"?

6. State and briefly define each of the three basic laws of logic.

7. What is the basic apologetic question we must ask of the unbeliever regarding universals and the laws of logic?

8. How is the scientific method problematic to the laws of logic in the unbeliever's worldview?

9. How is the unbeliever's ultimate commitment to chance problematic for the laws of logic?

10. How does the unbeliever's worldview involve internal tension and contradiction when it tries to affirm the laws of logic?

11. What is the problem with claiming the laws of logic are human conventions adopted by men?

12. What is the relationship between the laws of logic and God?

13. Cite some verses that affirm each of the three laws of logic.

4. Practical Applications

1. To the untrained mind, the laws of logic can seem to be saying the same thing from three different angles. Look up some explanations of the laws of logic on the Internet. Write a three page summation explaining and distinguishing each of the laws of logic, giving one page to each law.

2. Think of other Bible verses that affirm each of the three laws of logic.

3. Write a two or three lesson study on the importance of the laws of logic and their compatibility with Scripture. Teach these lessons to a small group interested in apologetics.

4. Once you have familiarized yourself with the laws of logic through the previous studies, discuss them with a non-Christian friend. After discussing these laws, ask the unbeliever how he can account for them. Be ready to point out their incompatibility with affirmation of a chance universe.

5. Read the materials at Christianlogic.com on how to study logic (www.christianlogic.com/articles/suggested_course_of_study_for_logic.htm). Take the recommended course of study outlined there.

6. Study Morris S. Engel's *With Good Reason* to improve your logic abilities.

5. Recommended Reading

Bahnsen, Greg L., "Apologetics in Practice": www.salemreformed.org/ApologeticsinPractice.html

Bahnsen, Greg L., "Tools of Apologetics": www.cmfnow.com/articles/PA101.htm

Hawkins, Craig S., "The Bible, Logic, and the Post-modern Predicament": www.apologeticsinfo.org/papers/logicpostmodern.html

Johnston, Patrick, "The Transcendental Refutation of Atheism" http://wherethetruthhurts.org/tractsbooksread.php?w=15&p=1#top

"Irrationality and the Eastern Mindset": www.christian-faith.com/religion/irrationality.html

12

Personal Freedom and Dignity

What is man, that Thou dost take thought of him?
And the son of man, that Thou dost care for him?
Yet Thou hast made him a little lower than God,
And dost crown him with glory and majesty!
(Ps. 8:4–5)

W<small>E NOW ARRIVE</small> at our last chapter in our study of the basics for defending the Christian faith. We have come a long way, having learned about the fundamental idea of and biblical warrant for the proper apologetic method; the impossibility of neutrality in thought; the meaning, importance, basic elements, and universality of worldviews; several alternative worldviews held among men; metaphysics, epistemology, ethics; and some of the basic problems crippling the unbelieving worldview.

This chapter will conclude our focusing on the problems inherent in non-Christian worldviews. In the three previous chapters we analyzed the problems of moral absolutes, the uniformity of nature, and the laws of logic. These are obviously issues of enormous significance, whose problematic character is catastrophic for the unbeliever's outlook on the world and life. We are now ready to consider these problems in accounting for personal freedom and dignity.

As we survey this problem area you should be encouraged to see once again that *only* the Christian truth claims can *account for* these huge worldview necessities. Remember: the fundamental argument

for the existence of God and confirmation of the Christian system is
"the *impossibility* of the contrary"—*not* "the *superiority* of Christianity over competing systems in handling discrete facts." The unbeliever
can't account for the fundamental issues of life *from within his own
system of belief*—indeed, he can't account for *anything*. Were he to be
epistemologically self-conscious he would be totally incapacitated.[1]
As Van Til puts it:

> It is the firm conviction of every epistemologically self-
> conscious Christian that no human being can utter a single
> syllable, whether in negation or affirmation, unless it were
> for God's existence. Thus the transcendental argument seeks
> to discover what sort of foundations the house of human
> knowledge must have, in order to be what it is.[2]
>
> * * * * *
>
> It is our contention that only the Christian can obtain real
> coherence in his thinking. If all of our thoughts about the
> facts of the universe are in correspondence with God's ideas
> of these facts, there will naturally be coherence in our think-
> ing because there is a complete coherence in God's thinking.[3]

So then, the presuppositional apologist is not content to declare
himself *neutral* and to argue for the *possibility* that *a god* might exist (as so many popular apologetic systems do). Rather he boldly
declares that the God of Scripture *does exist* and is the *necessary
precondition* for all reality and knowing. Therefore, Christianity is

---

[1] One who is **epistemologically self-conscious** engages life in a way that fully
comports with his theory of knowledge. That is, his behavior and reasoning are perfectly consistent with his basic commitments regarding the world and knowledge.
Bahnsen calls on Christians themselves to be "epistemologically self-conscious
about the character of their epistemological position, letting its standards regiment
and regulate every detail of their system of beliefs and its application." (Greg L.
Bahnsen, *Van Til's Apologetic: Readings and Analysis* [Phillipsburg, NJ: Presbyterian
and Reformed, 1998], 4).

[2] Cornelius Van Til, *A Survey of Christian Epistemology* (Phillipsburg, NJ: Presbyterian and Reformed, 1932) 11.

[3] Van Til, *A Survey of Christian Epistemology*, 2.

the *only* rational view available to man. This is rightly called "nuclear-strength apologetics." It is a take-no-prisoners approach to the war of the worldviews.

1. Central Concerns

In this chapter we will highlight matters of personal freedom and human dignity. We have already touched on the problem of personal freedom in the fourth chapter. You are encouraged to review that material in this connection. Here we will just briefly summarize the argument regarding human freedom, then we will turn our attention to the problem of human dignity.

The naturalistic worldview cannot account for freedom. If naturalism is true, then naturalists have no reason to believe in naturalism. The naturalist says that all thinking is but the electro-chemical response of the gray matter in the material brain, and that these responses are determined by our environment. Human thinking is on the same order as weeds growing. If naturalism is true, then the advocate of the naturalistic approach is only saying he affirms naturalism because nature has determined that he would. Naturalism contradicts freedom (and dignity). He has no reason for declaring naturalism to be true; he is just forced to say so.

The Worldview Importance of Dignity

Human "dignity" deals with notions of the ethical value, personal respect, and inherent worth of human life. The question of human dignity is of enormous practical significance in both our mundane lives and our theoretical worldviews. It not only impacts our daily attitudes and our interaction with others but serves as the very foundation for human rights and a stable society.

At the practical and social levels, basic assumptions about human nature lead most unbelievers to distinguish man from the animals. In doing this they are tacitly affirming the dignity of human life. They even attempt to do this from within their evolutionary viewpoint which places man on a continuum with the animals, just higher up the ladder. Or as Aristotle would express it: higher up the "scale of being."

One insightful way to illustrate our inherent sense of dignity is in our funeral ceremonies. Throughout history and around the world burial services have been used to show love, respect, and appreciation for the deceased, as well as sympathy, concern, and affection for the family left behind. The services themselves are almost invariably attended with some sort of ritual reflecting the belief system in the prevailing culture. As history shows, "funeral rites are as old as the human race itself. In the Shanidar cave in Iraq, Neanderthal skeletons have been discovered with a characteristic layer of pollen, which suggests that Neanderthals buried the dead with gifts of flowers."[4] So even with evolutionary assumptions, anthropologists acknowledge the idea of human dignity.

Another significant way in which we see the human race's assertion of dignity is through the establishment of law courts. Our legal system shows our inner realization of human dignity (believe it or not!). We underscore our sense of dignity and honor by creating social structures and framing legal codes designed to protect and encourage life, liberty, the pursuit of happiness, property rights, reputations, and so forth. In fact, "the science of law . . . is but one of the several sciences that are concerned with men living in a social state. Sociology, ethics, politics, political economy, as well as history, biology and psychology, all have a common ground, for they are all more or less related to each other, and all are necessary to a proper

---

[4]The *Wikipedia* entry on funerals surveys funeral customs in Ancient Rome, Japan, Africa, Scotland, and the United States. The study of funeral ossuaries (burial chests) are of great interest to archaeologists who have found innumerable ossuaries documenting funeral rites in ancient Persia, Babylon, Israel, and other cultures.

understanding of each science."[5] Our sense of dignity has enormous, wide-ranging implications for human culture.

Now how does this impact the apologetic argument? How shall we use this piece of information in order to perform an internal critique of the unbeliever's worldview?

The Unbeliever's Problem with Dignity

Let's begin our presuppositional critique of the unbelieving world-view with an interesting observation. Remember that only humans have a sense of dignity and that when we investigate the animal world, we do not see anything like a funeral for the deceased. Lions, for instance, have been known to sniff their dead relatives then consume them. Respect for the dead as evidenced in funerals and memorials is a distinctly human experience lacking any correspondence to animal activities.

As a presuppositional apologist, you must now ask the penetrating question: If man is an advanced animal, and if our practices may be traced back to our animal ancestry, why can't we discover any primitive behavior in the animal response to death that evolved into our more advanced ceremonies? Why have humans universally expressed the dignity of human life in this way? Funerals are not examples of man being a "superior" animal with an advanced intelligence, as with our developing calculus, building aircraft, producing written literature, composing music, and other such intellectual activities. Neither may we claim that funerals have any survival benefit for the species of *homo sapiens*, as per evolutionary views of animal instincts. Rather, funerals point to our sense of dignity and recognition of personal values, which are wholly lacking in animals.

As is invariably the case, the non-believer can't *account for* human dignity. If there is no God in whose image we are created, why

___

[5]John Maxcy Zane, *The Story of Law* 4, 2nd ed. (Indianapolis, IN: Liberty Fund 1998), 2.

do we have a sense of human dignity? Why have we developed social practices emphasizing our inherent worth? Why have we established rituals confirming it or legal codes defending it? What *accounts* for human dignity?

The unbelieving world today *generally* affirms the dignity of all human life. We say "generally" because in recent times and up into our own day, large groups have denied the universal dignity of man. The Nazis in World War II obviously did not affirm the inherent dignity of the Jews, denigrating them as "useless eaters." Japan's racist history is also well known.

The justification for chattel slavery as practiced in many Muslim lands today demonstrates their denial of universal human dignity. According to leading government cleric Sheikh Saleh Al-Fawzan: "Slavery is a part of Islam . . . . Slavery is part of jihad, and jihad will remain as long as there is Islam." This article went on to note: "Al-Fawzan is member of the Senior Council of Clerics, Saudi Arabia's highest religious body, a member of the Council of Religious Edicts and Research, the Imam of Prince Mitaeb Mosque in Riyadh, and a professor at Imam Mohamed Bin Saud Islamic University, the main Wahhabi center of learning in the country." Serge Trifkovic continues:

> Contrary to the myth that Islam is a religion free from racial prejudice, slavery in the Moslem world has been, and remains, brutally racist in character. To find truly endemic, open, raw anti-Black racism and slavery today one needs to go to the two Islamic Republics in Africa: Mauritania and Sudan. Black people have been enslaved on such a scale that the term black has become synonymous with slave. The mixed-race, predominantly Negroid but self-avowedly "Arabic" denizens of the transitional sub-Saharan zone have been indoctrinated into treating their pure-black southern neighbors with racist disdain. (To this day it can be danger-

ous to one's life to ask a dark-looking but Arabic-speaking Sudanese or Mauritanian Moslem if he is "black.").[6]

But almost certainly any person with whom you may come into contact in our culture today will have some general notion of human dignity, even if he breaches it by subtle racism or some other sinful attitude. We need to press home the problem of human dignity to the unbeliever. Is it simply a human convention? If so, it may be changed by society. Then on what stable basis may we establish our law system which is designed to protect our lives and our rights?

Uncontrolled Principle

The notion of dignity can't be reasonably controlled by principles of the unbeliever. Many popular views have even declared that *all* living things have dignity. For instance, the great humanitarian, theologian, and philosopher Albert Schweitzer (1875–1965) wrote *Reverence for Life* wherein he declared this very principle even in his title. In his *Philosophy of Civilisation* he succinctly stated his view: "True philosophy must start from the most immediate and comprehensive fact of consciousness: 'I am life that wants to live, in the midst of life that wants to live.'" His respect for "all" life led to absurd conclusions. Jack Coulehan, who annotated Schweitzer's biography, noted that "Schweitzer resisted modernization and didn't keep his hospital as cleanly as his critics would have liked, but this resistance was based largely on his philosophy of 'reverence for life,' which had apparently led him, insofar as was possible, to respect even the lives of insects and bacteria."[7]

Mahtma Gandhi (1869–1947) was committed to Ahimsa, which still remains as a principle of the Jainist religion:

---

[6]Serge Trifkovic, "Islam's Wretched Record on Slavery," *FrontPageMagazine. Com* (November 9, 2003) (http://www.jihadwatch.org/archives/000081.php).

[7]"Literature, Arts, and Medicine Database": http://endeavor.med.nyu.edu/lit-med/lit-med-db/webdocs/webdescrips/schweitzer11876-des-.html.

> Literally translated Ahimsa means to be without harm; to
> be utterly harmless, not only to oneself and others, but to
> all forms of life, from the largest mammals to the smallest
> bacteria. . . . In following this discipline Jain monks may be
> observed treading and sweeping in their temples with the
> utmost of care so as to avoid accidentally crushing crawling
> insects, or wearing muslin cloths over their mouths in case
> they should accidentally swallow a fly. [8]

Extreme environmentalists often fall into this camp when they
state such things as: "Respect for all life is also very important. This
means you respect Planet Earth. You care for the environment, and
you are *kind to all living things*."[9] But if that were true then even
being a vegetarian wouldn't make sense, for what of the dignity of
carrots?[10]

Animal rights advocates are complaining against our limiting
the notion of dignity only to humans. They are calling for laws that
affirm dignity for *all* animal life:

> The most commonly stated basis for international human
> rights is human dignity. The Universal Declaration of Hu-
> man Rights set the stage with Article I, to which all subse-
> quent human rights treaties refer. Article I states, "[a]ll hu-
> man beings are born free and equal in dignity and rights.
> They are endowed with reason and conscience and should
> act towards one another in a spirit of brotherhood. . . ."
>
> Human dignity traditionally has been defined by legal
> theorists and philosophers in a manner that derives from
> arrant human chauvinism. This is unfortunate for two rea-
> sons. First, relying on a speciesist definition of human dig-

---

[8]"Jain Living," on the B.B.C. website: www.bB.C..co.uk/religion/religions/jain-
ism/living/living2.shtml

[9]World Youth Network International, "IQ-EQ-SQ": www.worldyouthnetwork.
com/PDF/5th.pdf Emphasis added.

[10]A comedian once said: "I am not a vegetarian because I love animals but because I hate plants." Another pondered: "If God did not mean for us to eat animals,
why did he make them out of meat?"

nity undermines the cogency of human rights because it is scientifically and philosophically untenable. Second, basing human rights on irrational or metaphysical concepts makes it more difficult to debunk speciesism because of the subsequent recognition that legal rights are manufactured. With the goal of scientific and multi-cultural legitimacy, international human rights law might otherwise refer to non-metaphysical and permanent bases. This requires eradicating the species-based element.[11]

This article in a prominent law journal complains that "throughout most of documented history, humans have denied other animals legal rights and recognition as legal persons with two justifications: the 'theological basis' and a 'secular expression of species pride.'"[12] Notice the slam against our Christian worldview and its basis for human dignity. He laments that metaphysical considerations have not allowed for a proper valuation of animal worth, and calls for laws that meet evolutionary expectations in this regard: "Until recently, the metaphysical presupposition that humans are not animals has inhibited the interplay between human psychology, anthropology, and sociology with primatology and biological evolution— and vice versa."[13]

Materialist Impediments

In the materialist worldview we are just bundles of genetic information. What dignity inheres in a collection of DNA strands? Once again we are seeing the enormous (and dangerous!) complications arising from the disavowal of metaphysics and the dominance of

---

[11]Kyle Ash, "International Animal Rights: Speciesism and Exclusionary Human Dignity," *Journal of Animal Law*, Michigan State University College of Law (11) 196: www.animallaw.info/journals/jo_pdf/vol11_p195.pdf

[12]Ash, "International Animal Rights: Speciesism and Exclusionary Human Dignity," 197.

[13]Kyle Ash, "International Animal Rights: Speciesism and Exclusionary Human Dignity," 206.

pure empiricism in science, as we will now note. In reviewing a book by a bio-geneticist, Dinesh D'Souza observes that:

> In this view, the subjective preferences of those who seek to mystify human life do not square with the truths about human biology taught by science. The cells of human beings, Silver points out, are not different in their chemical makeup from the cells of horses and bacteria. If there is such a thing as human dignity, Silver argues, it derives exclusively from consciousness, from our ability to perceive and apprehend our environment. "The human mind," Silver writes, "is much more than the genes that brought it into existence." Somehow the electrochemical reactions in our brain produce consciousness, and it is this consciousness, Silver contends, that is the source of man's autonomy and power. . . . Genes fully control the activity of all life forms.[14]

This problem can be demonstrated over and again throughout technical literature. Cornell University Professor of Biology and leading historian of biology, William Provine writes: "The implications of modern science, however, are clearly inconsistent with most religious tradition. . . . No inherent moral or ethical laws exist, nor are there absolute guiding principles for human society. The universe cares nothing for us and we have no ultimate meaning in life."[15] His atheist worldview comes clearly to expression in this statement. This certainly precludes any justification of human dignity.

J. D. Bernal (1901–1971), past Professor of Physics at University of London and pioneer in x-ray crystallography, gave the following evolutionary definition of life: "Life is a partial, continuous, progressive, multiform and continually interactive, self-realization of the

---

[14]Dinesh D'Souza, "Staying Human: The Danger of Techno-utopia," *National Review* (January 22, 2001).

[15]William Provine, "Scientists, Face It! Science and Religion Are Incompatible," *The Scientist*, 5 (September 1988), 10.

potentialities of atomic electron states."[16] Are electron states dignified?

In his famous letter to William Graham on July 3, 1881, Charles Darwin (1809–1882) wrote: "But then with me the horrid doubt always arises whether the convictions of man's mind, which has always been developed from the mind of the lower animals, are of any value or at all trustworthy. Would any one trust in the convictions of a monkey's mind, if there are any convictions in such a mind?"[17] Renowned research psychologist B. F. Skinner put the matter pointedly: "To man [as] qua man [man as a human being] we readily say good riddance."[18] So much for human dignity.

Well-known biologist William Etkin writes that: "We are but fish made over . . . somewhat like the original design of a house that has been remodeled."[19] The more consistent unbeliever presses for a more fully self-conscious naturalism when *urging the removal of ethical constraints* upon scientific research. In the materialist worldview, life is not sacred and ethics is contra-scientific. Dinesh D'Souza explains:

> Nor are the techno-utopians worried about diminishing the sanctity of human life because, they say, it isn't intrinsically sacred. "This is not an ethical argument but a religious one," says Silver. "There is no logic to it." Biologist David Baltimore, a Nobel laureate, argues that 'statements about morally and ethically unacceptable practices' have no place in the biotechnology debate "because those are subjective grounds and therefore provide no basis for discussion." Silver and Baltimore's shared assumption is that the moralists

---

[16]J. D. Bernal, *The Origin of Life* (New York: Universe Books, 1967), xv.

[17]Rousas J. Rushdoony, *The Mythology of Science* (Nutley, N. J.: Craig, 1967).

[18]Schaeffer, *How Should We Then Live?* in *The Complete Works of Francis Schaeffer: A Christian Worldview*, 5 vols. (Westchester, IL: Crossway Books, 1985), 5:230.

[19]Bolton Davidheiser, *Evolution and Christian Faith* (Nutley, NJ: Presbyterian and Reformed, 1969), 157.

are talking about values while they, the hard scientists, are dealing in facts.[20]

Chance Confusion

In the final analysis, we must ask our standard apologetic question: What meaning does dignity have in a chance Universe? In a review of a book on the possibility of extra-terrestrial life (which was written by a Professor of Natural History, Paul Davies) we find a telling comment. Reviewer Gregory Koukl writes: Davies "has some interesting thoughts about the impact of the idea of evolution on the notion of human value and dignity. If you believe that we are the result of the natural processes of cause and effect, you end up with a serious problem with value, purpose, worth and dignity. *It is hard to argue that someone who is an accident of the universe has some kind of special destiny.*"[21]

Renowned Harvard University Professor of Paleontology, Stephen Jay Gould declared: "Human existence occupied but the last geological millimicrosecond of this history—the last inch of the cosmic mile, or the last second of the geological year. . . . If humanity arose just yesterday as a small twig on one branch of a flourishing tree, then life may not, in any genuine sense, exist for us or because of us. Perhaps we are only an afterthought, a kind of *cosmic accident*, just one bauble on the Christmas tree of evolution."[22]

Evolutionist J. W. Burrow, Professor of European Thought, Oxford University, wrote the introduction for a new edition of *The Origin of Species*: "Nature, according to Darwin, was the product of *blind chance* and a blind struggle, and man a lonely, intelligent mutation, scrambling with the brutes for his sustenance. To some the

---

[20]Dinesh D'Souza, "Staying Human: The Danger of Techno-utopia" *National Review* (January 22, 2001).

[21]"Chance and Dignity" (www.str.org/site/News2?page=NewsArticle&id=5202). Emphasis added.

[22]Stephen Jay Gould, *Wonderful Life* (New York: W. W. Norton, 1989), 44. Emphasis added.

sense of loss was irrevocable; it was as if an umbilical cord had been cut, and men found themselves part of 'a cold passionless universe.' Unlike nature as conceived by the Greeks, the Enlightenment, and the rationalist Christian tradition Darwinian nature held no clues for human conduct, no answers to human moral dilemmas."[23] Bertrand Russell saw man as a cosmic accident, devoid of meaning:

> Such, in outline, but even more purposeless, more void of meaning, is the world which Science presents for our belief. Amid such a world, if anywhere, our ideals henceforward must find a home. That Man is the product of causes which had no prevision of the end they were achieving; that his origin, his growth, his hopes and fears, his loves and his beliefs, are but the outcome of *accidental collocations* of atoms; that no fire, no heroism, no intensity of thought and feeling, can preserve an individual life beyond the grave; that all the labours of the ages, all the devotion, all the inspiration, all the noonday brightness of human genius, are destined to extinction in the vast death of the solar system, and that the whole temple of Man's achievement must inevitably be buried beneath the debris of a universe in ruins—all these things, if not quite beyond dispute, are yet so nearly certain, that no philosophy which rejects them can hope to stand. Only within the scaffolding of these truths, only on the firm foundation of unyielding despair, can the soul's habitation henceforth be safely built.[24]

Nobel Prize winning, Harvard University Professor of Biology George Wald (1906–1997) was once asked who in his view was Shakespeare? He answered: "A *chance* collection of molecules that

---

[23]J. W. Burrow, introduction in J. W. Burrow, ed., Charles Darwin, *The Origin of Species by Means of Natural Selection* (Baltimore, MD: Penguin, 1974), 43. Emphasis added.

[24]Bertrand Russell, *A Free Man's Worship: Mysticism and Logic* (New York: George Allen and Unwin, 1917), 46

existed 400 yrs ago."[25] Highly respected anthropologist Loren Eiseley (1907–1977), who headed the Anthropology Department of the University of Pennsylvania, once commented: "Man did not have to be any more than a butterfly or a caterpillar. He merely emerged from that infinite void for which we have no name."[26]

We must recall that chance can't account for morality or universals. Consequently, it can't affirm human dignity. What is the meaning of dignity in a chance Universe? Chance destroys the very possibility of meaning and significance, taking down with it the notion of dignity. Gregory Koukl highlights the problems of materialism and chance in accounting for human dignity:

> Why does science rob human beings of their dignity? Science has limited its area of study to the area of natural occurrences. Not only has it limited its search to that area, but it has essentially said that that is the only area that really exits. This is called philosophic naturalism. If only nature exists, then it turns out that we are merely parts of the machinery in the workings of nature, and we are the unwitting victims of the machinery of cause and effect happening over time without any plan. That robs human beings of their dignity. Clearly, if we are the product of chance, then we have no purpose. It seems hard to argue that we are anything different than anything else on this earth that has resulted from the process of evolution.
>
> The claim that we have some kind of peculiar dignity turns out to be a kind of species-ism. We arbitrarily view our species as qualitatively more valuable than other species, but the fact of the matter is that in nature that just isn't the case. Davies acknowledges that if we are stuck with philosophic naturalism, we are robbed of unique value and dignity, and we become one of many living organisms that are qualitatively indistinguishable.

---

[25]Schaeffer, *How Should We Then Live?*, 5:230. Emphasis added.
[26]Cited in Davidheiser, *Evolution and Christian Faith*, 149.

One might argue that we are more sophisticated in our evolutionary accomplishment, but what separates us from the rest? Nothing. That's a value judgment, and there are no value judgments like that that make any sense in nature because nature is value-less. Values are a philosophic construct. They are a theological and moral notion and have no place, strictly speaking, in a world that is simply defined by scientific law.[27]

Dignity does not rest on anything in the evolutionary Universe. It defies the law of gravity, so to speak, and just hangs there—if it is affirmed at all. As it has been put, an atheist is someone with no *in*visible means of support. At best, dignity is simply a human convention. And when affirmed, it becomes a contradiction in the unbeliever's worldview. Our Presuppositionalist challenge must point out this dialectical tension. Nancy Pearcey observes the destruction of freedom and dignity in the evolutionary worldview, mentioning its contradictory implications:

> Similar self–contradictions are endemic in the literature on evolutionary psychology. A prime example is *The Moral Animal*, where author Robert Wright spends hundreds of pages describing human beings as "robots," "puppets," "machines," and "Swiss watches" programmed by natural selection. He insists that "biochemistry governs all" and that free will is sheer illusion. He unmasks our noblest moral impulses as survival "stratagems of the genes," as mere devices "switched on and off in keeping with self–interest." But then, in a grand leap of faith, Wright insists that we are now free to choose our moral ideals, and he urges us to practice "brotherly love" and "boundless empathy."
>
> This persistent inner contradiction stems from the fact that evolutionary psychology is essentially a search for a secular morality. Darwinism cut the modern world loose from

---

[27]Gregory Koukl, "Chance and Dignity": www.str.org/site/News2?page=NewsArticle&id=520

religious traditions and systems of meaning; the result is a culture adrift in a sea of relativism. Now Darwinism is itself being plumbed as a source of meaning, a cosmic guide for the problems of living. Yet the Darwinist view of human nature is so negative, so counter to traditional notions of human dignity, morality, and reason (not to mention common sense), that there is an almost irresistible impulse to take a leap of faith back to those traditional notions, no matter how unsupported by the theory. For who can live with a theory that tells us that "ethics is illusory," and that 'morality is merely an adaptation put in place to further our reproductive ends,' in the words of Michael Ruse and E. O. Wilson? Who can live with a theory that tells us that if 'natural selection is both sufficient and true, it is impossible for a genuinely disinterested or "altruistic behavior pattern to evolve,' in the words of M. T. Ghiselin?[28]

The Christian View

The Christian view of man's dignity is affirmed in our Declaration of Independence, which rightly declares that men are "endowed by their Creator with certain unalienable rights." Scripture repeatedly establishes the firm basis of human dignity, declaring that man exists as the image of the eternal God (Gen. 1:26–27; 9:6; 1 Cor. 11:7; Eph. 4:24; Col. 3:10; James 3:9). The psalmist declares that God made man "a little lower than God" (Ps. 8:5).

Our value is underscored by the fact that the Son of God took upon Himself true humanity in order to redeem us from our sins. "Since then the children share in flesh and blood, He Himself likewise also partook of the same, that through death He might render powerless him who had the power of death, that is, the devil; and might deliver those who through fear of death were subject to slavery all their lives" (Heb. 2:14–15; cf. Rom. 8:3; Phil. 2:7–8).

---

[28]Nancy Pearcey, "Singer in the Rain," *First Things* 106 (October 2000), 57–63: www.arn.org/docs/pearcey/np_ftreviews1000.htm

Our holy God even provided for us in Scripture a system of morality and of law that establishes special protections for man, affirming his dignity. The fundamental law in this regard is the Sixth Commandment: "You shall not murder" (Ex. 20:13; Deut. 5:17). This law is specifically established on the underlying reality of the image of God within: "Whoever sheds man's blood, by man his blood shall be shed, for in the image of God He made man" (Gen. 9:6). This core law is applied in numerous ways in the case laws of the Old Testament and the moral principles of the New Testament. Jesus even applies it to hatred of another human (Matt. 5:21–22).

Scripture speaks of the high value of reputation and a name, even preferring them over gold. "A good name is to be more desired than great riches, favor is better than silver and gold" (Prov. 22:1). "A good name is better than a good ointment" (Eccl. 7:1). It also laments shame, which strikes at one's dignity and honor (Ps. 31:17; 69:19; Prov. 13:18; 1 Cor. 11:22).

Robert Reilley expresses the unbeliever's problem well in *Intercollegiate Review*: "The problem is that, by denying the possibility of a relationship between God and man, atheism also denies the possibility of a just relationship between men. . . . Human life is sacred only if there is a God to sanctify it. Otherwise man is just another collection of atoms and can be treated as such."[29] Philosopher Patrick D. Hopkins summarizes the non-believing view of man:

> This view essentially represents humans as moderately smart, moderately conscious, moderately creative, physically weak, emotional, social, and mortal animals participating in an ongoing evolutionary process absent any grand purpose or design. We are born, live, eat, excrete, think, feel, create, emote, organize, rank, compete, cooperate, and die. Although we are certainly more intelligent, and probably

---

[29]Robert R. Reilly, "Atheism and Arms Control," *Intercollegiate Review*, 24 (Fall 1988), 15.

more conscious and much more self-conscious than other animals, we are essentially the same as animals, differing only in degree and not kind, and not differing as much as we typically think. We are not metaphysically unique; we do not rank between angels and beasts; we are not embodied souls.[30]

In short, we can see clearly "the impossibility of the contrary." Only Christianity provides "the preconditions for intelligibility." The unbelieving worldview destroys even the dignity of human life, thereby undermining even the motive to argue against the Christian. In fact, he can't even account for his argument with the believer over the matter of human freedom, for in his view we are just subject to the laws of physics.

2. Exegetical Observations

In our twelve chapters we have had many opportunities to refer to Genesis 1 and the creation of man. The book of Genesis is extremely important to the Christian worldview in that it declares the origin of man and the Universe by the sovereign power of God. It also speaks to the very essence of what it is to be human and to possess dignity. Let us reflect briefly upon man's creation and its implications for his exalted personal dignity.

In Genesis 1 and 2 we find the Creator's account of man's origin. Rather than researching the genetic code for his ascension from mud, you should be reading the Genesis record for his creation by God. Genesis speaks eloquently of man's honor and dignity as the creation of the rational God contrary to his evolution by irrational chance. Let us survey some of the angles in Genesis pointing to man's dignity.

---

[30]Patrick D. Hopkins, "Transcending the Animal: How Transhumanism and Religion Are and Are Not Alike," *Journal of Evolution Technology* 14:1 (August, 2005), 13–14: www.jetpress.org/volume14/hopkins.html#_edn2

Man is the apex of creation. In the creation account we discover a well-ordered, flowing narrative outlining six days of God's creative activity. Old Testament commentator Derek Kidner states that "the march of the days is too majestic a progress to carry no implication of ordered sequence; it also seems over-subtle to adopt a view of the passage which discounts one of the primary impressions it makes on the ordinary reader."[31] In fact, Days 1 through 5 establish the environment for man in which he will live. The vegetation is for his food (Gen. 1:29); the animals are for him to rule over (Gen. 1:26).

Day 6, then, appears as the last stage of the rapidly unfolding creation process. Man forms the special climax to God's creative activity. The sixth day is therefore the grand finale of creation, setting man off as the goal and high point of God's labor of love.

Man is created after the inter-Trinitarian counsel. After God creates all else by His mere spoken word, He prepares to create man. And He does so with a distinctive inter-Trinitarian counsel: "Let us create man in our image" (Gen. 1:26). The plural expression "let us" alludes to persons of the Trinity and not to angels, in that: God alone is the Creator (Gen. 1:1; Neh. 9:6); man is created in only God's image (Gen. 9:6; James 3:9); God the Son (John 1:3; Col. 1:17) and God the Spirit (Gen. 1:2) are associated with God the Father in creation. This deliberative counsel underscores the significance of man's creation for the narrative.

Man is created as the image of God. The text clearly establishes man's distinctiveness in his being the very image of God: "Then God said, 'Let Us make man in Our image, according to Our likeness; and let them rule over the fish of the sea and over the birds of the sky and over the cattle and over all the earth, and over every creeping thing that creeps on the earth.' And God created man in His own

---

[31]Derek Kidner, *Genesis: An Introduction and Commentary* (Downers' Grove, IL: InterVarsity, 1967), 54–55.

image, in the image of God He created him; male and female He created them" (Gen. 1:26–27).

Scripture shows various ways in which man images God. God speaks ("then God said," 1:3, 6, 9, 11, 14, etc.); man speaks (Gen. 3:9–10). God makes things (Gen. 1:7, 16, 31; 2:3); Adam cultivates the garden (Gen. 2:8) and his sons make things (Gen. 4:20–24). God "names" the elements of creation ("God called," Gen. 1:5, 8, 10); man names the animals (Gen. 2:19) and his wife (Gen. 2:23). God exercises dominion (Gen. 1:1, 31); man is given dominion over the creatures (Gen. 1:26, 28). God rests from his labors (Gen. 2:2); man follows that pattern of rest (Ex. 20:9–11). Man images God.

Man is created in intimacy by God. In Genesis 1 *Elohim* (translated "God") appears throughout the creation account. *Elohim* acts as "the mighty one" who accomplishes the creation of the entire universe (Gen. 1:1; 2:1, 4) effortlessly by His mere word (eight quick fiats spread over six brief days). But in Genesis 2, rather than emphasizing the power of the Creator, Moses emphasizes his intimate relationship: God and man are in covenant. This is indicated by Moses' importing the covenant name ("Jehovah," translated as "Lord") into the context of the creation of man (Gen. 2:7). Furthermore, God lovingly forms man's body and breathes into him the breath of life (Gen. 2:7), whereas animals were massed produced (1:20, 24).

Man is created to commune with God. In Genesis 3 we find the casual remark that God was "walking in the garden in the cool of the day" and looking for Adam (Gen. 3:8–9). God conversed with man when He informed him of His abundant provision (Gen. 2:16), moral limits (Gen. 2:17), and when He sought him out in the garden (Gen. 3:9–11). As the psalmist effused: "What is man, that Thou dost take thought of him? And the son of man, that Thou dost care for him?" (Ps. 8:4). Throughout Scripture we see God not only communing with man, but preparing a means whereby man might approach Him in worship, prayer, and fellowship (e.g., Ps. 42:2; 96:8).

Man is created as a moral person. With creation accomplished in Genesis 1:1–2:3, we read Genesis 2:4. The first words of Genesis 2:4 introduce a new section that focuses on man and his moral probation in the garden: "This is the account of the heavens and the earth when they were created." Genesis 2:4b begins with the Hebrew expression, "in the day that" which is an idiom for "when." Thus 2:4b reads: "When Jehovah God made the earth and the heavens." The author is assuming the creation of the earth and heavens has been completed. Indeed, he has just finished narrating the account of the creation in chapter 1. So with the creation in the background he begins to set up the story of man—and his moral fall.

Rather than plunging right into the story, though, he begins by giving some background information about the events of Day 6. The first thing he tells about the creation up through Day 5 is that there were no wild desert shrubs growing on the earth nor was there any cultivated grain. A reason is given for the absence of both. There were no wild shrubs because God had not sent rain and no cultivated grain because there was no man to work the soil: "Now no shrub of the field was yet in the earth, and no plant of the field had yet sprouted, for the Lord God had not sent rain upon the earth; and there was no man to cultivate the ground" (Gen. 2:5).

In Genesis 2:5 Moses is not saying that there was no vegetation at all during this time, but that there was an absence of *specific kinds* of vegetation. He had previously told us that God created seed-bearing plants and fruit-bearing trees on the 4th day (Gen. 1:11–12). Here he informs us that there were no wild desert shrubs and cultivated grains. When Adam's creation is narrated just after this remark, we discover that he did not have to hack through wild weeds and brambles, nor did he have to break his back by hoeing. Rather, God created a productive, peaceable, pleasant environment for Adam (Gen. 2:8–14). Only later will brambles appear and hoeing become necessary—*after Adam rebels against his Creator* (Gen.

3:17–18). God had warned him of the death-dealing consequences of moral failure (Gen. 2:16–17).

Man is created to rule responsibly. In Genesis 1 we note that the animals are not appointed to "rule." Only *man* is to rule. In fact, he is to rule *over the sea, air, and land creatures* (Gen 1:26, 28). God *expressly* declares this. The psalmist praises God for putting man over the creatures (Ps. 8:6–8). Nowhere is man to share rule with the animals; man names the animals (exercises authority over them) as he begins ruling them (Gen. 2:20). In fact, an important feature in the historical fall of Adam is his allowing an animal (the serpent) to exercise rule over him (Gen. 3:1–7, 14–15).

Thus, man has both a basic constitutional urge to exercise dominion as a result of his being created in God's image *and* a fundamental responsibility to do so as a result of his being commanded in the Creation Mandate. Man's distinctive task in God's world in accordance with God's plan is to develop culture. Therefore, we learn that:

Man is created as an inventive being. Interestingly, early fallen man was driven to cultural exploits well beyond the expectations of humanistic anthropologists and sociologists. We see the effect and significance of the Creation Mandate very early in history in the culture-building exploits of Adam's offspring. In the Bible man is seen acting as a dominion-oriented creature, righteously subduing the earth and developing culture as a steward under God, despite the entry of sin. Man quickly developed various aspects of social culture: raising livestock, creating music, crafting tools from metal, and so forth (Gen. 4:20–22). Upon his very creation, not only was man commanded to develop all of God's creation, but he actually began to do so.

In all of this, we uncover clear and compelling evidence of man's *dignity*. He is the God-intended apex of creation. He is created after special inter-Trinitarian counsel. He is created as the very image of God and for the purpose of communion with Him. He is distinctly a moral person called to rule in the earth and develop culture to the glory of God. Christianity affirms man's dignity and provides its necessary preconditions for intelligibility.

3. Questions Raised

Attempt to answer the following questions on your own before looking at the text or consulting the **Answer Key**.

1. What does the phrase "epistemologically self-conscious" mean? Why is it significant as an apologetic tool?

2. Define the concept of "dignity" as it relates to "human dignity." How is it important for our daily lives? For our social lives?

3. What two illustrations of human dignity are presented? Explain the use of them in apologetics.

4. Though most Americans accept the notion of human dignity, not all people do. List some samples of widespread disavowal of human dignity.

5. State some historical examples of the problem of overstating the dignity of life (without Christian worldview constraints).

6. How does materialism destroy the notion of human dignity?

7. What is the ultimate problem the unbelieving worldview has in attempting to affirm human dignity?

8. Outline the Christian case for human dignity.

4. Practical Applications

1. Try to think of some contemporary issues that are affected by one's view of human dignity. Jot down a list and write a paragraph on how the Christian view resolves the issue. Samples would include euthanasia and abortion.

2. Read a few of the news items at The Center for Bioethics & Dignity. Copy three articles for your files that are directly related to the worldview debate over the dignity of man. (http://www.cbhd. org/news/index.html).

3. Research the Internet and find evolutionist statements that affirm human dignity. Read the articles and draw out from them the means by which the evolutionist attempts to establish human dignity. Jot down some of the problems you see in their reasoning. File these into your apologetics file.

4. Review our "Exegetical Observations" above. See if you can draw up other lines of evidence underscoring the Christian foundation for human dignity.

5. Research various websites calling for human rights as a concern for civil government. Develop two lists. In one list include all those sites that bring God into the equation. In the other list include those that make no mention of God or religion. File these into your apologetics file.

6. Using your research from point 5 above, read over the statements that do mention God and religion. Jot down the type of religion or "god" mentioned in the statements. Make a list of the problems in trying to establish human rights on a generic view of God or religion in general.

5. Recommended Reading

Clark, John D., "Some Philosophical Implications of the Theory of Evolution" *Origins* 3(1):38–45 (1976): www.grisda.org/origins/03038.htm

Flashing, Sarah J., "The Myth of Secular Neutrality: Unbiased Bioethics?": www.cbhd.org/resources/bioethics/flashing_2005-08-12.htm

Harrub, Brad, "The Inherent Value of Human Life": www.apologeticspress.org/articles/132

Koukl, Gregory, "Chance and Dignity": www.str.org/site/News2?page=NewsArticle&id=5202

Major, Trevor, "The Value of Early Human Life": www.apologeticspress.org/articles/259

"Social Apologetics": http://members.aol.com/VFTfiles/social_apologetics.htm

Schaeffer, Francis, *How Should We Then Live? The Rise and Decline of Western Thought and Culture* (Old Tappan, N.J.: Revell, 1967),

Trivcovic, Serge, "Islam's Wretched Record on Slavery," *FrontPageMagazine.Com* (http://frontpagemag.com/Articles/ReadArticle.asp?ID=4686)

Zacharias, Ravi, *The Real Face of Atheism* (Grand Rapids: Baker, 2004).

Answer Key

Chapter 1

"The Myth of Neutrality"

1. What is "apologetics"? Define the term and explain the derivation of the word "apologetics."

Answer: Apologetics is the vindication of the Christian philosophy of life against the various forms of the non-Christian philosophy of life. The word "apologetics" derives from the combination of two Greek words: *apo* ("back, from") and *logos* ("word"), meaning "to give a word back, to respond" in defense.

2. What is the central point of the first chapter?

Answer: To demonstrate that human thought and conduct are not neutral and that claims to neutrality are either mis-informed or fraudulent. Consequently, it discourages Christian attempts to develop apologetic systems on the basis of a supposed neutrality in that it contradicts the Christian worldview.

3. How is the very principle of evolutionism (even apart from the scientific/biological statement of evolutionary theory) opposed to the Christian faith?

Answer: Evolution is committed to the notion of relentless change and therefore is opposed in principle to the concept of absolutes. For the Christian, absolutes are essential, and God's Word is the ultimate absolute.

4. What is "deconstructionism"? Where did this philosophy first arise? How does it conflict with basic principles of the Christian faith?

Answer: Deconstructionism began as a form of literary criticism started in the early 1970s by Jacques Derrida. It states that no communication can have any set meaning or reliable message because of various influences on the person attempting the communication. This eventually moved beyond pure literary criticism to become a philosophy of absolute relativism. This directly conflicts with the biblical revelation in Scripture which claims two important truths in this regard: (1) God communicates with us by revealing the Scriptures to us so that we can understand, believe, and obey Him. (2) We are His images who reflect Him when we communicate with our fellow man in an intelligent, coherent way.

5. List some passages of Scripture that assert the certainty and authority of God's Word.

Answer: "The words of the Lord are pure words; as silver tried in a furnace on the earth, refined seven times" (Ps. 12:6); "The Scriptures cannot be broken" (John 10:35b); "All Scripture is inspired by God and *profitable* for *teaching*, for *reproof*, for *correction*, for *training* in righteousness; that the man of God *may be adequate, equipped* for every good work" (2 Tim. 3:16–17).

6. How does the unbelieving college professor's worldview subtly confront your faith, even when the professor is not directly mentioning Christianity per se?

Answer: (1) By selective consideration whereby he decides what questions are important, which options are serious, what evidence should be set forth in the class. (2) By claiming neutral tolerance of all views but being intolerant of "narrow" Christian views on homosexual conduct, abortion, feminism, and so forth. (3) By censorship, wherein he omits reading material arguing the Christian view while promoting books that counter it.

7. What is the meaning of "the myth of neutrality"?

Answer: No one can approach the issues of life from a purely neutral perspective. This is because the Bible teaches that man is a sinner who is opposed to God, not simply indifferent to him. Romans 1:18–21 speaks of the sinner's active suppression of the truth resulting from his darkened heart. Colossians 1:21 speaks of the sinner's hostility toward God. Paul pictures our outreach by images of warfare in 2 Corinthians 10:4–5.

8. What statements by Christ discount the possibility of neutrality?

Answer: Christ teaches that "everyone who hears *these words of Mine,* and *acts upon them,* may be compared to a wise man, who built his house upon the rock." He goes on to warn that "everyone who hears these words of Mine, and does not act upon them, will be like a foolish man, who built his house upon the sand" (Matt. 7:24, 26). "He who is not with Me is against Me; and he who does not gather with Me scatters" (Matt. 12:30).

9. Where in Scripture do you first see neutrality regarding God and his Word attempted?

Answer: In Genesis 3 where Satan presents Eve with the option to obey God or to dismiss His command. She was to assume a position of neutrality toward God's word.

10. Is the attempt at neutrality simply a methodological issue, or is it a moral one as well? Explain.

Answer: It is both. It is a moral issue because God demands in Scripture that man is to "fear him and keep his commandments" (Eccl.

12:13). The neutrality postulate is an attempt "to be as God" (Gen. 3:5). The Bible teaches that "whatever is not from faith is sin" (Rom. 14:23) for "without faith it is impossible to please him" (Heb. 11:6).

Answers to Chapter 2

"Destroying Philosophical Fortresses"

1. Why is the unbelieving mind actually "hostile" to the Christian worldview? What evidence is there to support this claim?
Answer: Since this is God's world, we are His creatures, are under His control, and will be judged by Him, there can be no neutrality in word, thought, or deed. All things belong to God and man owes his all to Him. To claim neutrality in thinking is to deny God's universal authority. In that Christianity is true, the world is as God created it—consequently, claims to neutrality are false despite being a widespread, modern secular myth.

2. On the subject of neutrality, what are two important truths about the unbeliever's claim of neutrality in reasoning?
Answer: The first is "the unbeliever is not neutral." The second is "the Christian *should not* attempt to be neutral."

3. What statements by Christ discount the possibility of neutrality?
Answer: "No one can serve two masters; for either he will hate the one and love the other, or he will hold to one and despise the other" (Matt. 6:24); "He who is not with Me is against Me" (Matt. 12:30).

4. Why do we say that men cannot be neutral toward God? Provide at least three biblical lines of argument supporting your answer.

Answer: (1) God created all things (Gen. 1:1; John 1:3), thereby giving meaning to the created order. He created all things for Himself
(Rom. 11:36; Col. 1:16d), thereby leaving nothing outside of His concern for His own glory. He owns all things (Ps. 24:1; 1 Cor. 10:26,
28), thereby having an inalienable right to man and all his property.
God governs all things (Isa. 46:10; Col. 1:17), thereby giving purpose
to all things under His wise plan. For man to claim neutrality in
thought is to deny God's creatorship, goal, ownership, and plan. (2)
We are positively commanded to fear God in order to gain knowledge in that "the fear of the Lord is the beginning of knowledge"
and "wisdom" (Prov. 1:7; 9:10). (3) God's universal lordship requires
submission to Him. God is the universal lord over all the universe,
from its smallest atomic particle to its farthest flung galaxy. Both
God and Jesus are spoken of as "the Lord of lords" (1 Tim. 6:15; Rev.
19:16). The authority of the Triune God is absolute and demanding,
so that to deny His authority in deference to "neutrality" is to deny
His lordship.

5. What do we mean by the "noetic effect" of sin?
Answer: The Greek word *nous* means "mind." The noetic effect of
sin is the effect of sin on man's mind and thinking processes. Man
is not fallen in only one dimension of life, but is sinful in *all* areas of
his life and being, including the mind.

6. Does Scripture teach that even the mind of man and his rea-
soning processes are affected by sin? Prove your answer by citing
Scripture.
Answer: Yes, man's mind is affected by sin, just as all other areas
of his human condition. Scripture speaks directly to the issue of
man's sinfulness in thought and mind. In Romans 1:18–21 Paul highlights man's resistance to God in "suppressing the truth" so that he
becomes "futile" in his "speculations." In Ephesians 4:17–18 Paul

strongly declares fallen man's "futility" of mind and the "ignorance" in them.

7. In that unbelievers have contributed much to human thought, science, and culture, what does it mean that faith in God is a prerequisite to truly understanding?

Answer: The only rational foundation for human thought and experience is the Creator God speaking in His Word. The unbeliever knows this true God deep in his heart, even though he denies God. The unbeliever's accomplishments are due to his suppressed knowledge of God, rather than his public denial of God which can't account for rationality, order, and so forth.

8. Read 2 Corinthians 10:4–5. With Christian friends, discuss its meaning and significance for apologetics.

Answer: This passages teaches that you are to hear the call to obedience *in your very thoughts*: "We are destroying speculations and every lofty thing raised up against the knowledge of God, and we are taking every thought captive to the obedience of Christ" (2 Cor 10:5). You are to challenge "every lofty thing" which is raised up "against the knowledge of God" so that you take "every thought captive" to "the obedience of Christ." This plainly and forcefully calls you to obey Christ in the entirety of our thought processes—including your method for defending the faith of Christ.

Answers to Chapter 3

"Defining Worldviews"

1. Define "worldview."

Answer: A worldview is a network of presuppositions (which are not verified by the procedures of natural science) regarding reality (metaphysics), knowing (epistemology), and conduct (ethics) in terms of which every element of human experience is related and interpreted.

2. Why is it important that we understand the idea of a world-view?

Answer: A worldview governs the way we view reality, knowledge, and morality, the most basic issues of life. We need to be able to articulate our own worldview, so that we may more consistently live and promote the Christian life and more ably challenge the unbeliever's worldview to show his error and the glory of the Christian system.

3. Does everyone have a worldview? Or is this just a Christian concept? Explain your answer.

Answer: By necessity all sane men have a worldview, because they all must live in the world. Worldviews govern the way we view reality, think and reason, and live morally. These are key issues for any life system.

4. Why is understanding our worldview as a "network of beliefs" important to a biblical approach to apologetics?

Answer: As biblical apologists we want to challenge the unbeliever's whole system of life, to show him that he has no foundations for the way he lives. We want to show him the necessity of having Christian foundations in order to make life intelligible. Piece-meal criticisms do not get to the root of the matter and are easily side-stepped.

5. What is a "presupposition"?

Answer: A presupposition is an elementary assumption in one's reasoning or in the process by which opinions are formed. . . . [It] is not just any assumption in an argument, but a personal commitment that is held at the most basic level of one's network of beliefs. Presuppositions form a wide-ranging, foundational perspective (or starting point) in terms of which everything else is interpreted and evaluated. As such, presuppositions have the greatest authority in one's thinking, being treated as one's least negotiable beliefs and being granted the highest immunity to revision.

6. How do your presuppositions fit into your "network of beliefs"? That is, what role do they play in your worldview network?

Answer: Presuppositions are the foundations for all your other beliefs. They give meaning to all of your life issues.

7. Are presuppositions easily changed or dismissed? Why do you say this?

Answer: No, they are not easily dislodged. Given that they are your core commitments and govern all other issues in life, they are more securely established beneath a whole host of secondary assumptions. Without presuppositions your other assumptions cannot stand.

8. What are some presuppositional issues that we have latent in our thinking and generally do not think about, but which are absolutely essential to rational living?

Answer: The reality of an objective external world; the reliability of memory; the relationship of the immaterial mind and the material body; your continuing personal identity over time; and the reality of cause-and-effect relations.

Answers to Chapter 4

"Worldview Features"

1. What are the three leading issues for any worldview to answer?

Answer: Questions regarding the nature of reality (metaphysics), how we know (epistemology), and how we must act (ethics).

2. From what do we derive the word "metaphysics"? What is metaphysics?

Answer: "Metaphysics" is derived from the Latin word *metaphysica*, which is based on the compound of two Greek words: *meta* ("after, beyond") and *physika* ("physics, nature"). It literally means "beyond the physical," that is, beyond the physical world of sense perception. It is the study of the ultimate nature of reality, the origin, structure, and nature of what is real.

3. What are some key metaphysical questions?

Answer: What *is it* to exist? What sorts of things exist? What is the nature of man? What is the nature of the universe? Is it objectively real? Does God exist? What is His nature? What is God's relation to the universe? Is there change or development? How do things change? What is the character of the laws or concepts that govern reality? Are they changing? Universal? What are the limits of possibility?

4. Do all people have a metaphysical program? Explain your answer.

Answer: Whether the average person is even aware of metaphysics or not, he most definitely has a metaphysical program or outlook at work in his life. This is because he has at least a general understanding of what he believes the world is all about. If he did not, he wouldn't be able to make sense out of his experience and couldn't function in the external world.

5. What is the difference between "neutral ground" and "common ground"?

Answer: "Neutral ground" requires that there be no commitment one way or another on any given issue being debated. "Common ground" speaks only of a "point of contact" that you share with your debater.

6. In the Christian view, what are the two levels of reality?

Answer: The uncreated, eternal God, and all else (the created, temporal order).

7. What do we mean when we say that God is "self-contained"? How is that significant for our apologetic?

Answer: God needs nothing outside of Himself to prolong His existence. He is absolutely self-sufficient; He alone is self-definitional.

8. From what do we derive the word "epistemology"? What is epistemology?

Answer: "Epistemology" is based on two Greek words: *episteme* ("knowledge") and *logos* ("word, discourse"). It is the study of the nature and limits of human knowledge; it addresses questions about truth, belief, justification, etc. It investigates the origin, nature, methods, and limits of knowledge, discovering what we know and how we come to know it.

9. What are some key epistemological questions?

Answer: What is the nature of truth and of objectivity? Of belief and of knowledge? What are their relationships? Can we know and yet not believe? What are the standards that justify beliefs? How do we know what we know? What is the proof or evidence that is acceptable? What are the proper procedures for science and discovery? How are they evaluated? What standards do they offer?

10. Why do we say that all the universe reveals God?
Answer: Because God created it for His own glory and created man to know Him. Furthermore, the world works according to the all-organizing plan of God and necessarily reflects his wisdom and order.

11. What are the three forms of revelation in the Christian epistemology? Briefly explain each one.
Answer: (1) General Revelation, which is the revelation of God's existence and glory as seen in creation. (2) Special Revelation, which is God's direct revelation to man to instruct him in what he should believe and do, which is recorded for us in Scripture. (3) Incarnational Revelation, which is found only in Christ in that He came to earth as God in the flesh.

12. What are some key ethical questions?
Answer: What is the nature of good and evil? What are the standards for ethical evaluation? The questions of guilt and personal peace. How do we attain or produce moral character?

13. Discuss Exodus 3:14 regarding its insights into God's being.
Answer: God calls himself "I am Who I am," which is based on the verb "to be" and is found in the imperfect tense in Hebrew. The imperfect tense indicates uncompleted action, an ongoing reality: God continually is. The repetition of the verb ("I am/ I am" in "I am that I am") emphasizes uninterrupted continuance and boundless duration. This name reveals that God determines from within His own being. "I am that I am" signifies there is no cause back of God. As the Absolute One, He operates with unfettered liberty. He

is not moved by outward circumstances or resisted by countervailing forces.

14. What are the two principal Bible passages that clearly assert the Bible is "inspired" revelation from God? What do they teach us?

Answer: Second Timothy 3:16–17 and 2 Peter 1:20–21. They both teach that Scripture is the direct revelation of God and is authoritative.

Answers to Chapter 5

"Alternative Worldviews"

1. What are some key issues you must understand in dealing with Hindus? What aspects of Hinduism comport with several contemporary Western views?

Answer: You must understand monism (which teaches that all is one), maya (which asserts that all experience is illusory), and relativism (which denies absolutes). In several important respects, Hinduism comports well with several leading Western perspectives, and especially the New Age movement. It has no problem with evolution in that the Hindu religion itself involves an ongoing adaptation of other religions and a spiritual evolution upwards. Much of modern psychology affirms the inherent goodness of man, while Hinduism speaks of man's basic divinity. Relativity of all truth claims, so widespread in our culture, fits comfortably enough with the Hindu view of illusion, god being a part of everything (both good and bad), as well as its practice of absorbing various beliefs (all other religions are *yoga*, "paths"). Its hyper-spirituality (elevating the spiritual to the exclusion of the material) is alluring to many who are disenchanted with the materialism in Western culture.

2. What are some key issues you must understand in dealing with those influenced by Behaviorism?

Answer: Materialism (which teaches that all that is real is material), mechanism (which teaches that all human action is the result of environmental stimuli), the denial of free will (resulting from inherent materialistic mechanism).

3. What is Marxism's view of the progress of history? What is "dialectical materialism"?

Answer: It follows the Hegelian view of thesis, antithesis, then synthesis. This means that struggle is the necessary condition for development to a higher and better life. Dialectical materialism is the interpretation of reality that views matter as the sole subject of change and all change as the product of a constant conflict between opposites arising from the internal contradictions inherent in all events, ideas, and movements.

4. What is the key idea involved in Existentialism?

Answer: Personal freedom leading to self-expression. This requires the priority of living over against knowing, willing over thinking, action over contemplation, love over law, personality over principle, the individual over society. The religious existentialist seeks the "personal encounter" with God over "propositional understanding" of God. The secular existentialist rids God altogether.

5. Discuss two biblical reasons justifying philosophical reasoning.

Answer: (1) God created man in his image, which includes rational thought, so that man has an innate desire from his creation to know. And (2) God specifically calls man to seek and to learn, so that man has a moral obligation from his Creator to discover.

6. Name the five core worldview presuppositions surveyed.

Answer: Monism, dualism, atomism, pragmatism, and skepticism.

7. What is the central principle of Monism?

Answer: All is one. Reality is made of only one ultimate substance or principle. Monism denies the multiplicity of things.

8. What is the central principle of Dualism?

Answer: Dualists hold there are two ultimate realities: mind and matter.

9. What is the central principle of Atomism?

Answer: All reality is material, with matter being composed of infinitesimally small particles.

10. What is the central principle of Pragmatism?

Answer: Pragmatists teach that the meaning of an idea or proposition lies in its observable practical consequences. They argue that we must live to solve our problems, even though we do not need to theoretically account for explanations. We must be able to adapt to the environment, solve our problems and get ahead in life. Pragmatism shuns the traditional problems of philosophy. Instead they say: "We do not need certainty, but utility."

11. What is the central principle of Skepticism?

Answer: Skeptics teach that we do not know anything for certain at all. All human knowledge is so deficient that at best it can only be probably true. Because of this, knowledge is deemed to be simply opinion.

Answers to Chapter 6

"Worldviews in Collision"

1. What is the concept of "antithesis" in apologetics?

Answer: "Antithesis" speaks of opposition or a counter point. As Christians we must recognize the fundamental disagreement between biblical thought and all forms of unbelief at the foundational level of our theory of knowing and knowledge. Worldview apologetics is an all-or-nothing-at-all proposition in which it denies a basic, general agreement between the non-Christian and the Christian. To give up the antithesis in seeking neutral ground, is to give up that which makes the Christian faith distinctives.

2. Where do we see the problem of antithesis begin in Scripture? What is the key verse that sets the pattern of antithesis throughout Scripture?

Answer: In Eden when Adam rebels against God. This sets up God's curse upon the world and Adam's race which continues through history. Genesis sets the pattern of antithesis found thorughout the rest of the Bible.

3. How does Genesis 2 set up the character of Adam's Fall in Genesis 3?

Answer: It shows the loving, intimate creation of Adam and Eve by God, and God's abundant provision of a peaceful environment. Adam and Eve lacked nothing they needed, but they sinned against God.

4. Where do we see the ultimate antithesis?

Answer: In Hell where men are forever separated from God and His common grace.

5. Why is it important to understand the Bible in order to bring a *philosophical* challenge against the unbeliever?

Answer: A philosophical challenge arises from our biblical worldview. We are setting one worldview over against the other. Consequently, we must understand our own worldview in order to present an adequate challenge to the unbeliever. We must promote the Christian faith *particularly*; and our faith is contained in the Bible.

6. Give some samples of evidence of contradiction within the unbeliever's worldview as it plays out in his life.
Answer: The unbeliever proclaims a materialistic worldview, but attempts to have some form of (non-material) ethics. He promotes sexual liberty, gay rights, and abortion rights as a matter of freedom and in resisting imposing morality, but then he responds in moral indignation at Hitler's holocaust, America's "unfair" wealth, various wars, and so forth.

7. What is the basic image of sin which the Bible employs to describe its catastrophic nature?
Answer: Sin is presented as a warfare, an active, destructive, hostile rebellion of man against God.

8. What biblical passage shows that unbelievers do know God but that they actively suppress that knowledge?
Answer: Romans 1:18–20 where Paul states that unbelievers suppress the truth.

Answers to Chapter 7

"Overcoming Metaphysical Bias"

1. What is the modern mind's pre-disposition toward metaphysics? When did this begin?
Answer: The modern mind tends to discount metaphysics as distracting, outmoded, and unnecessary. This became a special prob-

lem during the Enlightenment of the seventeenth and eighteenth centuries.

2. Among those who tolerate metaphysics, which do they deem more basic, metaphysics or epistemology? Why?

Answer: Metaphysics is subordinated to epistemology. This results from the great success of scientific and technological achievement. Science has brought us so much, that the scientific "method" has become the dominant ideal in modern thinking.

3. State five of the eight responses that are provided against the anti-metaphysical bias of today.

Answer: (1) Epistemological method is not neutral because it either presupposes the truth or error of the Christian worldview. (2) Metaphysics is essential to epistemology in that how one reasons depends on the nature of reality. (3) Anti-metaphysical arguments are uncritical in that they make metaphysical assumptions about reality. (4) Metaphysical presuppositions are necessary to human experience in that they provide a starting point for reasoning. (5) Anti-metaphysical arguments are mistaken in not realizing that the principles of the scientific method themselves are non-observational. (6) Anti-metaphysical arguments are self-contradictory in that they specifically disallow non-observational experience, but this very principle is based on non-observational assumptions, as is the principle of the uniformity of nature (which is absolutely essential to science). (7) The anti-metaphysical bias is anti-Christian in that it precludes the Christian answer at the outset. (8) The anti-metaphysical bias is sinfully motivated, for Paul informs us that men seek to suppress the truth in unrighteousness.

4. Explain why epistemology is not neutral. What are the two basic epistemological methodologies available to man?

Answer: The Bible calls man to begin with the fear of God for knowledge and wisdom; the unbelieving mind denies this at the very foundation of its operating principles. In the final analysis, there are only two positions: the Christian and the non-Christian approaches. All non-believing approaches are simply variations on the principle of suppressing the truth in unrighteousness. Every method presupposes either the truth or the falsity of Christian theism.

5. How does the record of Adam and Eve help us see that epistemology is non-neutral?

Answer: God sovereignly and unambiguously commanded that Adam and Eve *not* eat of the Tree of the Knowledge of Good and Evil. But Satan challenged God's direct command and told Eve the decision was hers to make. Eve took it upon herself to weigh the two options before her: "Shall I follow Satan who sees no wrong in this? Or shall I follow God who simply declared it wrong without any justifying reasons?" This is the same method the unbeliever chooses: He asserts for himself *the right to determine proper method*. And he does so without reference to God.

6. In the Christian worldview, what are the two levels of reality? Explain why the "two levels of reality" are important.

Answer: The two levels of reality are: the eternal God and created reality. The "natural man" assumes "the ultimacy of the human mind." His *method* is to operate in the world in a way that reduces all reality to one level, denying the authority of God as absolutely determinative. The unbeliever's method does not bow to the absolute authority of the Creator but claims all authority to reason on his own terms without reference to God.

7. Why is metaphysics necessary to epistemology, so that our scientific method itself must involve a basic metaphysic?

Answer: Our theory of knowledge is what it is because our theory of being is what it is. We cannot ask *how* we know without at the same time asking *what* we know. Epistemology cannot be divorced from metaphysics in that metaphysics studies such questions or issues as the nature of existence, the sorts of things that exist, the classes of existent things, limits of possibility, the ultimate scheme of things, reality versus appearance, and the comprehensive conceptual framework used to make sense of the world as a whole. These issues *necessarily* impact epistemology.

8. In what way is anti-metaphysical hostility considered to be "uncritical" and naive?

Answer: If you do not know something about the universe to begin with, you cannot devise a method for separating truth and error (epistemological concerns). Everyone begins with an *integrated worldview* involving metaphysics *and* epistemology. The contemporary anti-metaphysical bias is naively uncritical in overlooking this.

9. Given the Christian's starting point with God, explain how we can avoid the charge of circular reasoning?

Answer: (1) We are not engaged in special pleading for the Christian worldview. We are simply asking which system makes human experience intelligible? For sake of argument, we will grant the unbeliever his system with whatever foundations he adopts in order to see if it can justify its truth claims. But then he will have to grant us ours (for sake of argument) to see if we can justify our truth. (2) All systems must ultimately involve some circularity in reasoning. For instance, when you argue for the legitimacy of the laws of logic, you must employ the laws of logic. How else can you justify laws of logic? In the Christian worldview, however, the Christian apologetic is *not* engaged in a *viciously* circular argument, a circular argument *on the same plane*. We appeal above and beyond the temporal realm.

God's self-revelation in nature and in Scripture informs us of the two-level universe: God is not a fact like other facts in the world. He is the Creator and Establisher of all else. (3) Circularity in one's philosophical system is just another name for 'consistency' in outlook throughout one's system. One's starting point and final conclusion cohere with each other. (4) The unbeliever has no defensible standard whereby he can judge the Christian position. His argument either ends up in infinite regress (making it impossible to prove), has no justification (rendering it subjective), or engages in an unjustifiable same-plane circularity (causing it to be fallacious).Without a self-verifying standard, he has no epistemological way out. And only the Christian worldview has such a self-verifying standard.

Answers to Chapter 8

"Approaching the Unbeliever"

1. What specific Bible passage sets up the two-fold structure of the apologetic challenge to the unbeliever?
Answer: Proverbs 26:4–5: "Do not answer a fool according to his folly, Lest you also be like him. Answer a fool as his folly deserves, Lest he be wise in his own eyes."

2. What does the Bible mean when it speaks of a "fool"?
Answer: In the Bible a fool is not necessarily one who is a mentally deficient, shallow-minded ignoramus. The fool is one who "trusts in his heart" (Prov. 28:26; cf. Jer. 9:23), who rejects God, the ultimate source of wisdom and truth: "The fool has said in his heart, 'There is no God'" (Ps. 14:1; 53:1). He is a fool because "the fear of the Lord is the beginning" of "knowledge" (Prov. 1:7) and of "wisdom" (Prov. 9:10).

3. What are the two particular aspects of the biblical apologetic challenge to unbelief? Briefly explain each of the two steps of apologetics.

Answer: (1) Presenting the truth. That is, presenting the Christian worldview on its own terms. (2) Warning of folly. That is, entering into the non-Christian worldview on its own terms in order to provide an internal critique of its showing its internal inconsistency.

4. In what limited circumstances should you adopt the unbeliever's worldview?

Answer: Only for providing an internal critique of its systemic errors, not in adopting it as a valid option.

5. Why should you avoid arguing that Christianity is the "best" position to hold? What should you argue instead?

Answer: Because this implies the unbelieving worldview has some merit. The truth is that God exists, and He alone provides the preconditions for the intelligibility of human experience.

6. In the final analysis, what phrase by Dr. Van Til encapsulates the biblical proof of God, displaying the very essence of our argument?

Answer: "The impossibility of the contrary." This is an indirect argument for God which demonstrates that without God nothing whatsoever can be known.

7. What do we mean when we speak of the "preconditions of intelligibility"?

Answer: These are the most basic assumptions that provide for the very possibility of knowledge. These assumptions or presuppositions can only be accounted for in the Christian system in its commitment to the Creator God.

8. How is our very self-awareness an argument for God's existence?

Answer: The very fact of self-awareness distinguishes man from rocks. But how can the unbeliever account for human self-awareness as a fundamental factor of life? Where does it come from? How is it that man is self-aware? In the unbeliever's naturalistic, materialistic conception of the universe, all must be accounted for in terms of the material interaction of atoms. Point out that this forces us to view ourselves as simply matter-in-motion. Ask him how matter can be self-aware. What view of the world makes self-awareness intelligible? Ask the unbeliever to explain where inert matter comes from, then how it becomes living matter, which eventually becomes self-aware, which eventually becomes rational, which eventually becomes moral—and all by the evolutionary mechanism of time plus chance.

9. Explain how the Christian worldview establishes logic while the non-Christian worldview can't.

Answer: The unbeliever's view of origins presents a chance-based worldview which can have no laws, no necessity, no logical principles, but only randomness. According to cosmic evolutionary theory all is ultimately subject to random change and is in a constant state of flux. But our very rationality requires laws so that things may be distinguished, classified, organized, and explained. Rational comprehension and explanation demand principles of order and unity in order to relate truths and events to one another. Consequently, on the basis of the non-believer's worldview rationality itself has no foundation.

10. How would you respond to someone who claims to use the "scientific method," which asserts that all knowledge comes by way of observational analysis through sense experience?

Answer: This method holds that knowledge must be limited to observation and sense perception. Once an unbeliever has committed to this procedure he is involved in epistemological self-contradiction: If all knowledge is governed by observation, then how did he come to know *that*? That is, how did he come to know that "all knowledge is governed by observation"? Did he *observe* that in the lab? Did he measure, weigh, or count it? Did he detect *that* conceptual limitation by exploring nature? And furthermore, does he observe that this principle is a *universal* limitation on knowledge in all places and at all times so that he can confidently trust it?

11. How would you show the futility of unbelief by the unbeliever's declaring child abuse or oppressing the poor to be morally wrong?

Answer: He cannot declare that it is absolutely wrong on his chance-based, relativistic worldview. Moral evaluations require an absolute standard, which the unbelieving worldview can't produce from the perspective of his chance universe. Why shouldn't some people take advantage of a child? Why shouldn't the rich oppress the poor?

12. How can a flower be used to show the incoherence of the non-Christian worldview?

Answer: In the biblical apologetic all facts testify of God, even the existence of a flower. Various problems arise in considering the flower: (1) The unbeliever can't account for the existence of matter. Where did it come from? (2) He can't explain induction. That is, he is unable to explain the flower's history and development, since his system is materialistic and the process of induction is not. (3) He can't explain the flower's conception which requires logic in order to even talk about flowers, in that it requires the universals of "flowerness" and "dirtness." (4) He can't account for value judgments about flowers. He has no account for aesthetic or ethical values. What do we do about the flower? (5) He can't explain the flower's adaptation to its environment. Why is it related to anything else in the random world? Why can things outside of me be made suitable to my purposes? (6) He can't explain the explanation of flower. In a chance universe of ultimate randomness, he can't account for unity, differentiation, and classes of things in order to explain what he means by "flower." (7) He has no way to explain our consciousness of flowers. We are self conscious, the flower is not. How is this so since I am but matter-in-motion?

Answers to Chapter 9

"The Problem of Moral Absolutes"

1. Why is morality an important issue in defending the existence of God?

Answer: Moral concerns are inescapable in human life. You will find that anytime your forgo beating up your neighbor, he will be grateful for your moral restraint. And what would society be if "every man did what was right in his own eyes" (Judges 17:6; 21:25)? We would all fear going out in public—or even staying at home with morally unpredictable family members. Every waking moment of life involves moral challenges as we choose one action as preferable over another.

2. List some extreme moral positions in the modern world that are helpful for showing the absurdity of attempting to establish ethics without reference to God.

Answer: Animal rights which forbid eating animals and even go so far as to provide the same rights to animals as they do for man; environmentalism which prohibits using the earth for the good of man.

3. State three moral positions for which modern Christians are denounced, showing the antithesis between the Christian and non-Christian worldviews.

Answer: (1) Pro-life defense of the unborn. (2) Defense of capital punishment to protect the innocent. (3) Opposition to the immorality of homosexual conduct.

4. Define what we mean by "ethical relativism."
Answer: The view that moral standards are relative from culture to culture, from time to time, or even from person to person so that we cannot assert any absolute standard of right and wrong.

5. What is the contradiction involved in asserting that no one should declare absolute moral values?
Answer: This assertion of relativism is absolutistic.

6. What is the standard apologetic challenge which we make against the unbeliever: Re-phrase that challenge for use in the debate over moral absolutes.
Answer: The standard challenge is: What worldview can account for this or for that. Regarding morality: What worldview can account for moral values that condemn child abuse, oppressing the poor, and so forth?

7. What is the absolute standard for good in the Christian worldview?
Answer: God's holy character as we come to know it by his self-revelation in Scripture.

8. One school of unbelieving ethics asserts that "good" is what evokes approval. Explain this position, being careful to note the two divisions in this approach.
Answer: That which is good is that which evokes either social approval or personal approval. Social approval is a society-wide con-

viction whereas personal approval may differ from person to person.

9. State five historically-held, reprehensible practices that have been held in various societies, which show the absurdity of the view that good is that which evokes social approval.

Answer: Genocide, infanticide, cannibalism, human sacrifice, child molestation, widow immolation, and community suicide.

10. What is the problem with claiming that ethical values are intuited?

Answer: You cannot argue about good: you just intuit what is good. Therefore, you cannot have a rational discussion about right and wrong, because you have no way to resolve differences of opinion. This reduces morality to subjective preferences that bind no one, not even the subjectivist who may change his view at any moment. In fact, you have no predictable way to say that a person's intuition about good is good itself. You end up having to intuit that your intuition is right, then intuit that your intuition about your intuition is right. On and on through an infinite regress which results from not having an absolute, self-verifying standard.

11. How would you respond to the claim that good is that which evokes personal approval?

Answer: This reduces ethics to personal preference. It cannot even declare something good, for such merely explains that the "good" is something that so-and-so prefers, rather than pointing to something objectively good.

12. How would you respond to the claim that good is that which achieves desired ends?

Answer: If good is that which achieves chosen ends, this leads to certain consequences. Utilitarianism teaches that good is that which produces the greatest happiness for the greatest number. By *why* is the greatest number determinative of good? And what happens when the numbers change? Does good change? Hedonists teach that our own individual happiness and well being are the goals of good.When then are sado-masochists, cannibals, and child molesters routinely denied having their happiness fulfilled?

13. Defend from Scripture the claim that God's law is our revealed standard of absolute good.
Answer: Romans 7:12 and 1 Timothy 1:8 declare that the law of God is "good." The law of God is given the same attributes as God himself: It is good, righteous, just, holy, and perfect.

Answers to Chapter 10

"The Uniformity of Nature"

1. How is the idea of the "universe" bound up with the notion of "uniformity of nature"?
Answer: That we live in a *uni*verse indicates that we exist in a single, unified, orderly system which is composed of many diversified parts. These parts coordinately function together as a whole, rational, predictable system.

2. Explain the meaning of the uniformity of nature using the two basic elements involved.
Answer: (1) Uniformity is valid in all places. The character of the material universe is such that it functions according to a discernible regularity. Natural laws that operate in one place of the universe will uniformly operate throughout the universe so that the same physical cause will in a similar circumstance produce the same physical result elsewhere. (2) Uniformity is valid at all times. We may expect the future to be like

the past in that natural laws do not change over time. Consequently, even changes in the universe caused by such super-massive events as exploding supernovas, colliding galaxies, and so forth, are predictable, being governed by natural law. These laws hold true at all times, from the past into the future.

3. Why is the uniformity of nature important to human experience and to science?

Answer: Science and human experience are absolutely dependent upon this uniformity because without it we could not infer from past events what we can expect under like circumstances in the future. Physical science absolutely requires the ability to predict the future action of material entities. Scientific experimentation, theorizing, and prediction would be impossible were nature non-uniform. Scientific investigation is only possible in an orderly, rational coherent, unified system. If reality were haphazard and disorderly we would have no basic scientific laws governing and controlling various phenomena. For instance, medical labs do controlled experiments to create procedures and medications that cure and prevent disease, and so forth.

4. State the apologetic challenge you should present to the unbeliever regarding nature's uniformity.

Answer: We must ask which worldview may reasonably expect that causal connections function uniformly throughout the universe or that the future will be like the past? We are asking, in other words, which worldview makes human experience intelligible and science possible?

5. The unbeliever argues that the scientific method operates on the basis of observation and experience. How does this present a problem for defending his worldview?

Answer: We have no experience of the future, for it has yet to occur. Therefore, on this experience-based scientific method, how can we predict the future will be like the past so that we may expect scientific experiments to be valid? Neither is it possible to observe and experience the scientific method. The validity of the method is presupposed.

6. Respond to the claim that we can know how things will operate in the future because we have seen how they operate in the past.

Answer: This statement still only tells us about the past, not the approaching future we now must anticipate. Furthermore, you can't expect the future to be like the past apart from a view of the nature of reality that informs you that events are controlled in a uniform way, as by God in the Christian system and not by chance in the unbelieving system.

7. What problem arises in the unbeliever's worldview when he claims he knows the universe is uniform?

Answer: How do we know assuredly that the universe is in fact uniform? Has man investigated every single aspect of the universe from each one of its smallest atomic particles to the farthest flung galaxies and all that exists in between, so that he can speak authoritatively? Does man have totally exhaustive knowledge about every particle of matter, every movement in space, and every moment of time? How does man know uniformity governs the whole world and the entire universe?

8. List some Bible verses that provide a foundation for our knowledge of the uniformity of nature.

Answer: Ephesians 1:11; Colossians 1:16–17; and Hebrews 1:3.

9. How would you show that the Christian system easily accounts for the uniformity of nature?

Answer: Since God created the rational, coherent universe by His sovereign, willful plan, and since He created man in his image to function in that world, we see clear revelatory evidence for the foundation of that which scientists call "the uniformity of nature."

Answers to Chapter 11

"The Problem of Universals"

1. What do we mean when we speak of "universals"?
Answer: In philosophy, any truth of a general or abstract nature—whether it be a broad concept, law, principle, or categorical statement. Such general truths are used to understand, organize, and interpret particular truths encountered in concrete experience.

2. Is the concept of universals practical to our everyday lives? Explain.
Answer: Yes, it is absolutely essential. Without them every fact would stand alone without reference to any other fact. Nothing could be understood in terms of relationships.

3. What three notions are involved in universals that define them?
Answer: Philosophers note that a universal involves three notions:. (1) By definition, a "universal" must apply to multiple things (otherwise, they would be particulars). (2) They are abstract rather than concrete (therefore, they do not appear in the material world). (3) They are general truths rather than specific.

4. Are laws of logic in the category of universals? Explain.
Answer: The laws of logic are universals. They are the most general propositions one can possibly hold. They are used every single time you think or talk about anything whatsoever. They are the abstract,

universal, invariant rules that govern human rationality. In fact, they make rationality possible by allowing for coherent meaning, rational thought, and intelligent communication.

5. Why should the laws of logic not be called "laws of thought"?
Answer: You should not say that these are "laws of thought," as if they were matters of subjective human psychology informing us how people think. We know, of course, that people actually breach the laws of logic regularly. The laws of logic are not laws of thought, but *presuppositions* of (coherent) thinking.

6. State and briefly define each of the three basic laws of logic.
Answer: (1) The Law of Identity states that "A is A." This means that if any statement is true, it is true; it cannot be both true and not true simultaneously. That is, anything that exists in reality has a particular identity and is not something else. The thing is what it is. (2) The Law of Contradiction states that "A is not not-A." That is, no statement can be both true and false in the same sense at the same time. (3) The Law of Excluded Middle states that "A is either A or not-A." That is, every statement must be either true or false exclusively, there is no middle ground. Or to put it differently: if a given statement is not true, then its denial must be true.

7. What is the basic apologetic question we must ask of the unbeliever regarding universals and the laws of logic?
Answer: "Which worldview makes sense of universals and the laws of logic?" The recurring problem for the unbelieving worldview arises once again: He cannot *account* for universals and the laws of logic.

8. How is the scientific method problematic to the laws of logic in the unbeliever's worldview?
Answer: The unbelieving empiricist cannot account for the laws of logic which regulate human reasoning. The laws of logic are not

physical objects existing as a part of the sense world. They are not the result of observable behavior of material objects or physical actions. Do the laws of logic exist in the natural world so that they can be empirically examined? If we are materialists, then only that which is objective in the realm of sense experience is real. What sense do the laws of logic make for unbelievers? What are the laws of logic? If they are just the firing of nerve endings in the neural synapses, then logic differs from person to person and are therefore not laws at all. The inherent materialism in the modern world cannot account for laws of logic.

9. How is the unbeliever's ultimate commitment to chance problematic for the laws of logic?
Answer: In a chance universe, all particular facts would be random, have no classifiable identity, bear no pre-determined order or relation, and thus be unintelligible to man's mind. Chance can't account for law. Universals and the laws of logic are inimical to chance and randomness:

10. How does the unbeliever's worldview involve internal tension and contradiction when it tries to affirm the laws of logic?
Answer: On the assumptions of the natural man, logic is a timeless impersonal principle, and facts are controlled by chance. It is by means of universal timeless principles of logic that the natural man must, on his assumptions, seek to make intelligible assertions about the world of reality or chance. But this cannot be done without falling into self-contradiction. About chance no manner of assertion can be made. In its very idea it is the irrational. And how are rational assertions to be made about the irrational?

11. What is the problem with claiming the laws of logic are human conventions adopted by men?
Answer: In the first place, the laws of logic are not agreed upon by all people. Hindus affirm monism which denies differentiation. Since

all is one, obviously there can be no law of contradiction. If the unbeliever states that the laws of logic are agreed upon conventions, then they are not absolute because they are subject to "vote" and therefore to change.

12. What is the relationship between the laws of logic and God?
Answer: The Christian holds as a basic presupposition that God is the Creator of the world and of the human mind, so that all intelligibility is due to Him. He is the author of all truth, wisdom, and knowledge. Christians see the laws of logic as expressions of God's thinking, His own consistent personal nature, not as principles outside of God to which He must measure up. The laws of logic reflect the nature of God, for in Him we find perfect coherence.

13. Cite some verses that affirm each of the three laws of logic.
Answer: (1) The law of identity is affirmed by God when he identifies Himself: "I am that I am" (Ex. 3:14). God is Himself and not something else. (2) The law of non-contradiction lies beneath the command to "Let your yes, be yes, and your no, no so that you may not fall under judgment" (James 5:12). (3) The law of excluded middle appears in the notion of antithesis, as when Jesus says: "He who is not with Me is against Me; and he who does not gather with Me scatters." Obviously, one is either "for" Christ or "against" Him. There is no middle ground—according to Christ Himself.

Answers to Chapter 12

"Personal Freedom and Dignity"

1. What does the phrase "epistemologically self-conscious" mean? Why is it significant as an apologetic tool?

Answer: One who is "epistemologically self-conscious" engages life in a way that fully comports with his theory of knowledge. That is, his behavior and reasoning are perfectly consistent with his basic commitments regarding the world and knowledge.

2. Define the concept of "dignity" as it reltes to "human dignity." How is it important for our daily lives? For our social lives?

Answer: Human "dignity" deals with notions of the ethical value, personal respect, and inherent worth of human life. The question of human dignity is of enormous practical significance in both our mundane lives and our theoretical worldviews. It not only impacts our daily attitudes and our interaction with others but serves as the very foundation for human rights and a stable society.

3. What two illustrations of human dignity are present? Explain the use of them in apologetics.

Answer: Funerals for deceased persons and law courts for defending rights. Animals have nothing in their activity that expresses any notion of dignity or of standards of right and wrong in society. Funerals and law courts exhibit our notion of human dignity.

4. Though most Americans accept the notion of human dignity, not all people do. List some samples of widespread disavowal of human dignity.

Answer: The Nazis denied the dignity of Jews in World War II. Muslim chattel slavery discounts the dignity of blacks.

5. State some historical examples of the problem of overstating the dignity of life (without Christian worldview constraints).

Answer: Albert Schweitzer refused to sanitize his hospital because it killed bacterial life. Janists make preparations to insure they do not accidentally kill flies.

6. How does materialism destroy the notion of human dignity?

Answer: In the materialist worldview we are just bundles of genetic information. What dignity inheres in a collection of DNA strands? Dignity is an immaterial, meta-physical concept.

7. What is the ultimate problem the unbelieving worldview has in attempting to affirm human dignity.

Answer: What meaning does dignity have in a chance Universe? We must recall that chance can't account for morality or universals. Chance destroys the very possibility of meaning and significance, taking down with it the notion of dignity.

8. Outline the Christian case for human dignity.

Answer: (1) Scripture repeatedly establishes the firm basis of human dignity, declaring that man exists as the image of the eternal God. The psalmist declares that God made man "a little lower than God" (Ps. 8:5). (2) Our value is underscored by the fact that the Son of God took upon Himself true humanity in order to redeem us from our sins. (3) Our holy God even provided for us in Scripture a system of morality and of law that establishes special protections for man, affirming his dignity. (4) The Scriptures speak of the high value of reputation and a name, even preferring them over gold. "A good name is to be more desired than great riches, favor is better than silver and gold" (Prov. 22:1).

Glossary of Terms and Phrases

Apologetics: The vindication of the Christian philosophy of life against the various forms of the non-Christian philosophy of life. The word "apologetics" derives from the combination of two Greek words: *apo* ("back, from") and *logos* ("word"), meaning "to give a word back, to respond," i.e., in defense. (1)

Antithesis: Antithesis is based on two Greek words: *anti* ("against") and *tithenai* ("to set or place"). "Antithesis" speaks of opposition or a counter point. As Christians we must recognize the fundamental disagreement between biblical thought and all forms of unbelief at the foundational level of our theory of knowing and knowledge. (13)

Atomism: A form of materialism which holds that the material Universe is composed of indestructible particles. In fact, the word "atom" is from the Greek *a* ("no") and *temnein* ("cut"), which speaks of the smallest material particle that can be cut down no smaller. Atomism necessarily denies Monism in that it affirms infinite atomic differentiation in reality. (84)

Autonomy: Autonomy derives from two Greek words: *auto* ("self") and *nomos* ("law"). It effectively means "self law," or "self rule." Human autonomy asserts that man's reasoning is the ultimate criterion of knowledge. (133)

Begging the Question: Begging the question (technically known by the Latin phrase *petitio principii*) is a fallacious manner of reasoning wherein your premise includes the claim that your conclusion is true, that is, your argument assumes the very point to be proven. (123)

Brute Fact: An uninterpreted fact that stands alone without reference to some other fact, principle of interpretation, and especially to God. Presuppositional Apologetics denies brute factuality in that all facts are created and controlled by God according to his plan and for his glory. (43)

Circular Reasoning: Circular reasoning (technically known by the Latin phrase *circulus in probando*) occurs when one assumes something in order to prove that very thing. Circular reasoning is often very subtle and hard to detect. (123)

Deconstructionism: Deconstructionism is a principle of modern language analysis which asserts that language refers only to itself rather than to an external reality. It challenges any claims to ultimate truth and obligation by attacking theories of knowledge and ultimate values. This philosophy attempts to "deconstruct" texts to remove all biases and traditional assumptions. Deconstructionists argue, therefore, that no written text communicates any set meaning or conveys any reliable or coherent message. (9)

Deism: A natural religion view which was very prevalent in the 17th and 18th centuries. This belief about God is derived solely from natural revelation and reason and not special revelation. The God of deism created the world, but does not interfere with it by means of providence, miracle, incarnation, or any other Christian affirmation. (29)

Dialectic: Dialectic (from the Greek *dialogo*, "to discourse") is the philosophical process (the "dialogue") whereby truth is arrived at by the exchange of ideas between opposing viewpoints. (78)

Dialectical Materialism: The Marxian interpretation of reality that views matter as the sole subject of change and all change as the product of a constant conflict between opposites arising from the internal contradictions inherent in all events, ideas, and movements. (78)

Discursive Reasoning: Analytical reasoning that proceeds by moving from fact to fact, point by point, in a logical fashion, rather than by intuition. (81)

Dualism: Dualism holds that there are two ultimate realities, usually designated as mind and matter. The Greek philosopher Plato (428–348 B.C.) was a Dualist in dividing reality into the ideal world of eternal "Forms" and the perceptual world of temporal sense experience. In the eternal world beyond the spatio-temporal world exist ideal Forms in perfection as unchanging realities. The world of experience is populated with dim, imperfect particular copies of those ideal forms (which are known to us only through intuition). (83)

Economic Trinity: The Economic Trinity looks at the Trinity in terms of the scheme of salvation, the plan of redemption: The Father elects us and sends the Son, the Son becomes incarnate and dies for us, the Spirit calls and sanctifies us. The notion of the economic Trinity focuses on the roles of each member of the Trinity. Neither the Father nor the Spirit died on the cross, only the Son. (83)

Egoism: This ethical system holds that self-interest is the proper motive for human conduct. This should not be confused with "egotism" which is conceit. (84)

Empirical: Knowledge that is observational, relying on sense perception. It is guided by experience rather than theory. (154)

Enlightenment: The European intellectual movement of the seventeenth and eighteenth centuries in which ideas concerning God, reason, nature, and man were blended into a worldview that inspired revolutionary developments in art, philosophy, and politics. Central to Enlightenment thought were the use and celebration of reason. For Enlightenment thinkers, received authority, whether in science or religion, was to be subject to the investigation of unfettered minds." (7)

Epistemological Self-consciousness: One who is "epistemologically self-conscious" engages life in a way that fully comports with his theory of knowledge. That is, his behavior and reasoning are perfectly consistent with his basic commitments regarding the world and knowledge. (216)

Epistemology: Epistemology is based on two Greek words: *episteme* ("knowledge") and *logos* ("word, discourse"). It is the study of the nature and limits of human knowledge; it addresses questions about truth, belief, justification, etc. It investigates the origin, nature, methods, and limits of knowledge, discovering what we know and how we come to know it. (61)

Ethics: The branch of philosophy known as moral philosophy. It studies right and wrong attitudes, judgments, and actions, as well as moral responsibility and obligation. (66)

Existentialism: A philosophy concerned above all else with freedom and self-expression. It exalts the experience of living over against knowing, willing over thinking, action over contemplation, love over law, personality over principle, the individual over society. (79)

General Revelation: General revelation is the doctrine that God reveals himself in nature. This form of revelation is directed to all men (thus it is called "general" revelation). Though God's revelation in nature does not show man the way of salvation, the Trinitarian nature of God, and many other such divine truths, it does show that God exists, that he is powerful, and that man is responsible to him. (62)

Generation X: Generation X consists of those whose teen years were touched by the 1980s, i.e. those born in the 1960s and 1970s. The term was popularized by Douglas Coupland's novel *Generation X: Tales for an Accelerated Culture*. In Coupland's usage, the X referred to the difficulty in defining a generation whose only unifying belief was the rejection of the beliefs of their Baby Boomer parents. Although not the first group of Americans to grow up with television, Gen Xers were the first group that never knew life without one. (12)

Incarnation: Incarnation derives from the Latin *incarnare*, "to become flesh." This is based on two Latin words: *in* ("in") plus *carn* ("flesh"). It speaks of the coming of the invisible, spiritual God in bodily form in Jesus Christ. (65)

Infinite Regress: The result when a suggested explanation or purported standard is challenged, causing the argument to point back further to a more basic commitment that sustains the explanation, and when that commitment is challenged, it points to an even more basic commitment, on and on ad infinitum. (122)

Marxism: Marxism is based on the philosophy developed by Karl Marx (1818–1883), a Jewish philosopher and social critic who lived in

Germany. It is an inherently atheistic, socio-political scheme holding that the material world is the ultimate reality and that religion is an illusion. (78)

Metaphysics: Metaphysics is derived from the Latin word *metaphysica*, which is based on the compound of two Greek words: *meta* ("after, beyond") and *physika* ("physics, nature"). It literally means "beyond the physical," that is, beyond the physical world of sense perception. It is the study of the ultimate nature of reality, the origin, structure, and nature of what is real. (56)

Monism: Monism is derived from the Greek word *mono*, "single." Monism is a metaphysical system asserting only one ultimate substance or principle in the Universe. Monism denies the multiplicity of things, holding that those many things we deem real are simply phases of a one and are somehow illusions. (83)

Nihilism: Nihilism teaches that the world and man are wholly without meaning or purpose. The world and man are so absolutely senseless and useless that there is no comprehensible truth. The word "nihilism" is derived from the Latin *nihil*, which means "nothing." (9)

Noetic: Noetic is derived from the Greek word *nous*, which means "mind" (see: Luke 24:45; Rom. 7:23; Phil. 4:7). The "noetic effect of sin" is one aspect of the doctrine "total depravity," which declares that the fall reaches deep down into a man's very being, even to his mind, his reasoning processes. (28)

Omnipresence: Omnipresence is derived from the Latin words *omni* ("all") and *praesens* ("present"). It speaks of God's personal, simultaneous presence everywhere throughout the universe.

Ontology: The study of the nature of being. (63)

Ontology: Ontology is the branch of metaphysics that deals with the nature of being. (190)

Ontological Trinity: The Ontological Trinity is God's triune being in itself, the one being of God the Father, Son and Holy Spirit. (82)

Polytheism: Polytheism is derived from the French, *polythiesme*, which is based on the combination of two Greek words: *polu* ("many") and *theos* ("god"). Polytheism is the belief in many gods, wherein particular gods are thought to govern specific aspects of the world and life. (50)

Pragmatism: The philosophical system which holds that the meaning of an idea or proposition lies in its observable practical consequences. Pragmatists argue that we must live to solve our problems, even though we do not need to theoretically account for explanations. We must be able to adapt to the environment, solve our problems and get ahead in life. Pragmatism shuns the traditional problems of philosophy: We do not need certainty, but utility. (85)

Predication: Predication is a logical concept borrowed from grammar. In logic predication is either the affirming or denying of something. It is the attributing or negating of something to the subject of a proposition. For instance, consider the following two statements of predication: "The sun is hot"; "The dark side of the moon is not hot." The first affirms (predicates) hotness of the sun; the second denies hotness of the dark side of the moon. (38)

Presupposition: An elementary (or foundational) assumption in one's reasoning or in the process by which opinions are formed. It is not just any assumption in an argument, but a personal commitment that is held at the most basic level of one's network of beliefs. Presuppositions form a wide-ranging, foundational perspective (or starting point) in terms of which everything else is interpreted and evaluated. As such, presuppositions have the greatest authority in one's thinking, being treated as one's least negotiable beliefs and being granted the highest immunity to revision." (44)

Proletariat: Proletariat derives from the Latin *proles* ("offspring"). In ancient Rome this signified the lower class poor in society. In Marxian theory it speaks of the working class which does not possess capital or the means of production. (78)

Reformed Theology: Reformed theology is the strongly Calvinistic, covenantal theological branch of evangelicalism. A good summary of the Reformed view of theology may be found in the famed doctrinal formulation known as the Westminster Confession of Faith (drawn up in the mid 1640s in England). (149)

Relativism: Relativism teaches that knowledge is relative due to the limited state of the mind and that there can be no absolutes to give a set meaning or value to any human thought or action. (9)

Skepticism: Skepticism says we do not know anything for certain at all. All human knowledge is so deficient that at best it can only be probably true. Because of this, knowledge is deemed to be simply opinion. These last two worldview cores are generally quite familiar to us today, though not always as formal schools of philosophical thought. (85)

Special Revelation: Special revelation is that disclosure that is given to God's people (hence, it is "special"). It comes from God by means of direct, personal, verbal (or visual) communication, either through special, prophetically endowed messengers or through the written record of those messengers. (64)

Subliminal: "Subliminal" derives from two Latin words: *sub* ("below") and *limmen* ("threshold"). It speaks of that which is below the threshold of consciousness, that which is just out of conscious perception. Advertisers have discovered that people unconsciously pick up on and are influenced by flashes of information just below the normal limits of perception. (11)

Teleological: The word "teleological" is derived from the Greek word *telos*, meaning "end" or "purpose" and *logos* ("word" or "study of"). A teleological argument argues for the existence of God based on evidence of order, purpose, design and/or direction in the created order. (60)

Transcendental Reasoning: Transcendental reasoning seeks to discover what general conditions must be fulfilled for any particular instance of knowledge to be possible. It asks what view of man, mind, truth, language, and the world is necessarily presupposed by our conception of knowledge and our methods of pursuing it. (124)

Universal: In philosophy, any truth of a general or abstract nature—whether it be a broad concept, law, principle, or categorical statement. Such general truths are used to understand, organize, and interpret particular truths encountered in concrete experience. (200)

Utilitarianism: The ethical system which holds that men must seek the greatest happiness for the greatest number. (85)

Worldview: A worldview is a network of presuppositions (which are not verified by the procedures of natural science) regarding reality (metaphysics), knowing (epistemology), and conduct (ethics) in terms of which every element of human experience is related and interpreted." (1)

Index